Grief Diaries

SURVIVING LOSS OF A CHILD

22 True stories about finding hope and healing
in the aftermath of losing a child

LYNDA CHELDELIN FELL
with
DEANA L. MARTIN
ERICA GALE BELTZ
ANNAH ELIZABETH
MARILYN ROLLINS

FOREWORD BY R. GLENN KELLY

A portion of proceeds from the sale of this book is
donated to Cry For Me, No More, a nonprofit organization
offering an experiential program to honor and support
bereaved families. For more information,
visit www.cryformenomore.com.

Grief Diaries
Surviving Loss of a Child – 1st ed.
True stories about finding hope and healing in the aftermath of losing a child.
Lynda Cheldelin Fell/Erica Gale Beltz
Annah Elizabeth/Deana L. Martin/Marilyn Rollins
For more information on Grief Diaries, visit www.GriefDiaries.com

Cover Design by AlyBlue Media, LLC
Interior Design by AlyBlue Media LLC
Published by AlyBlue Media, LLC
www.AlyBlueMedia.com

ISBN: 978-1-944328-00-9
Library of Congress Control Number: 2015917763
AlyBlue Media, LLC
Ferndale, WA 98248
www.AlyBlueMedia.com

PRINTED IN THE UNITED STATES OF AMERICA

GRIEF DIARIES

TESTIMONIALS

"CRITICALLY IMPORTANT . . . *I want to say to Lynda that what you are doing is so critically important.*"
–DR. BERNICE A. KING, Daughter of Dr. Martin Luther King

"DEEPLY INTIMATE . . . Grief Diaries *is a deeply intimate, authentic collection of narratives that speak to the powerful, often ambiguous, and wide spectrum of emotions that arise from loss. I so appreciate the vulnerability and truth embedded in these stories, which honor and bear witness to the many forms of bereavement that arise in the aftermath of death.*" -DR. ERICA GOLDBLATT HYATT, Chair of Psychology, Bryn Athyn College

"MOVING . . . *We learn from stories throughout life. In Grief Diaries, the stories are not only moving but often provide a rich background for any mourner to find a gem of insight that can be used in coping with loss. Reread each story with pen in hand and you will find many that are just right for you.*" -DR. LOUIS LAGRAND, Author of Healing Grief, Finding Peace

"A FORCE . . .*The writers of this project, the Grief Diaries anthology series, are a force to be reckoned with. I'm betting we will be agents of great change.*" -MARY LEE ROBINSON, Author and Founder of Set an Extra Plate initiative

"INCREDIBLE . . .*Thank you so much for doing this project, it's absolutely incredible!*"-JULIE MJELVE, Founder, Grieving Together

"STUNNING . . . Grief Diaries *treats the reader to a rare combination of candor and fragility through the eyes of the bereaved. Delving into the deepest recesses of the heartbroken, the reader easily identifies with the diverse collection of stories and richly colored threads of profound love that create a stunning read full of comfort and hope.*" -DR. GLORIA HORSLEY, President, Open to Hope Foundation

"POWERFUL . . .*I'm so glad that I have been a part of something so powerful.*"
-MARY SUTHERLAND, participant in *Grieving for the Living*

"WONDERFUL . . .*Grief Diaries is a wonderful computation of stories written by the best of experts, the bereaved themselves. Thank you for building awareness about a topic so near and dear to my heart.*"
-DR. HEIDI HORSLEY, Adjunct Professor, School of Social Work, Columbia University, Author, Co-Founder of Open to Hope Organization

"OUTSTANDING . . .*Lynda and her team did an outstanding job of moving all contributors through the process in a gentle, yet efficient way. Most importantly, the project team set up questions for contributors that were fashioned to elicit thoughtful and insightful answers.*"
-MARY LEE ROBINSON, Author, The Widow or Widower Next Door

"HOPE AND HEALING . . . *You are a pioneer in this field and you are breaking the trail for others to find hope and healing.*"
-KRISTI SMITH, Bestselling Author & International Speaker

"AMAZING . . . *This is so amazing that after all these years of dealing with all the issues I've had in my life, I'm finally feeling like I'm not alone in all this.*" - DEBBIE PFIFFNER, Contributor to *Grief Diaries: Grieving for the Living*

"GLOBAL . . .*One of The Five Facets of Healing mantras is together we can heal a world of hurt. This anthology series is testimony to the power we have as global neighbors to do just that.*"
-ANNAH ELIZABETH, Founder of The Five Facets of Healing

"GRATEFUL . . .*This journey, while the intent has been to guide and encourage others through this path of darkness, has provided invaluable insights into my feelings, allowing validation of those feelings by the person who matters most - - me! I am grateful for this opportunity.*" -NANCY HAMMINK REDMOND, participant in *Loss of a Spouse & Loss by Homicide*

"HEALING . . . *This was one of the hardest journeys I have led myself on and yet I would do it all over again. Healing is a hard process, of so many emotions but there is no time frame on how long it will take and through this project I have come closer to feeling healed.*"
-TERESA BROWN, participant in *Loss of a Parent & Grieving for the Living*

"REWARDING . . .*This experience has been very rewarding for me. Just being able to talk with others who have walked this road.*"
-MONICA MIRKES, contributor to *Surviving Loss of a Child*

DEDICATION

To our beloved children:
Corinne Joy Berndtson
Jenna Rose Cruz
Emily Detwiler
Alyssa Victoria Yvonne Fell
Poppy Gato
Lydia Marie Greer
Marisa Mirkes Haag
Taylor "Tayla" Marie Have
William Hayes Holesapple
Scott Michael Jessie
Luke Jordan
Krystle Cherie Kimbler
Kyle Lawson
Gavin Michael
Amanda Suzanne Mills
Logan Robert Mills
Randy Robert Rollins
Sara Marie Rollins
Nicholas Shelton
Dominique "Deedee" Faith St. George
Tariq "Jay" Strong
Megan Lynn Serrao Wellington

CONTENTS

FOREWORD

We are all so much like snowflakes, every one of us crafted one by one to be wondrously unique in our own way. We are then set upon our passages drawn by a mysterious and unseen force, often blown about wildly by the harsh and unpredictable winds of change. When one considers the influence of a snowflake, it seems that the impact of that single creation toward anything in life would matter little. Yet you need only to awaken on a crisp winter's morn to witness the beauty and grandeur on the landscape, once barren, brown, and dormant before Mother Nature decided to send down and gather a multitude of her fragile creations. That lonely, very fragile and unique flake, its blustery sojourn taking it to and fro, came together with many other unique flakes to create a new splendor and outlook on life in a gorgeous, clean blanket of thick snow.

Like that newly painted landscape, *Grief Diaries: Surviving Loss of a Child* gathered many snowflakes, each having been tossed about by the frigid and brutal winds of the unthinkable and heartrending loss of a child. Like those snowflakes, grief too is as unique and personal to the parent, as no two will ever grieve alike. Yet many have come together within this diary to share their uniqueness in order to provide a changed viewpoint for themselves and others.

No matter where the reader finds him or herself along the dark pathways of grief, this diary provides the wisdom earned though not only searing pain and anguish, but also self-discovery and a level of healing.

Each Grief Diaries writer is on a personal and deliberate path toward healing, albeit with the somber resolve that a complete recovery can never be championed. They will never be complete again. The best that can be reached is a modified normal, although one that can certainly be filled with joy, hope, and a strong purpose in life.

Some may wonder why a grieving parent would contribute to this project; their loss so painful and at the forefront in their hearts. Perhaps each writer shares my own understanding that in a small way, it allows us to bring our dear children back to the present. Words are much like a photograph: once taken, they immediately become a printed snapshot of life. Photos can be pulled from an album and bring a hint of "living in the moment," and so too can our written words as they memorialize our lost loved ones.

Is it possible there is a greater reason for sharing the loss of our children, other than the brief ability to live in the present? Absolutely. We grieve, after all, because we loved someone so very deeply, and the physical loss of someone so interwoven into the very fabric of unconditional love leaves us with a bruised but very, very compassionate heart. When one reads the offerings contained within this diary, it becomes obvious that each writer shares an unselfish love for others, as well as a devotion to imparting their experiences, regardless of the pain to themselves. It is their hope that by doing so, it will bring comfort to others who find themselves somewhere along the same path of loss.

Lynda Cheldelin Fell provided the visionary insight for the Grief Diaries and served as the compiler of stories from the selfless writers. In coordinating the efforts to bring forth such a powerful resource, she instills a confidence that calls out that we can, and must, survive. With the amazing collaboration of all those who participated, we find many messages of both deep sorrow and amazing hope in the stories to follow.

It is my contention that the one message that stands out so prominently is the unquestionable awareness that we do not move forward without our precious, lost children. Instead, we move forward *with* the unconditional love and joy of their spirit dwelling deeply within our very being. In what will seem to them to be just the gentle beat of a heart, we shall hold them once again.

Until then, we can live with peace and purpose.

R. GLENN KELLY
Author, Speaker, Grief Support Advocate
Board Member, National Grief & Hope Coalition
www.GrievingMen.com

PREFACE

One night in 2007, I had one of those dreams, the vivid kind you can't shake. In the dream, I was the front seat passenger in a car and my daughter Aly was sitting behind the driver. Suddenly, the car missed a curve in the road and sailed into a lake. The driver and I escaped the sinking car, but Aly did not. My beloved daughter was gone. The only evidence left behind was a book floating in the water where she disappeared.

Two years later, on August 5, 2009, that horrible nightmare became reality when Aly died as a back seat passenger in a car accident. Returning home from a swim meet, the car carrying Aly and two of her teammates was T-boned by a father coming home from work. My beautiful fifteen-year-old daughter took the brunt of the impact, and died instantly. She was the only fatality.

Just when I thought life couldn't get any worse, it did. My dear sweet hubby buried his head — and grief — in the sand. He escaped into eighty-hour work weeks, more wine, more food, and less talking. His blood pressure shot up, his cholesterol went off the chart, and the perfect storm arrived on June 4, 2012. In an instant, my husband felt a strange warmth spread inside his head. He began drooling, and couldn't speak. My 46-years-young soulmate was having a major stroke.

My husband survived the stroke, but couldn't speak, read, or write, and his right side was paralyzed. He needed assistance just to sit up in bed. He needed full-time care. Still reeling from the loss of our daughter, I found myself again thrust into a fog of grief so thick, I couldn't see through the storm. Adrenaline and autopilot resumed their familiar place at the helm.

In the aftermath of losing Aly and my husband's stroke, I eventually discovered that helping others was a powerful way to heal my own heart. The Grief Diaries series was born and built on this belief. By writing books narrating our journeys through life's challenges and hardships, our written words become a portable support group for others. When we swap stories, we feel less alone. It is comforting to know someone else understands the shoes we walk in, and the challenges we face along the way.

Which brings us to this book, *Grief Diaries: Surviving Loss of a Child*. Losing a child of any age forces you on a journey unlike any other. It can steal your soul and leave you feeling lost, broken, and hopeless. Further, you might encounter others who don't understand your journey. This is where the Grief Diaries series can help.

Helen Keller once said, "Walking with a friend in the dark is better than walking alone in the light." This is especially true in the aftermath of a life-changing experience. If you've lost a child, the following true stories are written by courageous people who know exactly how you feel, for they've been in your shoes and walked the same path. Perhaps the shoes are a different size or style, but may you find comfort in their stories and the understanding that you aren't truly alone on the journey. For we walk ahead, behind, and right beside you.

Wishing you healing, and hope from the Grief Diaries village.

Warm regards,

Lynda Cheldelin Fell
Creator, Grief Diaries

BY LYNDA CHELDELIN FELL

THE WAILING TENT

Dear grieving mother,

Welcome to the sisterhood of the wailing tent. Although with profound condolences, I know this greeting will soon be forgotten, for your heart and soul have sustained a terrible blow. The shock known as "the fog" will accompany you for some time, greatly impacting your memory. So I offer you this written welcome to refer to when your recollection falters.

The wailing tent is an honored place where only mothers with a broken spirit can enter. Admittance is gained not with an ID card bearing your name, but with the profound sorrow freshly etched on your heart. Membership is free, for you have already paid the unfathomable price. The directions to the wailing tent are secret, available only to mothers who speak our language of everlasting grief. No rules are posted, no hours are noted. There is no hierarchy, no governing body. Your membership has no expiration date; it is lifelong. The refuge offered within its walls does not judge members based on age, religious belief, or social status. You can hang your mask outside and, if you can't make it past the door, we will surround you with love right where you lay.

The wailing tent is a shelter where mothers shed anguished tears among their comforting sisters. It is a haven where all forms of wailing are honored, understood, and accepted. In the beginning, you will be very afraid, and will hate the wailing tent and everything it stands for. You will flail, thrash about, and spew vile words in protest. You will fight to be free of the walls, wishing desperately to offer a plea bargain for a different tent, learn a different language. Those emotions will last for some time.

Your family and friends cannot accompany you here. The needs of the wailing tent are invisible to them and, though they will frantically try, they simply cannot comprehend the language nor fathom the disembodied, guttural howls heard within.

In the beginning, your stays here will seem endless. Over time, the need for your visits will change and eventually you will observe some mothers talking, even smiling, rather than wailing. Those are the mothers who have learned to balance profound anguish with moments of peace, though they still need to seek refuge among us from time to time. Do not judge those mothers as callused or strong, for they have endured profound heartache to attain the peace they have found. Their visits here are greatly valued, for their hard-earned wisdom offers hope that we too will learn to balance the sadness in our hearts.

Finally, you need not flash your ID card or introduce yourself each time you visit, for we know who you are. You are one of us, a lifelong sister of the wailing tent.

Welcome, my wailing sister.

Fondly,
The Sisterhood of the Wailing Tent

CHAPTER ONE

THE BEGINNING

Tears have a wisdom all their own. They come when
a person has relaxed enough to let go to work
through his sorrow. They are the natural bleeding of
an emotional wound, carrying the poison out of the
system. Here lies the road to recovery.
-F. ALEXANDER MAGOUN

Grief and sorrow is as unique to each individual as his or her
fingerprints. In order to fully appreciate one's perspective, it is
helpful to understand one's journey. In this chapter each writer
shares that moment when they lost their precious child to help you
understand when life as they knew it ended, and a new one began.

*

ERICA GALE BELTZ
Erica's 5-year-old son Luke Jordan died in 2005
from a fallen banister in his aunt's driveway

Luke died on a Tuesday. It was nine days after Christmas, and
I remember so clearly sitting on the front porch waiting for him and
his sister to get off the bus. Luke was several steps ahead of his
older sister, Lakin, and I could tell that he was extremely happy. He
was trying to get to me as fast as he could and tripped several times.

He finally reached me, out of breath but smiling so big. He said "Guess what, Mama? I am Star Student this week!"

He was only in kindergarten, but to him this was an honor worthy of a king. He was beaming. His older sister stood back, letting him have his moment. He pulled out a piece of butcher paper and unfolded it, and said "See, it's a poster about me, for my party tomorrow!" I can still see the light that was around him, still feel his excitement and still feel the incredible moment that the three of us shared that day.

We went over to my sister's house, Luke's favorite place to be. He wanted my niece, Ashley, to help him with his poster. I remember he got to ride in the front seat for the first time and he had the window rolled all the way down. He was not tall enough to see over the dash, but he could see out the passenger side window. He looked so proud and so grown up. His short crew cut blew in the wind, and it was really the perfect day.

We arrived at my sister's house to discover that they had only wood glue to stick his pictures to his poster. He said to his cousin, "I can't use wood glue, Ashwee, I'll stick to my poster!" Ashley agreed to go to the store to get the right glue and supplies. I'll never know how I could have left at that moment to go to the gym, but I did. It was just after New Year's and I was going to start working on a new healthier me. After walking into the gym, I panicked because it was crowded. Adam, my boyfriend, and I left and instead went to the store to get snacks for Luke's "All About Me" party the next day at school.

Cousin Ashley returned from the store and pulled to the top of the driveway to park. Luke had been watching from inside and ran outside when he saw their SUV pull up. Ashley's girlfriend, Brittany, was driving. My nephew Tyler was sitting on a skateboard at the bottom of the driveway, wrestling with one of the neighbor boys. The neighbor's oldest son had wedged himself between the garage and some kind of banister structure that separated him from the others. Luke ran down to the boys so he

2

could spread the word that the glue had arrived. The banister weighed about 300 pounds and when Luke stepped on the base of the structure, the combined weight caused it to start to teeter. The banister then fell on Luke, pinning him to the ground.

Ashley and Brittany were already in the driveway when the banister began to fall. My nephew ran inside to get help while Brittany lifted the banister off Luke. My sister Christy was there within seconds, and said she could tell Luke was really hurt. Luke was so tough and so strong. She said he lay there perfectly still. Christy screamed for Shannon, Luke's uncle, and 911 was called immediately. Christy said Luke was trying to say something, but his voice was a faint whisper and she couldn't make out what he said. All Luke's cousins and his sister Lakin stood watching, frozen in place, the oldest was just nine.

The 911 operator asked if Luke was breathing, Shannon didn't think so. They could hear the ambulance close by. Shannon asked if he should start CPR but was instructed not to move Luke. When the EMTs arrived they confirmed that Luke wasn't breathing and his heart was not beating. They began CPR. Life Flight was called and the CPR continued. Still no sign of life. Life Flight arrived but then left. CPR was continued, and Luke was rushed by ambulance to the hospital. My sister rode up front, watching through the window as the EMTs did everything they could. She begged them not to stop. "He is so strong, he will make it! I am not his mommy. Please, please, you can't give up on him!"

The ER doctor met the team outside and got the news that the window without any sign of life had passed. My sister again begged them not to give up. She told the doctor that I didn't yet know about the accident, and that they were looking for me. They took my son into the hospital and went above and beyond the call of duty and continued their effort to save his life.

When I returned to my sister's house, a deputy was waiting for me in the driveway. The deputy asked if I was Luke's mom. I'm not sure if I spoke words or just nodded my head. The deputy said there had been an accident, that Life Flight was called, but not to panic because it was called off. She said Luke's heart was not beating on his own but again not to worry because they were doing that for him and they were helping him breathe. We followed the deputy to the hospital.

When we pulled up it seemed like twenty people were waiting for us, hurrying us out of the car, most of them crying. The chaplain opened my car door. I was taken to a tiny room with two nurses and my sister. They told me what was happening, their voices soft and tears streaming down their faces. I was allowed to go in as they worked on Luke. I honestly had no idea that Luke was dying. I still cannot believe he's gone. They were still doing manual chest compressions and using a handheld pump to breathe for him. The doctor suspected that Luke had internal bleeding, and put a tiny hole in his chest to confirm. Luke was given blood, but it quickly emptied from the tube into a tray outside his chest. The doctor said he could try again, but after that he will have done all that he could do. I asked for my family. They all stood so close around Luke's little body. I told them there was nothing else that could be done. They called the time at 7:30 p.m. Time stopped for our family that day. It was as if our hearts stopped beating at that moment too. I know for certain that mine had.

*

STACY BERNDTSON
Stacy's daughter Cori Joy died in 2003, the day before her
fourth birthday, from an undiagnosed genetic disorder

In April 1999, after nine years of marriage, infertility treatments and failed adoption attempts, I discovered I was pregnant. We were overjoyed that after all this time and effort it had happened without any intervention!

My pregnancy went very well. Other than some gestational prediabetes, there were virtually no problems. On November 15, 1999, I was induced two weeks before my due date because of the diabetic issue. Things went very well at first. When it was time to push, Cori's head came out but her shoulders got stuck. Things quickly got scary. My husband was told to turn off the video camera, and unfortunately he thought they said to leave the room. So I was alone at the most terrifying moment of my life.

Because Cori had little hands, the doctor was able to pull her out but it was believed that perhaps her neck had been broken. It was determined that although it was not broken, she did have a brachial plexus injury. Brachial plexus injuries are caused by damage to nerves in the spine, shoulder, arm and hand. Perhaps due to the traumatic birth, Cori also had some issues with breathing. The first five days of her life were spent in the neonatal unit even though she weighed nine pounds eight ounces at birth! When Cori was released, they told us they did not know how bad the injury was and when or if she would be able to use her left side.

She recovered quite well, however, and really didn't show a favoring of one arm or a pain response those first few weeks at home. At her six-week check, the pediatrician noticed that Cori did not have the typical muscle tone of a newborn. He told us to make an appointment with the pediatric neurologist in town. After spending only five minutes with Cori, the doctor said, "Your daughter has cerebral palsy. This is a birth injury. Get her involved in Early Intervention Services, take her home and love her." At the time this was a devastating diagnosis for us. Years later I would say that I wish it had only been cerebral palsy. Cerebral palsy is a static disorder, which means that it doesn't change nor does it get worse.

This doctor's very snap diagnosis prompted us to take Cori for a second opinion. The new doctor had a different opinion. He believed that it could take up to a year for her to heal completely from her traumatic birth. Cori received Early Intervention Services from the time she was three months old, and over the course of her life we were blessed with many dedicated professionals who took to heart the task of helping her reach her full potential.

At a year old, Cori had not developed much more muscle tone. She could not sit up on her own and she never crawled or walked. So began what would be a three-year journey in search of a diagnosis. That journey took us from USC Hospital to Children's Hospital-Seattle and many laboratories and specialists in between. Our beautiful daughter endured many tests, MRIs, brain scans and EEGs.

An MRI confirmed that Cori did NOT have cerebral palsy. An EEG confirmed she was having myoclonic seizures. A seizure disorder was the only condition that was ever conclusive for Cori, but it did not explain all the other issues she faced nor give us a diagnosis. All the while Cori's therapists believed that she was completely on track cognitively, and she woke each morning with the biggest smile on her sweet face.

When she turned three, we were told that Cori was not getting enough nutrition by mouth. Without muscles it is hard to eat, swallow and digest food. It would often take three hours to feed her one meal. They suggested a feeding tube.

We now believe this was the beginning of the end. After the tube was placed we had a few weeks where life was not completely focused on getting Cori fed. Then she began to have foam coming out her mouth. This obviously affected her ability to breathe. So we had to lay her down on her side so the foam could drain out and keep her airway clear. She was no longer able to be in a sitting position.

Doctors thought it could be acid reflux, but reflux medications did not stop the foaming. Then they suggested a procedure to change her G-tube into a GJ tube which would deposit nutrition from Cori's stomach farther down the intestinal tract. On November 13, 2003, we had an appointment at Children's Hospital in Seattle to go over the process with a GI doctor. Cori had a really good day. When we got home I held her in the chair beside her bed for a short time. We were able to have her sitting upright for only a small amount of time before the foaming would start. Steve stood beside the chair. This was not our typical routine, but for some reason we did this that night.

Cori knew the hand signs for "yes" and "no." I asked her, "Cori do you know how much Mommy and Daddy love you?" She formed her little hand into a fist and pumped up and down, the sign for "yes." I then asked, "Cori do you love your Mommy and Daddy?" She pumped her fist up and down again, "yes." We kissed her and laid her down on her side. We placed the oximeter on Cori to signal us if her oxygen level dropped, meaning a possible airway obstruction.

The next day, November 14, 2003, was the day before Cori's fourth birthday. Steve got up at 6 a.m. to take a shower. He checked on her; she was awake and gave him a smile. He adjusted her in bed and went into the bathroom. While in the shower, Steve heard a beep from the monitor we took everywhere with us. He said it was a different sound than what we would hear when her oxygen saturations dropped. He went into Cori's room. She was not breathing and was bluish, 911 was called. They worked on her for what seemed a long time. They were able to get her heart started and took her to the hospital.

At the hospital Cori was intubated and not breathing on her own. They did various tests which did not really give us any answers. We were able to gather family around, as well as her pediatrician. While they were arranging an air flight to Seattle, there came a time when I knew from just looking at her that she was already halfway to heaven at 6 o'clock that morning. I told them to give me my baby. So they took all the machines off and gave her to me. I rocked her and sang to her, and I believe that in those moments she took her first steps as she ran from my arms into the arms of our Lord Jesus.

*

KARI BROWN
Kari's 2-year-old daughter Dominique (Deedee)
died in 2014 from obstructive sleep apnea

Dominique Faith was born two months early as a late Christmas gift on December 28, 2011. She weighed only three pounds ten ounces. We fell in love with her immediately. Deedee stayed in the NICU for four months, undergoing battles with viruses and subsequent surgeries to help her survive. She eventually was discharged from the NICU on May 3, a day after Brandon's (my fiancé, her father) birthday.

Deedee struggled to eat and speak but picked up her own talents in other ways. She communicated through American Sign Language since she was hard of hearing like myself. Brandon is also deaf, so we were elated to see that Deedee was comfortable with signing as the means of communication. Every night, Deedee would have to sleep at an angle because she had obstructive sleep apnea. I always worried that she would somehow pass away during the night because her airway became constricted. Our worries faded away as her survival rate increased. We fell so much in love with this bundle of joy that I decided to stay home and provide all her care, since she needed extra attention. We still didn't feel right for Dominique to be sleeping in her own bed with all the problems she had, so we had her sleep with us, in the middle.

One morning, while Brandon and Dominique were still asleep, I woke up and noticed that Deedee was breathing funny. I woke up Brandon, we both checked Deedee and thought she was okay. Brandon returned to sleep, and I got up to make coffee. As I was putting away Deedee's toys in her bedroom, she got down from bed and ran toward me with her little hands around her fragile neck. Her precious face was turning blue, and she attempted to cry, but nothing was coming out of her mouth. When I bent down to pick her up, she collapsed.

It felt as my heart stopped beating for that whole day when she collapsed. I ran over to Brandon with her in my arms and woke him up. We both laid her down and attempted CPR. Nothing was working. We screamed her name, we cried out loud, we called 911. but nothing was bringing her back. And then Deedee took one last attempt to breathe, and stopped. It felt like I could feel her soul leaving her body. Like she was already gone. I couldn't accept that, I couldn't comprehend that. I needed her and she needed me. She was my world, the light of my life, the reason to live.

The ride in the ambulance to the hospital felt like we were going five miles per hour. The EMT driver attempted to keep me calm, but something was telling me that she was already gone. That she would never come back into my arms again. We arrived at the hospital, but the nurses kept us at a distance. Brandon sat down in a chair because he felt sick, crying and pleading. I never felt so numb, wailing, screaming for my baby to come back to me. After some time, one of the nurses came over to us with tears in her eyes. Right then and there, I knew our baby Dominique was forever gone. I disagreed, I denied the fact that she was gone. I begged the nurse to do something, anything to save her. The nurse couldn't respond, but offered to let us hold Dominique one last time. We held her. And cried, cried and cried. I kept begging Dominique to please wake up and come back to us. But she never did.

An autopsy later revealed that she had suffered from a constricted airway. Our biggest fear actually came true. I blamed myself for not doing more for Deedee, for not disagreeing with the doctors and taking action when I knew something was still wrong. For not waking up Dominique that morning when she was breathing funny.

*

TANISHA CALDWELL
Tanisha's 23-year-old son Tariq (Jay)
died in a car accident in 2015

I will never forget the day: June 29. It started out as a normal day, warm, bright, and the sun was shining brightly! My husband had a doctor's appointment, so I took him to work and then came home to lay down awhile. My daughter came to me and asked, "Ma! Have you talked to Jay?" I replied no, I called him Sunday but he didn't answer. I then asked her why. As the words came from her mouth I felt as if I had walked into a nightmare! Jay had been in a car accident.

My son was of age, and didn't live at home so police didn't contact us. His phone was damaged, so I believe his contacts couldn't be retrieved. There were three other people in the car, and their families were notified. The accident was on the news and in the newspaper. We found out on the internet. Sad but true. My daughter saw it and informed me. I jumped out of bed to reach for my phone to check, and it was as if my world was crumbling. This can't be true! This cannot be happening! Not to me! Not my family! Lord, please don't let this be true! Please! No! I scrambled to call my husband at work. I just didn't know what to do. I felt lost. I wanted time to stop and go back, so this would not be real. I called the authorities, trying to get information. When the officer asked who was with me, and then said he was going to send over an officer, I knew my worst fear was a reality. My sweet baby Tariq was gone.

We gave him a beautiful homegoing service on July 9, 2015. One of the hardest days of my life.

*

LYNDA CHELDELIN FELL
Lynda's 15-year-old daughter Aly
died in a car accident in 2009

August 5, 2009, dawned like any other lazy summer morning, with a serene sunrise that created little rainbow prisms in the fresh morning dew. Our fifteen year-old teenage daughter, Aly, rarely slept in. A competitive swimmer, she rose like clockwork at 5 a.m. six days a week for early morning practice. Wrapping her favorite fuzzy blue blanket around her small five-foot two-inch frame, she grabbed her bulky swim bag and crept downstairs to wait for her daddy.

The drive into town every morning was a treasured father-daughter time. Classic rock from the truck radio played softly in the background while Aly rested her sleepy head on Lammy, her favorite stuffed animal she favored as a pillow. On this morning, the seventeen-minute trip to the pool was nothing out of the ordinary. "Bye-bye, daddy, love you," she softly murmured as she and her bulky swim bag slid out the truck door, leaving Lammy and the fuzzy blue blanket to fill her empty seat. "Bye-bye, Lovey. Love you. Have a good day," my husband tenderly replied. He watched fondly as his youngest daughter made her way across the parking lot before disappearing through the aquatic center door. My husband usually enjoyed their quiet morning trips to the pool together but this morning, as he drove away, a dreadful, ominous feeling swept over him. And it was there to stay.

The day's itinerary held promise and excitement for Aly. Following morning practice, a handful of senior swimmers planned to carpool to Seattle to watch the U.S. Open, a championship long course meet, home of the 1990 Goodwill Games. Aly had competed in this pool many times herself. But today she and her teammates would instead be spectators, watching the nation's top swimmers compete for a qualifying spot in the Olympics, one of Aly's life goals.

It was an exciting day, and I heard from Aly several times, her voice always full of giddy teenage excitement. Although glad the kids enjoyed the field trip, by day's end I was anxious for their return.

As day gave way to evening, and evening to dusk, a brilliant full moon eased its way over the horizon to hang high and bright in the dark summer sky. Our other kids were out that evening, offering my husband and me some rare quiet time.

At 10:20 p.m., Aly called home one final time. The two parent drivers had gotten the kids to within thirty minutes of our local pool, the planned rendezvous point. Aly and two boys, Donovan and Patrick, would continue the final leg home alone, with eighteen-year-old Donovan at the wheel. Aly had deep respect for Donovan, a quiet yet popular swimmer with a strong work ethic and, like Aly, greatly admired for a powerful butterfly stroke. Just weeks away from starting his senior year in high school, he was a solid team leader and well respected by all. Closer in age to Aly was Patrick, a favorite teammate both in the pool and out. He and Aly immensely enjoyed their spirited friendship and on that fateful night, rather than sitting "shotgun" next to Donovan, Patrick chose to sit next to Aly in the back seat, a move that would save his life.

Aly confirmed on the phone that they were just leaving Burlington, thirty minutes away, and we agreed to meet in the local pool's parking lot as planned. As always, I told her I loved her and would see her shortly. I hung up the phone, kissed my husband goodbye, and headed out into the night alone.

Because of the late hour, the drive to the pool was quiet and peaceful. Arriving in the deserted parking lot of the aquatic center, I sat in my husband's truck playing on my cellphone to pass the short time until the swimmers arrived.

As 11 p.m. drew near, the day's fatigue began to set in. I texted Aly to see how close they were, but received no reply. Waiting a few minutes more, I called her phone. She didn't answer. Waiting a few more minutes, I tried again, then twice, three times. Still no answer. Believing her phone battery had died from overuse during the long day, I had no choice but to sit and wait.

Suddenly, startling me in the dark, my cellphone rang from an unknown number. "Hello?" I answered, wondering who would be calling at that hour. "Lynda, this is Sean....Donovan's dad. There's been an accident. We are on our way now, 911 is guiding us." Sure that it was nothing more than a minor fender-bender, I didn't panic as I told Donovan's dad that I too would make my way to the kids. I drove out of the pool parking lot and was soon heading south on the freeway toward Burlington, a thirty-minute drive away. I called my husband. "Honey, the kids have been in an accident. I'm sure it's nothing, but I'm heading that way now." Panicked, my husband pleaded with me to come pick him up, but since that was in the opposite direction, it meant a delay of at least forty-five minutes. I told him that would take too long and I wanted to get to Aly as soon as possible, but promised to call him as soon as I was by her side. He pleaded again, but not wanting to waste precious time, I held firm and kept driving south.

I called Donovan's parents back to let them know I wasn't far behind, hoping they could tell me exactly where the accident was, but this time I received no answer. I tried again and again; no answer. I then remembered they had called 911 for directions. I decided to try the same. I dialed the number and calmly explained who I was and why I was calling. The emergency dispatcher was hesitant, but agreed to give me directions. I asked if she knew which hospital the kids had been transported to, but she wouldn't offer me any further information. I reassured myself that the accident was minor, and hospital transport probably wasn't warranted. The dispatcher then shared that support staff was on the scene. Support staff? How strange. Why in the world would support staff be dispatched to a fender-bender? My brain just simply didn't comprehend the possibility of anything more than a minor accident.

Despite the bright full moon, I soon got lost on the dark and unfamiliar roads, and once again called the 911 dispatcher for directions. Finally, in the distance, I saw the lights of multiple emergency vehicles. But this accident was far too serious, and didn't even remotely fit the scenario that played in my head. I assumed I had come upon the wrong accident but, feeling confused and having nowhere to turn the truck around, I approached the accident scene intending to ask directions. I slowly drove up to the emergency roadblock and an official stepped into the road to greet me.

From that moment forward, I recall the events as if in a dream, like little snapshots blending together as my world shattered with each spoken word. I rolled down my window, but my voice left me as the official and I stared at each other. Finally I managed to utter two tiny words: "My daughter." The words came out in a flat statement, not a question, and the officer stood outside my window staring at me. Finally, as his eyes searched mine, he quietly asked, "Fifteen?" "Yes," I confirmed. "Alyssa Fell?" he continued in our hesitant exchange. "Yes," I mumbled as I stared at him. The officer continued standing outside my window, his eyes piercing mine. He was unsure what to do with me. Others approached my window and at that moment, with all those faces gazing hesitantly at me, I knew.

That was the very moment when my treasured motherhood, as I knew it, became every parent's worst nightmare. The gathering group grew larger as I quietly mumbled my final query, "She's here….isn't she?" It was more of a declaration than a question, and all those faces continued to stare at me. The night became very quiet, but no one replied. "Take me to my daughter," I softly yet firmly commanded. Not one person moved, all frozen in place, as they watched my face for signs of hysteria. "Take me to my daughter," I repeated. Not waiting one second more, I opened the truck door, climbed out, and began making my way toward the two crumpled cars in the nearby field. I was vaguely aware that the group was following me, although no one dared stop me.

Instinctively, like a wild animal searching for her young, I knew where I would find my baby girl. On the ground, next to a rear passenger door, my precious teenage daughter with the smooth tan skin and long blonde hair, the strong swim shoulders and tiny waist, my stellar student with fierce determination and dedication to reach the Olympics, was strapped to a backboard and draped by a stark white sheet. I knelt down beside her as my eyes surveyed the car's blood-spattered interior. Reaching across her covered body, I searched for her hand under the sheet's edge. Finding it, I held it as I sat next to my beloved Lovey, too shocked to cry. My daughter's soft skin was still warm, and I could feel random muscles twitching through the sheet. I fought the urge to lift the white sheet from her sweet face for fear of what I might see. Instead, I looked down at her cute little feet peeking out. I thought to myself, "Where are your shoes, silly girl?" My brain failed to absorb the reality before me.

Behind me stood a large group of emergency responders and law enforcement officers, hushed respectively as they took in the scene. As I held Aly's small hand in mine, I could feel the powerful and raw compassion from those standing behind me. Then, for a brief moment, I looked up into nothingness, nothing but the dark field that stretched before us, and that is when I saw her. My beloved grandmother, who had passed thirteen years before and from whom Aly had inherited her small stature, had an arm around Aly and was gently leading her away. Aly was looking over her shoulder at me as she walked beside the great-grandmother she never knew. Walking away from me, forever.

My cellphone's intruding ring suddenly pierced the stillness. My robotic body automatically answered. It was Jamie. He was impatient, wondering why in the world I hadn't yet called him. In a monotone, I remember telling him Aly hadn't made it, that I was with her now in the field, next to the crumpled cars. I don't remember his reply or the rest of the conversation.

Everything from that point forward became a blur, and would remain so for many months. Like little snapshots of time, I only remember glimpses from the remainder of that night. Being led to the hospital by support personnel. Jamie arriving at the hospital, driven down by our brother-in-law. Sitting together in a small private hospital room, discussing Aly's organ donations with the coroner. Kissing Donovan and Patrick on their foreheads as they both lay crying. Telling them both that it will be all right, hoping I could convince myself of the same. Of walking out of the hospital door at 4 a.m. with an ER full of people watching, my legs threatening to give way as we exited into the night. Leaving for home. Together. Without our precious daughter. As the bright full moon gave way to dawn.

*

JACQUELYN CRUZ
Jacquelyn's 24-year-old daughter Jenna
died in 2012 from pulmonary edema

On November 16, 2012, I stood at the top of the stairs and hugged my daughter for the last time. I said all the usual parenting words: "Watch the speed limit, no texting and driving, call me when you get there," and of course "I love you, Jen." She did arrive safe and sound and did text me of their safe arrival.

You see, Jenna did not want to go on this weekend trip with her fairly new girlfriend of three months, but I talked her into it. Jenna suffered from social anxiety and meeting new people. I assured her the weekend would be fun. Her new friend Katie was very patient with Jenna's social anxiety. Katie's brother and sister-in-law would be there as well as cousins, all about the same age. I spoke to Jenna on the morning of the seventeenth and she sounded great! They were riding four-wheelers, and the house was so pretty and it reminded her of her grandparents' house in the country. I was relieved to hear she was having fun.

16

What I haven't told you about Jenna is that she wasn't in the greatest of health. She had high blood pressure, borderline type II diabetes, sleep apnea and she was overweight. Her father and I had numerous conversations with her about her health, but it always fell on deaf ears. The one action she did take was to get a CPAP machine to help her sleep better. Two weeks before the trip, her mask broke. Without the mask, her snoring was so loud. I begged her to call for the replacement mask, but she never did. When she didn't use the mask, she became very tired easily. My Jenna laid down for a nap on November 17, and never woke up.

Do I blame myself for talking her into going on the trip? Most days, yes. But, like any parent, I was encouraging my child to explore new things, meet new people and have fun. Never in a million years did I think she wouldn't come back to me. Two years, nine months, and two days, and I still have trouble breathing every day around 6:15 p.m., the same time Jenna passed away.

*

MICHELLE DETWILER
Michelle's 19-year-old daughter Emily
died in 2014 due to congenital complications

After giving birth to a son with medical challenges, my husband and I chose to provide foster care for medically fragile babies for the state of Washington. Emily was adopted into our family through that program, joining us when she was released from the hospital at six months of age. We were told that Emily would not live very long. We poured our life and love into that fragile baby and she grew into a beautiful teen despite her many medical challenges.

At age seventeen, Emily had surgery to correct lifelong problems with her bowels. The surgery was performed, but it didn't heal correctly. It split apart and the day before her planned discharge home, Emily needed emergency surgery to repair her bowel. That surgery was the first of many she endured over the next four months of hospitalization. Although not expected to live through the recovery of the first two surgeries, Emily made it into the ICU and continued on the very long road to recovery. She had a hole in her gut which took many months to heal. And there were many ups and downs during that time.

When Emily came home from the hospital she was not the same as she had been earlier in her life. Where there once was a smiling young lady sitting in her wheelchair, we now had a tired daughter who needed nutrition infused into her veins through an IV pump because her bowels still did not work. I think we knew at that time it was the beginning of the end.

Emily's health continued to waver for a year after that surgery, and then she began to decline. When she was in her last week of life, it was as if my eyes were opened and I realized how short her time actually was. I called the doctor and asked for hospice care. Although Emily did have nursing care at home because of her medical challenges, I did not know anything about death and dying and what to expect. I needed hospice there.

Unfortunately, due to confusion over payment for hospice services, we did not receive any hospice benefits for Emily until her last hour of life. In that last week before she died, when I fully understood that she was headed for heaven, I notified my family and friends. Some came to visit with her, and others sent notes via Facebook and email. I was in shock and could hardly believe we were actually coming to the end of her life. I couldn't think and wanted to hold her and tell her how much I loved her. We took pictures and some video, and filled her last days with favorite music and movies. My mother had made plans to come visit Emily at the end of the week. Emily loved her grandmother so much. But I didn't know if Grandma was going to be here soon enough to see Emily one last time. So I fixed up a Skype connection so they could talk to each other. That was the last time Emily had her eyes open and the last time she smiled. And I got a picture of that last smile! Oh, how I cherish that picture.

On Saturday when Grandma was to arrive, the hospice worker finally showed up…. late. Emily was breathing erratically and I knew it was going to be her last weekend, maybe even her last day with us.

Our family and two close friends joined us, along with her two favorite nurses. The nursing shift change was happening, and when hospice arrived they both stayed to get the new orders from hospice. I had stopped some of Emily's medications the day before, knowing that she didn't need them any longer. Emily was peaceful and not in need of any medical intervention for pain. My husband had gone to the train station to pick up Grandma. Our older sons came to visit their sister as she lay quietly in bed. The television played her favorite cartoon movies, and her brothers sat telling her about the exciting parts that she had always enjoyed.

As her breathing slowed and her heart monitor began to alarm we decided to just turn it off. My husband had not returned with Grandma yet, and I was beginning to worry that Emily would die before they arrived. We encouraged Emily for more vigorous breaths with "Grandma's coming! Grandma's coming!" And she made it, staying alive till my mother and husband arrived. One of the nurses ran to the driveway and told them to forget the luggage and just come into the house. Grandma sat by Emily's bedside and chatted with her for a few minutes while I whispered in Emily's other ear to go with Jesus when she saw him. I wanted to reassure her that it was okay, that we would be okay, and she could go.

Grandma said, "Well, Emily, it looks like you are getting tired now so I'll let you go to sleep. Good night, Emily, we'll see you in the morning." Dad sat down next to Emily and held her hand. He whispered sweetness to her as our family stood around. Emily took her last breath and then she moved on to heaven.

I could never imagine losing a part of my heart, and yet it's happened. There is nothing that can compare to the loss of a child. The only light in the dark tunnel of grief is my hope in the Lord who made heaven and Earth. I know that I will also go to where she has gone. I would not have the strength to carry on except for my faith in Jesus. Faith - it's a rock to stand on, an eternal anchor.

Our daughter's memory is always with me daily, moment by moment. Grief that has been so severe used to cut at me like a knife. I often wondered if I would ever stop hurting, stop crying. But it's happening little by little. I still have days that are hugely sad, but more and more days that are better. I know life isn't this way for everyone who experiences grief but I'm so thankful that mine is. My vision now is to be able to give some measure of hope back to families who are grieving and in the same spot I'm in. One can never truly know what the experience is like except by walking down the same path.

I'm here, I've survived the death of a child, and there's hope. You can go on. I'm living proof of that. You can go on.

*

ANNAH ELIZABETH
Annah's son Gavin Michael aspirated on his meconium
during the delivery and died 26 minutes following his birth

I recall three distinct childhood memories: I wanted to change the world, to end hate, injustice and suffering. I dreamed of being a writer. I wanted one day to be a mom, but not an old mom, so I was going to have those babies before I turned thirty.

Like most teenagers, I experienced the normal worries about not being good enough, not smart enough and not pretty enough. And like many a teenager, though most people never knew how I felt on the inside, I struggled to fit in. I graduated high school, went to college, found a job and met a boy.

A whirlwind romance later, I found myself five hundred miles away in another state with a new job and a failed relationship. My parents offered to come move me back home, but for some unknown reason, I chose to stay in this new town. Initially, I stayed because I hoped that my beau and I would work things out, but one day I woke up and realized I deserved so much more than the manipulation he'd offered. Afterward? I didn't give it a thought until years later. You see, I never believed in fate or destiny, and then a man came to fix the broken lock on my front door and my life was forever changed.

That handyman, Warren, and I quickly became friends. Nearly four months later we went out on our first date, and four years after that we were newly married and expecting our first child. I was twenty-six years old and life was rolling along right according to my master plan. That pregnancy progressed without so much as a hiccup, and I worked right up until the day before I delivered.

We thought we'd prepared for everything. We'd read parenting books, followed prenatal advice and I swallowed those enormous vitamins. We'd baby-proofed the house, prepared the nursery, pre-washed the clothing, sterilized the baby's things, picked out names and attended Lamaze classes.

In one of our later birthing classes, the instructor addressed the group like this: "I know you're all in happy places with even happier times ahead, but I want you to think about something. What would you do if something happened to the baby? I know it's not anything you want to think about, but you really should spend a minute or two discussing it." "What would you do if something happened to the baby?" I asked Warren on the way home that night. "I don't know. You?" he replied. "I don't know either," I responded. We didn't talk about it again. Until we had to.

On May 11, 1990, my labor progressed exactly as all the doctors and books had said it would. Shortly after the nurse hooked me up to the monitors, all of that changed. An emergency Cesarean section later, doctors discovered that my son had aspirated on his meconium, the baby's first stool. While Warren sat in the waiting room and I lay asleep under anesthesia, a medical team worked to save my son's life. Gavin Michael, unable to overcome his circumstances, died twenty-six minutes after he quietly entered this world.

Those early days, weeks and months are a blur, but I do remember one thing clearly. Even in those earliest mourning days as I recovered in the hospital, I knew I didn't want to spend a lifetime grieving my son. I didn't know what that meant, what it looked like on the other side, or how I was ever going to get there, but I knew what I didn't want.

The casseroles dried out. The well of visitors and sympathy cards dried up. I grieved. I cried. I smiled when I saw a rainbow. I felt like I'd betrayed my son's memory. I returned to work. I worried I'd forget my child. I pleaded with the universe for understanding. I asked questions. I found a few answers. I blamed myself.

I'd always known I was going to be a mom, so the second the doctor gave Warren and me the go-ahead, we began trying to conceive. I'm one of those "Fertile Myrtles." I've always joked that all Warren had to do was unzip his pants and voila! I was pregnant. Almost eight weeks into that next pregnancy, I miscarried. I went into an emotional tailspin. I questioned God, my own spirituality, my role as a woman, a mother, a wife and my place on Earth. And I stayed true to my plan. I was going to be a mom, one way or another. Warren and I signed on and began the lengthy, tedious process of becoming foster parents. When my obstetrician gave us the green light, well, you know, our bedroom came alive again.

Flash forward seven years. I'd had two more complicated but successful pregnancies, a second miscarriage, had spent six weeks in a psych ward for severe depression, and was seven months pregnant when I discovered that my best friend and my husband were having an affair. I sat slumped in a heap against my washing machine for hours. This is what I later wrote about that morning: "Every piece of hope I'd ever held onto before had just been shredded. My faith in people, my trust; my belief in God, in dignity--every spiritual, emotional, social, physical, and academic part of me lay in a heap to be tossed out with the garbage. It never made it to the garbage. I recycled it instead."

22

The part of me that knew I didn't want to spend a lifetime in mourning urged me to get up off that floor and it screamed at me to do something. I eventually did. I pulled myself up to a standing position and reached out, once again, for help.

All those unanswered questions I'd ignored when work and diapers and preschool and Scouts and sports got in the way came back with a vengeance. I knew that if I were to get to the other side I had to give those queries serious attention and I had to find those answers.

One main question stood above the rest. How can some people survive death or destruction or disease and go on to live happy, healthy lives, while others of similar circumstance succumb to despair or, worse, drugs or suicide, and are forever held back from living their best lives?

These are some of the realizations I discovered: Grief encompasses much more than death. Though we have countless resources to help us with our bereavement, we have little other than platitudes to guide us once we decide our grief is no longer serving us a purpose. We need to ADD the healing piece. Healing doesn't mean that what happened is okay; rather, it means that we can be okay in the face of it. We're all born with everything we need to heal. Though the details of our resources and our circumstances look different on each of us, the crux of the matter is the same: We have all encountered some event that has led to grief which wants to be healed. And right next door are neighbors who are also suffering and allies who can help us on our own journey to healing.

*

WENDY EVANS
Wendy's 21-year-old son Kyle died in 2009
from diabetes when his insulin pump malfunctioned

Kyle was diagnosed with type I diabetes when he was fourteen years old. Because of his age, the diabetes diagnosis was really not a part of his identity. His daily care was somewhat overwhelming with fluctuating blood sugars and numerous shots. Eventually Kyle's doctor prescribed an insulin pump for his care. Initially this medical device was a great part of his treatment plan. When Kyle was in college he worked in one of my offices part time and attended classes at campus nearby. One Sunday night he came over to do laundry, something he often did every week. He seemed fine and even helped us with a flooring project we were working on.

The next day Kyle called me after class and said he was not feeling well, and wanted to go home and sleep. He did not show up for work the next day or call. I went to his apartment and asked the management to let me in. We found Kyle dead on his kitchen floor.

*

BONNIE FORSHEY
Bonnie's 16-year-old son Billy died in 1993
from an overdose of prescription drugs

My son Billy never made it through his teens. Our world was turned upside down due to suicide. I still do not know if it was intentional or not. There are so many unanswered questions. Billy was a very kind and funny soul. He was always giving his belongings to others who were less fortunate than him. That is what I remember most, his generosity. He could light up a room with his smile and blue eyes. You could never have a bad day with him around. He was my practical joker. He was flesh of my flesh, blood of my blood, and was my heart and soul.

On October 30, 1993, I lost him. He was forever sixteen. I lost my sanity and my self-identity. The person that I am now is not the same person I used to be. I wear a mask, fake my emotions, pretend everything is okay, when it will never be okay again. Billy started sleeping a lot, he told me it was because he stayed up too late. I never knew that it was because he had taken antidepressants out of the trash can. His stepfather's old pills, Sinequan, was toxic and Billy was taking them. I never knew until it was too late. I was a nurse, I should have known, should have seen, but I didn't.

Approximately one week prior to the loss of my son, I began feeling very anxious. I had very bad premonitions and my heart knew that something was about to happen, but I never would have believed it would be the loss of my child. I worked the 3 to 11 p.m. shift that week, and I remember frantically calling my house at night to check on my son. I went as far as to clock out just to come home and check on him. It was out of my hands. Those dreaded events unfolded, and I couldn't do a thing to stop them.

We were at home when Billy came out of his room. He opened his mouth to show me all the pills and immediately drank a glass of water. He then ran into his bedroom, locking the door behind him. I got on the phone to call 911, and then called Billy's father. His father had left us when the kids were toddlers, and didn't want to be bothered. I heard a faint voice cry out on the extension phone, "Dad, you will never have to worry about me again. I am dying." CLICK. I kicked the door down and held Billy while waiting for the ambulance. I kissed him and told him how much I loved him.

My last memories are horrific: waiting for the ambulance, he becoming unconscious in my arms...it was all too late. We waited in the emergency room, and of course I thought it would all be fine. We treated overdoses on a daily basis and they all recovered and went home...it was the gunshot victims that didn't make it. Wrong! Then I remember the doctor taking us back to a quiet room. I thought he was going to tell me that Billy was fine...wrong again. My whole world came crashing down when the doctor told me they had done all that they could, but Billy coded three times and was gone. We were then led into a room where my precious child lay on a gurney. He was intubated and there was charcoal all over his face. Billy's clothing had been cut from his body and was handed to me. He was forever still. Never again would I hear his laughter or see his smiling blue eyes light up. I would never again hear the words, "I love you, Mom," or hear him call me "shorty," because he had towered above me and thought it was so funny. I was and forever will be changed. I miss the very essence of his soul.

When the doctor told me that Billy was gone, my mind could not process the words. I fell completely and totally apart. He told me that the medicine they had given Billy to reverse the effects of the ones he had taken had a synergistic (incompatible) effect, and my son had coded three times and died. Someone pulled the doctor aside to tell him that I was a nurse. He immediately tried to retract those words. He also told me that he would not give me a sedative, that I would have to go through the natural grieving process. I was so distraught and in shock, and was being treated terribly. The doctor really tried to push me over the edge by having me "Baker Acted." I was placed in four-way leather restraints. That was no way to treat a grieving mother. I was in that bed for twenty-four hours, crying my eyes out, unable to comprehend the horror of the events that had unfolded. The doctor told me that someone else would have to handle my son's funeral arrangements, because I would not be there.

The following day I was transferred to a psych facility where I was to be held for seventy-two hours. The van got into an accident, and they had to call another van to transport me. I couldn't believe what was happening. I felt as if I were outside of my body, watching everything unfold. Finally we arrived at the destination and they took me inside. There was no doctor there because it was a weekend and they refused to call one in. There were also no beds, so I had to lie on the floor with six other people who really did belong there.

The following day a psychiatrist did come in, and when he found out what had happened to me he was furious. He said I did not belong there and was very angry that no one had called him. Needless to say, I was released and went home to the place that screamed loneliness. Billy's scent was all around me. His clothing and belongings were there, never to be touched by him again.

I had to wait for the autopsy to be completed before I could lay my precious child to rest. Billy had been nicknamed "the peacemaker" by his friends. He never believed in gangs and always let everyone know that. I watched members from two gangs come together at his service. They all took off their colored bandanas and placed them in the casket with Billy. They kissed their index fingers and touched them to his heart.

When I received the autopsy report, it showed charcoal in both lungs as a result of the tube placement being wrong. I have been able to forgive that doctor. It took some time, but I know my son would want me to. I spend my time speaking with bereaved parents and also to troubled teens. I share my story and hope that it can help them, maybe even save a life.

*

TALIA GATO
Talia's 8-year-old daughter Poppy
died in 2009 in a car accident

It was a cold, sunny, ordinary winter day. It snowed earlier in the week, though most of it had melted away. I drove on that country road so many times. My two daughters were in the car with me, doing routine weekly errands. When my tires hit the same bridge we crossed nearly every day, we skidded into the path of an oncoming truck. So this is the part where I can't write the whole story of the accident. The accident was so horrific I can't write it. It is all in my head and I relive the story over and over again. I can see everything, smell it, taste it, and feel it. I see everyone there trying to help me, and me helping them. I even remember what I wore, and what they wore. My daughter Poppy wasn't moving. I prayed and prayed. One blonde EMT prayed with me. Please, God, don't take her! Please! I remember it like it happened yesterday. I called my husband to tell him what was happening. I didn't even recognize my voice. I didn't know this woman.

I relive it every day. It comes across my thinking daily. It is my private agony. I have learned to endure every day. It is an agony that I go to sleep on, and wake up with. Each time I wake up, I realize one daughter is gone. But it's not a dream. It's my new reality. I have never told my story completely, just parts of all the different things that happened that day. On the one hand, I believe death is sacred, as are the moments just before and after.

Maybe I will tell my complete story one day, when I am ready. But it would have to be verbally, in person, and only to the ones who have earned a free entry, the others who belong to this tribe of loss, the other parents who know this pain intimately. My story belongs only to the others who have fought this war in their own minds, and have to endure it.

Sometimes, not all the time, but I feel this world keeps turning and I am watching it like a movie. It continues to go round and round, and keeps turning, but I am standing still.

*

DAPHNE GREER
Daphne's 5-year-old daughter Lydia died in 2008 in a
car accident during a routine morning commute

It was a beautiful midsummer morning. The sun was peeking brightly over the tree tops as we drove down the highway. The fresh smell of summer was in the air. We had made this daily commute for years, the same stretch of twenty-mile highway en route to day care and my work. I enjoyed this time with the children, listening to their entertaining stories, questions about life, and hearing their sibling banter in the back seat. They would often hold hands, sing, or draw and color to pass the time.

But on this beautiful midsummer morning, just a few short miles from our home, we were involved in a two-vehicle accident. My five-year-old daughter Lydia passed away as a result. My son and I had minor injuries.

How was I to live this new life I had been given? I did not sign up for it, yet it unsuspectingly landed in my lap, as life so often does. In the midst of loss, especially when it is new, taking one breath at a time is often all we can do. As time would go on, I would somehow learn to manage the intense grief and pain, miraculously and subconsciously training myself to live with the "new normal." I never wanted a "new normal." I wanted my old life back.

My journey has been anything but easy. In the seven years since the accident, it has been difficult, challenging, immensely painful, yet all the while full of amazement and awe. I have changed both inside and out, and my passions and views on life have turned, making me appreciate every day I have been given.

*

KORBY HAVE
Korby's 17-year-old daughter Taylor (Tayla)
died in 2013 in a car accident

My daughter Tayla Marie was an outgoing seventeen-year-old who was just ending her junior year of high school. On May 13, 2013, Tayla and her boyfriend made plans to meet for a late movie to discuss their recent fight. Despite the fact that it was a school night, I allowed her to go. I helped her get ready by braiding her hair, told her I loved her and to drive carefully, and watched her drive away. I can still picture her face as she looked at me and waved while driving away.

The details of what happened while they were at the movies are still unclear but it is believed that they left the theater at around 11:35 p.m. At 11:48 p.m. I received a text from Tayla's boyfriend letting me know that Tayla was speeding. I didn't want to distract her while she was driving, so I decided to wait until she got home to talk with her. Unfortunately, she never made it home that night.

We live only about fifteen minutes from the theater, so when Tayla hadn't arrived home after thirty minutes I began to call her, thinking she might have stopped by a friend's house. But her phone went right to voice mail and she didn't respond to my texts, which was unusual for Tayla. After unsuccessfully trying to get hold of her, I contacted her boyfriend to see if he knew where she was, but he told me he hadn't seen her since they left each other at the theater. I decided to go look for Tayla, thinking that maybe her car had broken down. As I traveled down the freeway, I could see an accident on the opposite side of the freeway, but because of the barrier I couldn't really see any details. I decided to turn around and investigate. I will never forget the feeling of helplessness when I came upon the crash site and saw Tayla's car. Those images will forever be burned into my brain.

As I got out of the car, I was approached by a highway patrol officer who told me that I couldn't stop here. I explained that the car was my daughter's and I wanted to know where she was. The officer asked me to wait by my car and then left me standing there for what seemed like forever but probably was only about ten minutes. Finally another officer approached me and asked me again to identify myself, which I did, and then I again asked where my daughter was. I will never forget the next words: "I'm very sorry to inform you that your daughter didn't survive the crash." Those words still echo in my head. I remember thinking that they had the wrong family. The officer left me on the side of the road to process what he had just told me, but I couldn't understand how Tayla could be here one minute and gone the next. I remember calling my family and her dad to inform them of what I had just learned. And, in the heat of the moment I called her boyfriend and yelled at him that he was responsible for her death. When the officer approached me again I asked what happened and was told that Tayla was traveling at a high rate of speed – over 100 mph. For some reason, Tayla swerved and then overcorrected causing her to lose control. Her car spun several times before impacting the barrier, then rolled three times and Tayla was ejected.

I was told she wasn't wearing a seatbelt. I have never known my daughter to get into a car without putting on her seatbelt. She would always be the first person to remind others to wear their seatbelts. I am still unsure why she wasn't wearing one that night. I had always talked with Tayla about the dangers of speeding and not wearing her seatbelt, but like many teenagers, Tayla thought she was invincible and that nothing bad would ever happen to her. I too lived in a bubble where I believed that bad things happened to other families, but nothing like that would ever happen to mine. Tayla was my only daughter. Even though her accident happened over two years ago, I still struggle daily with everything I lost when I lost her.

*

DEANA MARTIN
Deana's only two children, 25-year-old Amanda
and 21-year-old Logan, died in a car accident in 2011

On January 18, 2011, my children's stepmother died. We lived in Georgia, and my children made plans to drive to Indiana for the funeral. My daughter's fiancé, Anthony, moved up from Florida to live with us just two weeks prior, and he agreed to drive them. My three-year-old granddaughter was also in tow. The drive went fine, and they made it to Indiana with no problems. The night of the showing, my son Logan called to thank me for the flowers I sent. My ex-husband had three children when I married him, so my children had three half-siblings. None of the children had money, so I sent flowers in their names. Logan and I had been fighting when they left for Indiana, but over the phone Logan thanked me and said he loved me. Less than sixteen hours later, both my children would be dead.

The morning of their stepmother's funeral was hectic. All the relatives from out of town, including my children, stayed with my ex-husband. My daughter's fiancé, Anthony, was the last to get up; he basically threw on his clothes and jumped into the car. Amanda told our three-year-old granddaughter, Armaya, to ride with Uncle Man and said, "It's okay, honey. We are all going to the same place anyway." The caravan of cars left for the funeral home a mere two miles down the road. It was snowing pretty heavily, and just a mile down the road my daughter's car hit a patch of black ice and spun into the path of a semi-truck which hit their car on the passenger

31

side where my daughter sat. The impact from the semi pushed the car down into a ravine where it crashed into a tree.

At 11 a.m. I was returning to my desk from a routine meeting with my boss. I noticed my cellphone had many missed calls from area code 317. I knew that whoever called had tried desperately to reach me; I must have had twenty missed calls. It turns out that the caller was Boo, my ex-husband's middle boy, whom I hadn't spoken to since our divorce fifteen years earlier. His words would change my life forever: "Deana, this is Boo." When I heard who it was, my brain could not compute why he would be calling me, yet I knew something very bad had happened. He said, "Deana, I need to tell you something." I immediately started screaming, "I can't hear this! I can't hear this!" Boo finally said there had been a terrible accident, and Amanda and Logan had died. I asked about Armaya and he said she was fine, that she was not in the car. I asked about Anthony, and Boo said that Anthony was dead too. I asked if Armaya knew what had happened to her mommy, and Boo said he did not know. As soon as I hung up, I called their half-sister Lisa who was at the mortuary with all the children. Most of them had witnessed the accident but were too young to know exactly what happened. I asked Lisa if Armaya, my three-year-old granddaughter, knew about her mommy. She said, "No." I asked Lisa to not let anyone tell Armaya; I needed to be the one to tell her.

My coworkers took me into an empty office. I had to do the inevitable, I had to call family. I called my sister, who could barely hear me through the sobs. All I remember of the conversation is "Jeana, Amanda and Logan are dead. I can't call Mom and Dad. What do I do now?" My sister's travel agent found us flights. Jeana would fly into Atlanta and then fly with me to Indiana. My neighbor came to get me, and I could barely walk so coworkers helped me to the car. My neighbor silently drove to my home, and then helped me get into my robe. I went around and took my children's pictures off the walls and held them while sitting in my mother's recliner. My mother, who lived with me at the time, was also in Indiana for a great-aunt's funeral the week before.

As I sat there in a daze, the rescue team was still trying to cut my children out of the mangled car. I had always asked not to know too much, not to be given details. But I heard enough to piece together an accident scene in my head. Apparently my son was partly ejected through the car's back window. The kids' sister-in-law was an R.N. She and another relative ran down to the scene and held my son as he took his last breaths. The truck driver put a blanket over Logan to protect him from the snow. I am sure Logan knew he was not alone at that moment. I know my daughter and Anthony died on impact, because no one could see them in the mangled car except for my daughter's hand. It took rescue workers six hours to cut my children free from the wreckage. My children died on January 20, 2011, at 9:58 a.m.

The accident was all over the news before I even reached Indiana. Several coworkers came to my home to help me prepare to travel Indiana to bury my children. They helped me pack and made lists of whom to call. Several people said I called them that day, but I don't remember speaking to any of them. My head was filled with nothing but "My children are dead, my children are dead. Now what? How do I do this?" I had the worst pain in my heart and abdomen. I could not eat, I could not drink. All I could do was hold my children's pictures and stare into space.

My friends got me packed and to the airport, and put me in a wheelchair. I don't remember checking bags. My sister met us, took the wheelchair from my friends, and we proceeded to the gate. I remember sitting next to my sister on the plane in silence, staring out the window into the darkness. My nipples hurt so bad, like when a mother is breastfeeding. I instinctively knew this was a physical manifestation of my mourning.

From that point forward, everything became a blur. I remember thinking, "How am I going to do this?" It was similar to that first childbirth experience, when you think "How am I going to do this?" You don't have a clue but you are led innately.

*

MONICA MIRKES
Monica's 30-year-old daughter Marisa
died in 2013 due to Cesarean complications

Having had two energetic boys, we were more than ready for a little girl to complete our family. It was then that my husband was diagnosed and treated for testicular cancer. Our life plans were derailed. There were thoughts of mortality, things that young couples never dream of. We set our goals on Terry getting well and that our life would go on as planned.

When our little girl arrived, we were complete. She was beautiful and her big brothers were in awe of this tiny creature who invaded our home with bows, dolls and dainty dresses. We were perfect. But it was short-lived, for Marisa went into heart failure at two months and was taken to Children's Hospital in Dallas. We were told she had a heart defect, and the goal was to stabilize her until she was big enough for a heart catheterization. Marisa weighed five pounds at birth and had gained only one pound over two months. Ten pounds was the doctor's ideal weight for catheterization; she wouldn't reach that weight until she was eight months old. Marisa was put on digoxin, a drug that would help her heart beat stronger to pump the blood through her body. We were ready to take her home or at least a hotel close to the hospital, as we didn't want to be very far from help. But we never made it out. Marisa started to have a reaction to the medication. What was going on? A resident came in and asked if Marisa's kidneys had been checked. No, there hadn't been any concerns there. He asked me to follow him, and away we went for an x-ray. I sat on a bench while he whisked my baby away. I sat there for what seemed like hours. One nurse came out, another doctor went in, and then another. Two doctors came out talking, unaware of who I was. I heard one say, "We have a grave problem. Her cardiologist has to be brought in." I've entered the Twilight Zone, and I am alone.

I am asked to return to Marisa's room and told the doctors will be in shortly. Her nurse knows nothing, so she holds my hand while we wait for someone to tell us something. They bring Marisa back along with what seems like everyone. The room is full. I sit there while they tell me my daughter has less than half of a kidney, and she is missing the second one. We are in trouble. Marisa was having a toxic reaction to the heart medication; it would have to be reduced to almost nothing. We just wanted to buy time for her to get bigger so we could fix her heart. We were told she would need a kidney transplant because her stunted kidney couldn't last. When would the ax fall? It would all depend, and would be a roll of the dice for the next seventeen years.

It took Marisa longer to get over simple colds. She had no stamina. She actually wore out her clothes because it took forever for her to grow out of them! One good perk was always the front row for class pictures.

Fast-forward through complications, illnesses, noncompliant school districts, hospitalizations, and relatives who kept telling me to give Marisa cranberry juice. She was in high school when her kidney started to fail. We were lucky that Marisa could have a transplant and not have to go on dialysis. She underwent a kidney transplant in March 2000. I donated the first kidney but she lost it, and we almost lost her due to complications. Her older brother Aaron donated his kidney two weeks later. Now life is looking good, and Marisa gets to come home. She is amazed at how good food tastes; she has energy! She starts driving to high school with her younger sister. And then Marisa starts getting tired, she can't walk even short distances without sitting to catch her breath. What is happening? Five months after her transplant Marisa is diagnosed with PTLD, post-transplant lymphoproliferative disorder, cancer caused by the medication she was taking. A sad complication of transplants. My daughter has non-Hodgkin's lymphoma. A tumor the size of a grapefruit is in Marisa's chest constricting her breathing. Anything that could go wrong did in fact go wrong.

Again fast-forward through your worst nightmares. Six months of chemo and home schooling, but Marisa makes it her goal to graduate with her class. And she does. She then starts college and follows her dream of becoming a social worker. But once again, she is hit with a second diagnosis of cancer, and eighty percent of her liver must be removed.

Marisa meets someone, marries, and earns a Master's in social work. She is doing so well that her doctor feels a pregnancy is possible. Marisa has a beautiful healthy baby boy delivered by Cesarean due to complications. She takes her baby home. Her life goals have been met, hard won, but not without a price. Marisa struggles with infection after infection. The Cesarean surgical site will not heal. She is in and out of the hospital, the last time for eight months. She goes home to plan her son's second birthday. She is again hospitalized and goes into a coma. We are told there is no hope. Her brothers are called in. How do you take your child off life support? Marisa dies, surrounded by family and close friends, the day after her son's second birthday. I held one hand and her husband held the other. It was hard to let go. I relive that day and the decision every day. I ache when her father and I are doing things with her son that she should be doing. His first steps, first day of school, the park or just plain cuddling. People say life goes on...they just don't know how hard it is.

*

DENISE PURCELL
Denise's 27-year-old daughter Megan died
in 2011 from an accidental overdose

It was four years in November. It was Thanksgiving Day, 2011. I was busily, cheerfully preparing for our Thanksgiving feast. I was calculating the different times required to make each dish so they would all be ready at the same time, around 2 to 3 p.m. It was about 11 a.m. when the phone rang. I half expected it to be Megan, as she usually called on Thanksgiving to ask for my stuffing recipe. I wondered why she didn't just write it down, but then Thanks-

36

giving wouldn't be the same without her phone call. But this year I didn't expect the words I was about to hear as I picked up the phone. It was my son-in-law, Jasen. He said "Mom?" I said "Yeah?" with surprise in my voice. He said "It's about Megan." Without letting him finish his sentence, I asked what happened. Was she hurt? Was she in the hospital? There was silence for what seemed an eternity, although it was only a few seconds. "Megan died this morning about 7 a.m." It was a two-hour difference, since she lived in Colorado. His words echoed in my ears. My heart sank, my legs gave out from under me, and I heard myself scream. It seemed so far away, so unreal. I dropped the hazelnut creamer from my other hand as I fell to the floor. I dropped the phone. I was sure my heart stopped beating. I couldn't comprehend anything. I stared blankly at my other three daughters as they huddled around me. My oldest picked up the phone and gave it back to me. I said "I'm here, Jasen." He started explaining. "I woke up this morning and found it strange that Megan had not been up yet. I went and checked the other bathroom and found her lying on the floor with froth that had formed in the corner of her mouth. She wasn't breathing. I called the police and the emergency response team showed up with them. She had passed sometime during the early morning." The medical examiner did an autopsy the next day. I requested a copy of the report. Her death was determined to be accidental. She had toxic amounts of different drugs in her system including bipolar medication, antipsychotic medication, and anxiety medication along with a narcotic pain killer that was prescribed for the ankle surgery from which she was recovering. There was also alcohol in her system. That was the day my worst fear came true. My and the lives of my four other daughters have never been the same. Thanksgiving has never been the same. Megan's birthday and holidays arrive with a deep sadness.

Our second tragedy was waiting a week for Megan's body to be released and come home. We had a service, though she was cremated and her ashes delivered to me two days later. I slept with her ashes next to me for a week.

I sifted through Megan's photos, journals and letters, but it wasn't enough. It will never be enough. Her sisters were going through their own hell, sibling hell. It was always us girls, no matter what, and then we became separated by pain. For some reason, we could never quite understand what the others were feeling, so we didn't talk. We hid from the world and each other until we couldn't do that anymore, and we began grief counseling. That was the longest journey of our lives.

Going through Megan's belongings was also hard. Each of us took something to help us get through the day, something that would make us feel better. But we go day by day. We talk briefly, to the point, about anything concerning Megan. We deal with it in our own ways. Only recently have I been able to muster a smile when I look at her picture. I stare at her picture and try so hard to remember her voice, what a wonderful person she was, so giving and caring. She shone like a diamond.

I will forever have that piece of my heart broken, but it's time to cherish the daughters I still have with all their beautiful lives unfolding. Megan is forever with us. It will always be just "all of us girls."

*

MARILYN ROLLINS
Marilyn's 37-year-old son Randy and 16-year-old granddaughter Sara
died in a car accident in 2006 during a family camping trip

My son Randy came into this world a whopping ten-pound baby boy. His hair was so fine and blond that he looked bald. He used to go to sleep with his head buried under my arm. He was all boy, and from the day he said his first word he talked incessantly. Randy was a sturdy little boy who loved camping and fishing. His best friend was his little brother Rusty. Randy grew up strong, never giving us a moment of worry. He met the girl of his dreams in high school and married her shortly after their graduation. A year later they started their family with a beautiful baby girl they named Sara.

Sara had a perfect little heart-shaped red birthmark on her forehead. She loved music and she loved to laugh. Randy had another girl, Emily, two years later. She and Sara were best friends, just like Randy and his brother had been. Seven years later, little Adam came along. Randy finally had his boy and he was so proud of him. They did so much together and it was amazing for me to watch my child now raise three children of his own. Randy joined the volunteer fire department in his community, and when Sara turned sixteen she joined as a junior firefighter. She beat all the boys on the physical tests!

On September 22, 2006, Randy and his family were going camping with his in-laws. My husband, Bob, and I stayed home for the weekend, and were planning a cookout at home. That Friday night we went to our son Rusty's apartment for dinner and dessert. We played with his children for a while and then went home.

Shortly after we got home, the phone rang. It was someone from the campground, telling us that Randy and his family had been in an accident. Bob and I left very quickly, heading toward the town of Knox because that is the way we thought they had gone. Rusty had been a police officer, and made some calls to see what information he could find out. He called me on the cellphone, saying that Randy had been airlifted to South Bend. We turned and headed for South Bend. I knew that he had to have been hurt badly to be taken by helicopter. My friend Maryanne found directions for us on the internet and directed us by phone, at the same time trying to keep us calm. We reached South Bend, only to find that Randy was not there but our grandchildren, fourteen-year-old Emily and nine-year-old Adam, were. I was confused and I had a sick feeling in the pit of my stomach, as no one would answer my question, "Where is my son?" Bob stayed with Adam, and I stayed with Emily. They had severe injuries though not critical. A nurse came to tell us that the rest of the family was on their way by ambulance from Knox. I actually calmed down a bit, thinking that it was so confusing because there were two hospitals involved, but Randy would be with Sara and his wife, Kim, when they arrived in South

Bend. It seemed like forever before they got there. As we ran toward the door of the ER, they wheeled my daughter-in-law in, and I could see that she too was severely injured. Her father came toward me and said, "The coroner needs to know what to do with Sara's body." I think I screamed as I fell to my knees. Then he said to my husband, "Can we ask Randy?" I told him, "Randy isn't here." I knew at that moment that they were both gone.

A minister took us to a quiet room and finally confirmed our fears. My oldest son and sixteen-year-old granddaughter did not survive the accident. We decided that my daughter-in-law's father would break the news to Kim, and we would tell the other children in the morning. Whenever they asked us about Randy or Sara, we simply said that they were being cared for. We went back to the ER and Kim was told that her husband and oldest daughter were gone. I remember her screams so vividly.

After the children were taken up to a room, a doctor asked if we would like to go down to the morgue to see Randy. Sara's body had been taken to the Knox hospital. I said no, but my husband and youngest son went. They told me that Randy just looked like he was sleeping.

The next morning my daughter-in-law was brought to the children's room in a wheelchair, and our friends and family gathered around their beds. Their rooms were next to each other, with a large sliding glass door between them that could be opened. The nurses pulled the curtains on the windows to the rooms and left us in our grief. Kim told her surviving children that their beautiful sister and loving father were gone. Spontaneously everyone joined hands and said the "Our Father" prayer as we tried to comfort these suffering children and their mother. I remember looking out at the activity in the halls of the hospital and thinking, "Why are they still moving? How can they just keep going? My son and granddaughter are dead." It was a week before there could be a funeral, because the rest of the family was in the hospital.

We learned that the truck directly in front of them that night had crossed to the left of the center line and was hit by a semi-truck, which then lost control and hit Randy's vehicle. Kim was driving. Randy and Sara were both sitting on the passenger side. At first we thought the man was a drunk driver, but it was determined later that he had suffered a seizure at the wheel. He never regained consciousness and died a few weeks later. The truck driver was not hurt, and spent many hours at the hospital concerned about our family. I really felt bad for him. My husband and I stayed at the hospital with the other two children. There was a Ronald McDonald House in the hospital and we ate our meals there. Occasionally we would use the room they reserved for us. What a wonderful organization!

Randy and Sara went to the cemetery atop the firetrucks that they loved so much. "Amazing Grace" was played on bagpipes as their pink and silver coffins were carried to their graves. We all cried as last call came over the radio for Lieutenant Randy Rollins. One of the firefighters handed Adam his dad's fire helmet. Emily received Sara's fire helmet. My daughter-in-law received the flag that draped Randy's coffin. Roses were laid on Sara's pink coffin as people filed past, leaving kisses and tears in their wake. Then our grief journey began.

*

KATIE ROUSH
Katie's 26-year-old daughter Krystle
died in 2013 of accidental alcohol poisoning

Krystle's father had an emerging drug and alcohol problem, and we divorced after seventeen years of marriage. He also forgot to tell his girlfriends that he was married. I raised my children in Ashland, Kentucky, but moved to Columbus, Ohio, to start over. Krystle wanted to stay with her father, as she was daddy's girl. My eldest, Sami, moved with me. My middle child, Nikki, was in college.

Soon after, Krystle's father sued me for full custody. Why, I don't know, because we had shared parenting. He was trying to do it on the sly, saying he wanted all the money he could get out of me. So since Ashland was a small town, I lost. His lawyer knew the judge and, well, the rest you can figure out. Soon after, Kryssi started not showing up for school. The principal called me, since I used to teach there, saying he could never reach Kryssi's father. To make a long story short, her father was using crack cocaine and not staying home.

Kryssi started drinking. She called saying she wanted to move in with me so she could stop drinking and turn her life around. When I arrived to bring her home, she had to tell the police she wanted to come with me, so I would not be charged with kidnapping. Her father showed up and threatened me and the neighbor. Kryssi was scared, so she stayed there. She lived with her boyfriend from age fifteen on. Nobody would listen to me at children's services. I paid child support but nobody would help me get my daughter. Each time I tried, her dad would make it look like he was "dad of the year."

At age eighteen, my child dropped out of school. She was now doing drugs and was pregnant, living with her boyfriend. Kryssi ended up in jail, I bailed her out and made special arrangements for her to move with me to Columbus. Finally! But her father still had her wrapped around his little finger. She took my credit cards and maxed them out. She and her dad returned the merchandise and used the money to buy drugs. She was afraid to tell me, and ran back home to him. Two years later Kryssi asked if she and her little girl Olivia could live with me. I went and got them, and then paid for Kryssi to enter rehab. She did well too! She got her GED and enrolled in college to become a drug counselor. She also had a job. Then she met a boy. The problem returned. He drank, she started, and it got bad again, so much so that I put a warrant out for her arrest. This was my last chance to save my daughter. She had threatened me (while high) so I figured if she went to jail, this would get her to a rehab place to help her.

Four months later she looked great. It seemed she was back to her old kind, caring, funny self. We worked with the courts to get the charges dropped. She was not drinking and was off drugs and seeing a counselor. I got her a job at the tanning salon I managed. In the process of staying sober, Kryssi had given Olivia's dad custody so Kryssi could focus on getting her life together. We talked about getting Olivia back and enrolling her in school. Kryssi was so excited! She was still with that boy but was working and doing great. Then, I don't know when, why or how, my daughter started drinking again.

When you are addicted you become a different person. The drugs and/or alcohol take over. You will sell your soul for your next drink. Kryssi was at it again. She tried taking liquor out of my house. I cried and pleaded with her. I told her that whatever we needed to do to get her sober, we would do it. I told her she had so much goodness inside her, but she just did not realize it. The last time I saw my daughter was July 22, 2013. I told her I loved her. I was getting my grandson for the week and told her we needed to get together and make plans.

I was at work on the morning of July 30, when two detectives came to my workplace. The female asked if I knew Krystle Kimbler. I said, "Yes, that's my daughter. Is she in trouble?" When they didn't respond, I just knew. I asked her, "Oh my god, is she dead? Is my baby dead?" Her eyes told me everything. I hit the floor, shattered. My beautiful flower child, Krystle Cheri Kimber, was pronounced dead at 7:55 a.m. that day due to accidental alcohol poisoning.

What happened after that was horrendous too. Her father came out of the woodwork and put a hold on her body so I could not plan her funeral the way she wanted, as she and I had discussed. He was stoned, and the coroner could not understand him. He had no money, nothing. He wanted me to pay half of this huge funeral that Kryssi didn't want. I said no.

My daughter's remains sat in a steel drawer for a week until he finally figured it out. To keep the peace, I signed off on her remains. I was threatened and warned not to show up at her funeral. I didn't. I wanted my daughter's last day here on earth to be peaceful. I mourned my child here in Columbus. My other two kids took her father's side as well. My husband comforted me. I did get half of Kryssi's ashes, which I scattered on her beloved lake.

*

SARA RUBLE
Sara's 19-year-old son Scott died in 1994 from a combination of a seizure disorder, Strep throat and dehydration

When Scott was fifteen he suddenly suffered three seizures. They came from out of nowhere. He was a healthy young boy. He loved school, was a leader and a soccer player. He was our only child. When the seizures occurred, his dad and I were in shock and even fearful for Scott's future. We had never faced anything like this. Scott, on the other hand, took it seriously but never felt he was being held back by the seizure diagnosis. Soccer continued and he made the varsity team as a freshman. We were thrilled and relieved to see life move on more normally- even with Scott taking three Dilantin tablets daily to control his seizures.

Throughout high school Scott excelled, graduating fifth in his class. He was co-captain of the soccer team and senior class president. His dad and I were in awe of this child and his determination. He handled life as he did before - with strength and a trusting that he could do what he wanted and needed to do.

When it was time for college, Scott wanted to study environmental sciences so he could change the world in his own way. We had to let him go and not hold him back. As parents we could not let our fears over the seizures get in his way. He had a wonderful freshman year and absolutely loved college. Toward the end of the school year, Scott decided he wanted to work in a national park for the summer. He could even earn college credits writing about Native Americans and other topics he might be interested in. His dad and I both encouraged Scott to go to Colorado. It sounded perfect for him.

A week after school got out, Scott and his dad drove from Ohio to Colorado. His dad then flew home so Scott could have his car for the summer. He was very responsible and took his daily medication, but the seizures were a concern to us as parents. We wanted him to "fly" and thrive, yet we tried to keep him safe too. Knowing he had arrived safely in Colorado brought us greater peace of mind. Scott was to join other college students who were coming to the park. It would be quite an adventure living in a dorm on top of a mountain, camping, learning about the national park, and the great outdoors as well. And so the day after he arrived, Scott reported for training Monday morning with the adults who worked at the park year-round. As unbelievable as this is today, we had no cellphones in 1994. Scott assured us he would call us once a week and update us. We trusted that all would go well.

We did not know that no other students had arrived yet, so Scott was in the ten-room dorm by himself that first week. And we did not know he had to provide much of his own food, as meals were limited to lunch at the park's visitor center. Scott had not shared that information with us before he left. Most likely he assumed that the dorm would be filled with other kids and they would surely find ways to eat.

On Thursday night Scott called me and his words were, "Mom, I am so sick I wish you were here." Oh my God, what is happening? I listened to his every word, and not wanting him to sense my fear, took it all in. He had been sick since he arrived, throwing up and not eating much. "Oh, no…" Scott was slight to begin with, five-feet eight-inches and one hundred and thirty pounds. There wasn't much room for weight loss. I couldn't imagine how weak he must have felt. It sounded to me like he had Strep throat, even though neither of us had ever had it. But the Dilantin! Could that medication even be in his system after four days of being sick?

Oh, God. I asked about it, he said he and been taking it...but...

"I'm going to the doctor tomorrow morning," he said. He finally had to tell the adults who were training him just how sick he was. They made an appointment for him with a doctor who was in the nearby town. I was so relieved to hear that. Still not letting my deepest fears and concerns seep out, I had to let Scott feel he was in control of this. "Nineteen years old"...I reminded myself. "My only child..." Scott assured me he would call after the appointment. We said "I love you," and hung up.

I was jumping out of my skin! I had never felt this kind of fear for Scott's life, his safety. Oh, my God. I called my ex-husband, Scott's dad, and he knew too. He had spoken with Scott. We had to trust that Scott would be okay. Yes...trust. But I could not find peace of mind with that. I was scared. The next day, Friday, I worked only in the morning. I could not think of anything but Scott. I came home and called him...even though he said he would call me. I could not wait another minute.

He sounded better. Relief poured through me. Scott did have Strep throat. The doctor had given Scott a shot and some medication. And he was eating. He had gone to a grocery store and bought some food: chicken noodle soup, a peanut butter and jelly sandwich, and a banana. Definitely the best meal Scott had all week. I could feel his relief too. Everything felt better, for both of us.

We did not hear from Scott on Sunday. We figured he was busy, and we had just spoken with on Friday. Trust...

On Monday morning Scott did not report to his training class. A young man went to his room to get him. With indescribable horror, he discovered Scott had died. I cannot even imagine what happened then. A pathologist was called in and determined that Scott had died Friday night in his sleep, five days after arriving at the park. No one had checked on Scott over the weekend. No one.

Scott's body was not in good shape. His autopsy was a case of determining what it wasn't...to try to come to what had caused Scott's death. Strep throat, seizure disorder, elevation, dehydration. The perfect storm had invaded Scott's body. My biggest fear. The most unbelievable, unimaginable, horrific thing that could ever happen in our world...happened. We flew to Colorado the next day because we HAD to...to scream at the staff at the park...to ask them WHY? But their angst and tears, fears, opened us up to compassion. No one could have saved Scott, we learned. It was a perfect storm. And with the coroner's knowing words...his own son had died too...we did not see Scott. His death changed us forever.

*

DENISE SHELTON
Denise's 22-year-old son Nicholas died in 2010
when he struck a steel cable while riding an ATV

I had taken the week off from work to be with my sister who was in the ICU slowly dying from a rare disease. I was scheduled to go home that day to get ready for Easter. My sister had a setback, and I decided to stay another day. I called home to let my son, who was living at home, and my husband know what was going on. However, I had the worst feeling. I tried to shake it off as merely being upset about my sister, but in my heart I knew that wasn't it.

My son Nicholas answered the phone and we had such a wonderful conversation. He was home for lunch and told me he was going four-wheeling after work with some of his friends. I said he was trying to give me more gray hair. We laughed and he reassured me of his expertise. I said, "No, Nicholas, really. I have a bad feeling." He said, "Okay, Mom. I'll be careful. I always am." I started to cry a little, saying that I missed him so much. He told me that I'd been gone only several days and that he knew how my "feelings" were, so he would most definitely be extra careful. He told me how he knew Good Friday was a special day and that he had to work only half a day. We could have lunch together the next

47

day, when I got home. I agreed, and we both said "I love you." Before I went back in the hospital room, I sat and cried...for so many reasons.

Later, my husband called. The lump in my throat grew. Nicholas had been in an accident and they thought it had something to do with a fence. "What kind of fence? Like a little white picket fence?" "I don't know." "Is he okay?" "I don't know. " "Where is he? What do you mean you don't know where he is? How do you know this much?" "His girlfriend called." "Well, what did she say? Is he okay?" "I don't know." "How can you not know?" "They had to call an ambulance." "Why? Why did they have to call an ambulance? Why didn't one of the guys just drive him there?" "I don't know. I don't think it's good." Suddenly it was like I could no longer comprehend what he was saying. My heart sank. I felt like I was going to puke. No, no, it couldn't be anything bad. It just couldn't. "Maybe he broke his leg, like his femur. That can be very serious...but he'll still be okay. I'll call the hospital."

Because Nicholas was over eighteen, the hospital couldn't tell me anything. I asked if he broke his leg, like his femur, but she wouldn't answer me. I said wouldn't she want to know if it was her son? She said they were working on him. What did that mean? Were they operating on his leg? Putting on a cast? Or....? No, I couldn't think it. My sister told me to go even though her situation was grave. The two-and-a-half-hour drive back home was as if God opened the lane for me. I was praying. Petrified. Shaking. I was on autopilot. It's just a leg, probably. Right? The cellphone rang. My husband said they were airlifting Nicholas to another hospital. What? What did he say? Why would they airlift him for a broken leg? I knew. In my heart, in my soul, in my very being I KNEW what was happening, but my brain could not possibly comprehend how or why. "Wait, they're airlifting him? You have to be with him." "I'm just pulling up to the hospital. I can see the helicopter on the roof." "You can't let him go alone. He'll think we don't care. Hurry, catch the helicopter." "Okay. God, please."

At the hospital, they led me into a family room. I expected to see my husband. I saw Nick's aunts and uncles from out of town, cousins, friends… it was full. Who were all these people? They were all looking at me. I fell to the floor.

I don't know when my daughter and her fiancé arrived from 1,200 miles away. It's such a blur. Bits and pieces yet still so clear, as if it happened today. And then, hours upon hours that are just gone. I want to see him. Where is he? They are telling me to be prepared. Just take me there. I am frantic and start to look for Nick by myself when my husband takes my arm. He has been crying. It's all so surreal. We walked into the room. It is dim or else it is hard to see because of the tears running down my face. I have watched loved ones die before: tubes, ventilators and IVs. I stand there. My feet are frozen. I want to run and scoop him up and hold him in my arms, yet part of me is not sure that they haven't made a terrible mistake. I don't remember being shocked at how he looked. I wasn't scared of all the tubes, the ventilator, the IVs, the neck brace, the blood. It was him! It was my baby. It was my sweet funny, baby. My Nicholas. There he was. He was still here. See? Here he is. We can get through this.

The doctor wants to talk to us. He states that Nick's airway was crushed and although he was at first breathing on his own, he is no longer doing that. Oh! He was breathing on his own, I heard. That's a good sign. But then he got hit in the head and it knocked him unconscious immediately. They don't think he felt much pain. What hit him in the head? No one knows at this point. But it was so hard that it broke many bones in Nick's face and caused a shift in his brain. A midline shift. I'd heard of that. "Okay, so wait…wait…can't you just drain the extra blood off his brain and then he'll be okay?" "What do you mean that's not the problem?" Well, when Nick's airway was crushed, it deprived his brain of oxygen and he would be a vegetable if he lived. He would probably lose his eye. "Well, he can live with one eye."

The doctor put a hole in his head to appease us really. I had lost a loved one to a brain injury, and it took weeks. We had time. He could be okay. They said they needed to do a test to see if Nick's brain was working. It was not. But we had weeks yet, I thought.

I let friends and other family go and see Nick, two at a time, because I would have weeks with him. Then they called my family into a room. They wanted to know if Nicholas wanted to donate his organs. What? WHAT? He's not even dead. No one said he was dead. No one pronounced him dead. What are you talking about? That's when I found out that if we donated his organs, we could stay another day. If not, they needed his room.

*

CHAPTER TWO

THE AFTERMATH

Somehow, even in the worst of times, the tiniest fragments of good survive. It was the grip in which one held those fragments that counted.
-MELINA MARCHETTA

Following profound loss, the first questions we often ask ourselves are: How am I going to survive this? How can I function when I have no feeling or when those sensations are so strong they threaten to paralyze me? How can I cook and clean and cope? There we stand in the aftermath, feeling vulnerable and often ravaged with fear. How do we survive?

*

STACY BERNDTSON
Stacy's daughter Cori Joy died in 2003, the day before her fourth birthday, from an undiagnosed genetic disorder

Cori died the day before her fourth birthday. We had a cake ordered and a birthday party planned. Everyone was going to be in our home anyway, so we picked up the cake and everyone came. We sang "Happy Birthday" to Cori. I remember being in sort of a daze. I would try to be the hostess, but then I would go into my room and break down. I am younger than my brother and sister by about eighteen years. Both our parents died before Cori was even

51

born. My sister and sister-in-law took care of nearly everything that day. I remember my sister folding underwear and feeling like she shouldn't be doing that for me. Now I realize that anything anyone did that day helped them feel like they were helping us in some way. I realize that just by being with us they were helping, even if we didn't necessarily see that then.

*

KARI BROWN
Kari's 2-year-old daughter Dominique (Deedee)
died in 2014 from obstructive sleep apnea

I honestly don't really remember the first few weeks. But I remember feeling physically sick. I lost almost twenty pounds within two weeks; I did not want to eat nor could I sleep. I was lost. I wanted to curl up and die, to be with my Deedee. I built my life around her, we revolved around her. But when she passed, I lost my sense of purpose, like I had no one to take care of anymore. I became a stay-at-home mom so I could raise her, and give her my everything. We lived in San Antonio because of the great medical opportunities that assisted with Dominique's growth. But when she passed, there was nothing left for us in San Antonio. So three months later we returned to Austin where Deedee was originally born.

At first I was angry at the world. I was mad that people acted like my daughter's death did not matter, no one paid attention to myself or my fiancé. But later on, after changing perspective and trying to appreciate that not everyone understands, I started to see what impact Dominique had in people's lives. She brought some kind of light to them, and it touched their heart. It took some time, but I understood that Dominique's mission on Earth was done; that she had done what she came here to do. Sometimes I still struggle; she was gone way before she was supposed to.

I attended therapy and reached out to a couple of friends who had also lost children. I now understood the heart-felt pain they experience on a daily basis from not having their child with them. I wrote daily letters to Dominique in a notebook. I wrote about how much I missed her, and wished she were here with me.

I will be honest: I never saw myself as a survivor until the question asked how I survived the initial aftermath. I honestly thought that I wanted to die when Deedee passed. But I survived the tragedy of losing my only daughter. In doing so, I found a different sense of purpose: To help others and to share my experience, and try to teach people that life is precious.

*

TANISHA CALDWELL
Tanisha's 23-year-old son Tariq (Jay)
died in a car accident in 2015

I did a lot of praying. I cried a lot too. It was by God's grace that I made it this far. I also found a grief support group which has been extremely helpful!

*

LYNDA CHELDELIN FELL
Lynda's 15-year-old daughter Aly
died in a car accident in 2009

Looking back, I was on autopilot for a very long time. I actually remember very little of the first two and a half years, just little snippets of time, like frozen snapshots. I remember our house and front porch being filled with people for the first ten days. I remember Xanax prescription bottles bearing my and my husband's names magically appearing on the counter. I have no idea who prescribed them or how they got to our house, but they had our names on the bottles, one for each of us. I remember my sister kneeling in front of me and putting warm socks fresh from the dryer on my bare feet. I remember my brother-in-law lovingly preparing a beautiful display of freshly cut fruit on a plate just for me. Fruit was the only food I could stomach for days. It was all very strange, like watching a movie with me in the lead role. My husband and I would rise in the morning, make our way down to the front patio where family and friends stood guard. We sat there all day, getting up only to use the bathroom or retreating to our bedroom to escape.

Aly was such an active teenager. I remember wondering how in the world our lives could go from sixty miles per hour to zero in the blink of an eye. Our grandson was at that cute two-year-old stage, though I remember nothing of his adorable antics. I remember nothing of our children. It's as if two years were stolen from my life.

I remember feeling scared that the color and beauty would never return to my world. I remember hating nighttime, when the house was quiet and there was nothing to distract me from the overwhelming sadness. The dread would build starting at about 4 p.m. Nighttime was just horrid. The rest is a blur. It took two and a half years before the fog started to thin just a wee bit. And then my dear sweet husband suffered a major stroke. Once again, I found myself at square one.

*

JACQUELYN CRUZ
Jacquelyn's 24-year-old daughter Jenna
died in 2012 from pulmonary edema

I really don't know how I survived the first few weeks after Jenna's passing. I think it was a combination of a few things. When I look back, the one constant was my husband, David. He was really the only one who knew what to do for me. Nobody understood the pain but him. Jenna was a part of me and him. During the day family and friends came and went, but at night it was just the two of us. I couldn't image doing this alone. I know we slept a lot and stared at a television screen for most of the day.

Our bodies ached, psychically ached from head to toe; that's what grief does to you, I didn't know that then. My reason for living at that time was for my two other children, Danny and Chelsea. After reading about other mothers who lost children, I know it's natural for a grieving parent to have suicidal thoughts. My husband and I talked about it, but then realized the pain it would bring to our living children. I did get Xanax from my doctor for the first few weeks and it did help, but I was so afraid I would get addicted to it. I am now on an antidepressant and it really helps with the crying. I have no plans to come off it any time soon. People often ask me, "How do you do it?" I don't have an answer for them. I believe in miracles because I am one.

*

MICHELLE DETWILER
Michelle's 19-year-old daughter Emily
died in 2014 due to congenital complications

A couple of days before Emily died, our friends came to our home and stayed with us. They were so supportive, the wife having had a child that died eight years before. She knew the pain we were about to endure, the shock and the grief that was to come. Our friends brought food and supported us through the funeral home visits and planning her funeral. I don't know how we could have done anything if our friends hadn't been there to support us.

After Emily died I could not think. It was if someone stole my mind. I knew who people were, but it was as if time was passing without me. My family arrived and continued to support us as our friends were doing. What love we had around us! I could not have survived it if I had not had those friends there during that first week. I think I would have stayed in bed. I did not want to go to the funeral. I can't imagine why I felt like that. How could I not want to go to my daughter's funeral? But I didn't. However, with the support I had from family and friends, I did arrive at the funeral.

*

ANNAH ELIZABETH
Annah's son Gavin Michael aspirated on his meconium
during the delivery and died 26 minutes following his birth

My first experience with child loss came on an overcast, cold, dreary, yet otherwise truly magnetic day. I had awakened in the wee morning hours to what turned out to be real contractions, not those annoying Braxton Hicks pains. That labor progressed exactly as the books, doctors, and our Lamaze instructor had said it would. The room with its white walls and white linens, the bed with its stirrups, and the counter that held the doctor's plastic examination gloves were all part of the day's electric excitement. One minute I was chatting with the nurse, only to watch her race from the room, then return with what seemed like a posse of frantic people who informed my husband and me there was a problem with the baby and they were going to have to immediately perform surgery. Dragging myself awake from that emergency Cesarean section, I remember finally squeaking out these words: "Where's my baby?" "I'm sorry; he didn't make it," is the response forever burned into my brain. Most of what I remember of the next week is blurred by a drug-induced haze. I had a few visitors, but only recently found out when I reconnected with an old friend that I had refused well-wishers in those earliest hours following Gavin's death.

I remember reading condolence cards and weeping after I read the two Mother's Day cards that friends sent. Two days following my son's birth I should have been celebrating my new role as Mommy. In joy's stead, one whisper filled every fiber of my being, one that rooted itself like an umbilical cord into my days and nights for a long time to come: What kind of mother has no child? I survived the aftermath much like many of us do. I welcomed countless visitors that first week, then watched the well of company quickly dry up and the casseroles dry out. I cried buckets of tears and ate buckets of ice cream. I marveled at rainbows and hummingbirds and hated myself when I discovered I couldn't be happy for my sister, who gave birth to my beautiful niece two weeks after my son died. I sat on the floor with Gavin's unused garments and rocked myself to sleep in our childless nursery.

I went back to work, endured the panic-stricken looks from all those who didn't know or couldn't handle the fact that my son had died, and I welcomed the warm embraces from the few family and friends who could and would share in my sorrow. I immediately chose to begin trying to have another baby. Seven years later I'd survived two more miscarriages, three complicated but successful pregnancies, and a six-week psychiatric stay for severe depression.

One of the questions that plagued me right from those earliest days in the hospital following Gavin's death was this: "How is it that some people can go on to live happy, healthy lives following tragedy while others succumb to despair, drugs, a life of void – or worse, suicide – and are forever helped back from living their best lives?" Little by little I grew stronger, and found numerous answers to that query.

These are a few of the things I discovered. We reduce grief to three words: "Loss and healing" or "grief and healing," when in essence there are three autonomous components. Loss equals the event. Grief equals our response to that loss event. Healing equals our recovery from the conflicts that comprise our grief. When we eliminate "loss" or "grief" we deny either the event or our sorrow. The Chinese philosopher Lao Tzu once said, "The journey of a thousand miles begins with one step." Examining our daily language and understanding the autonomy between loss, grief, and healing are two of the first things we need to do on our road to recovery.

I realize our losses are often layered and I went on to identify five categories of loss: death, despair, disaster, disease and dysfunction. I also discovered that there are many nuances within each of those types of events. I discovered that each of us is born with everything we need to heal our big and small heartaches. I also noticed that, though the details look differently on each of us, we are all born with the same five traits: An academic ability to learn;

we are born in a body and into a physical environment; we all have an ability to feel emotion and an ability to socialize in some form or another. Lastly, we are all born with a spirit.

Once I had reconciled the last piece of my grief puzzle, I began assembling all the grief event recovery tools I'd gathered on my journey. Helping others when their grief begins to soften has continued to help me through other life obstacles that have come my way.

*

WENDY EVANS
Wendy's 21-year-old son Kyle died in 2009
from diabetes when his insulin pump malfunctioned

The aftermath of Kyle's death was horrendous. The pain was unimaginable. My husband, mother, brothers and best friend were at the ready for weeks. They did not know how to help and I did not know how to ask for what I needed. I did not know what I needed; I only wanted the pain to stop by having my son back. At Kyle's funeral service (which I barely remember) someone mentioned Compassionate Friends. The third week after Kyle's death I attended a meeting with my mother. But I think it was too soon, as I quickly became overwhelmed by the stories other attendees offered. My husband and daughter eventually felt that counseling might help, so they identified a therapist and we went for help. The first thing the therapist said to us was, "There is little I can do except bear witness to your grief." I began to understand that the grief journey is personal, difficult and has its own timeline. I have read countless books, and I wrote in a journal compulsively for three years.

*

BONNIE FORSHEY
Bonnie's 16-year-old son Billy died in 1993
from an overdose of prescription drugs

The loss of my son was the hardest thing I have ever had to go through. I was in deep shock and unable to comprehend what had happened. I beat myself up for not seeing any signs. I had failed as a mother, and as a nurse. I honestly don't know how I made it. I am unable to remember much because it was so traumatic.

*

TALIA GATO
Talia's 8-year-old daughter Poppy
died in 2009 in a car accident

I think how I survived was by taking some sort of pills for about eight months so I could sleep at night. I knew I had to wean myself off, because I didn't want to rely on them. I was surrounded with a season of friends. Someone was always around bringing meals and helping around the house. My sister-in-law stayed with us for two weeks, which was extremely helpful. They took care of me and were tolerant of my being a mess. There were two key ladies who organized meals for me for six months. This was helpful, not having to cook for months. I knew hundreds who were praying for us. I didn't do anything, but I did get up every day and tried to do things around my yard and take care of my daughter. She was a lost child, and it breaks my heart to remember.

We didn't do much as a family; we mostly stayed home. I remember it as a numbing fog. Lots of things happened, people avoiding us, saying weird things. Loss turned our lives upside down. I felt a deep emptiness that ached. It was very helpful to have people stop by and sit with my pool of loss. But when the year passed, my support left. I think they thought I was okay. But it was only the beginning of what I call the onion effect of loss.

*

KORBY HAVE
Korby's 17-year-old daughter Taylor (Tayla)
died in 2013 in a car accident

I think I survived the initial aftermath simply because I had no choice. I am a single mom with two other children to take care of. If I didn't take care of them, who would? I attended a few grief groups with my family, but was always uncomfortable sharing my feelings because it made my family sad, so I stopped going and kept my feelings to myself.

*

DEANA MARTIN
Deana's only two children, 25-year-old Amanda
and 21-year-old Logan, died in a car accident in 2011

I am not sure I survived the initial aftermath. I am not sure I was ever truly there. It all seemed so surreal and like an out-of-body experience. I received the call at work. I could not drive, and there was so much to do. A friend came to drive me home, and a couple of other friends from work took time off to help me pack for the trip to Indiana to bury my children. My children died in our home state of Indiana, only a mile or so from their father's home. They had traveled there from Georgia to attend their stepmother's funeral; she died of lung cancer. I had their remains placed in Indiana for family to have a place to mourn. I don't remember doing much at all, but yet so much at the same time. There we so many lists. All I did was speak and they were created and others carried them out. People said I spoke to them during those first few days, but I do not recall speaking to them. I felt as if I floated from place to place, not really walking or aware. It truly was surreal. At times I simply recall being there, not how I got there.

I was surrounded by family. My sister flew into Atlanta from West Palm Beach, Florida, to accompany me on the trip to Indiana to bury my children. She helped me make decisions at the mortuary, along with my father. But in a way it wasn't as if I was making the decisions so much as I was being led on what to choose and the arrangements to make. It all came very easily, without great effort. I do not recall being in mental anguish, for I was numb beyond recognition! I did not even know who I was. It was as if I was living someone else's experience. This could not be me, or my children's bodies we had to clothe, and it was not ceremonies for them that we were planning! Surely we were doing all this for someone else.

I don't remember eating, but I know I did. I don't remember much of anything; it all flashes through my mind like still film shots as I look back to those initial days. I do, however, recall in great detail having to tell my sweet three-year-old granddaughter about her mommy. She had seen the semi-truck destroy her mother's car, but at that age she could not conceptualize where her mommy was. I made everyone promise not to tell her. I knew in my heart that I needed to be the one to tell her when I got there. Until then they avoided her constant questions of "Where is Mommy and Uncle Logan?" Once I arrived, friends retrieved her from my ex-husband's family about an hour away. Several of us took her to a private room upstairs in my cousin's home and we sat in a circle, "crisscross applesauce," as she would call it. I then used the story of *The Lion King* and the death of Simba's father as an analogy to try to help her understand. I said that her mommy and Uncle Logan's bodies no longer worked after being hurt very badly, and their spirits had gone to live in the stars just like Simba's daddy. She climbed up and sat her tiny body in my lap after we told her, and she never spoke a word or shed a tear. It was very surreal. She has very strong attachment issues to this day and can't stand to be alone, and she will not let go of possessions even as small as a scrap of paper she found on the ground.

I was fortunate that I had great support at first from family and friends, and I was more led to do what needed to be done rather than doing them on my own. I did not experience the typical house full of people because we were in another state. We used a cousin's house as "ground zero" and we all stayed in hotels close by. I went back to work after two weeks, though I don't remember the actual day I returned to the office. I barely remember the return trip to Georgia after the funeral. None of it became reality for a very long time. Now, almost five years out, each day there is still more acceptance and reality to experience.

*

MONICA MIRKES
Monica's 30-year-old daughter Marisa
died in 2013 due to Cesarean complications

Do you ever really survive the loss of your child? Numbness. I have never been deep-sea diving, but it felt as if weights were attached and I was thrown overboard into arctic waters. Sinking and cold. You are existing, doing what you have to do to get through the day until you can get home and crawl into bed. The first year I was on autopilot. The second year, it all started to come back. Still, there is no time to sit and absorb what has happened. My husband will ask if everything is all right. NO! It is not all right. It never will be. But if it makes everyone happy, I'll go along with the game of "I'm okay now." My focus has to be Marisa's baby, keeping his world balanced. Maybe that is how I am surviving. Sleep for me is hard. A friend told me about Zentangle. It's basically doodling, but more. I keep a journal and before I go to bed I "doodle." For me, it is a way to relax and go through my thoughts.

*

DENISE PURCELL
Denise's 27-year-old daughter Megan died
in 2011 from an accidental overdose

I was in shock. My life just stopped. I was on autopilot because I had three younger daughters and an older one. I didn't cope. I escaped into my mind, and ended up in the hospital with a mental breakdown. I no longer cared about anything.

62

*

MARILYN ROLLINS

Marilyn's 37-year-old son Randy and 16-year-old granddaughter Sara
died in a car accident in 2006 during a family camping trip

Are we given a choice? I woke each morning feeling as if I had
been kicked in the stomach. The first thought was 'Oh my God, my
son and granddaughter are dead!' I know that sounds harsh. I
didn't think "gone, passed, in heaven, crossed over," etc. They were
dead.

We spent that first week at the hospital with the survivors: our
daughter-in-law, fourteen-year-old granddaughter and eight-year-
old grandson. It kept us busy, kept our minds occupied. I thought
so much about my granddaughter Sara. I was angry at God! She
was just a child, with her whole life before her. I watched Emily,
worried about how she was going to go on without her dad and her
best friend, her older sister. She just wanted to sleep, as if by
sleeping it would all be gone when she woke up.

Of course when you go home you have people coming by,
cards in the mail, phone calls, food. How I remember the food!
There was so much that it wouldn't fit in the fridge. As the days
went by though, I thanked God that it was there. I think the grief
really begins after the funeral is over. Then the emptiness comes.
The friends go home, phone calls taper off, and you have to begin
cooking for yourself again. This is when I finally begin to cry. A cry
and sometimes a wail, from somewhere deep inside. I hurt all over,
but mostly in my chest and around my heart. Was I having a heart
attack? It wasn't until much later that I learned that these physical
symptoms were real and part of a "broken heart."

Every day the events of that awful night played over and over
in my head like a videotape. I would physically poke my forehead
like a "stop" button, to try to get it to stop. I couldn't concentrate
on anything. I didn't sleep. I thought about suicide, but knew I
could never do that. My son was married and of course had his own
home, so I didn't really have anything physical of his. The one thing

that I had kept was a Winnie the Pooh teddy bear that he had as a child. I put that in the coffin with him. At the time it made sense, but I would give anything now to have that little teddy bear back! My husband found a jacket of my son's at work (they worked together), and he brought it to me. I still sometimes wrap up in it. I feel like he is giving me a hug when I have it on. I have pictures.

Today they are not just pictures, they are memories, each photo a gift that we have collected over the years. We look through them to see Sara as a baby, and as she grew into a beautiful young woman, until there are no more. No more memories, just dreams. Dreams of what she might have become, her career, her wedding, what she would look like now, what our great-grandchildren might have looked like. I pull out old and faded photos of my son, as a baby, as a child, as a teen, his senior pictures, his wedding pictures and one of my favorites, him standing in front of the nursery window at the hospital the night his beautiful Sara was born. He was so proud! I was so proud. Proud of the man I had raised. Once in a while someone will find a picture of him and give it to me. It is like they gave me gold! What an amazing gift!

The holidays were awful that year, though we tried for our other grandchildren. I remember that I bought a new tree, all new ornaments and lights. I wouldn't allow a package under the tree that wasn't wrapped in red, green or gold. Now when I think back, I have to laugh at how close to manic I was. But I think it was more a control thing. I had no control over all that happened, but I could control what my Christmas tree looked like! January started a whole new year of firsts for us.

*

KATIE ROUSH
Katie's 26-year-old daughter Krystle
died in 2013 of accidental alcohol poisoning

I wrote to my daughter. I kept a journal. I also started a book of memories for her daughter, my granddaughter, so she can know her mom. I hugged my dogs and cried into their fur. My husband was my support system.

*

SARA RUBLE
Sara's 19-year-old son Scott died in 1994 from a
combination of a seizure disorder, Strep throat and dehydration

After Scott died so suddenly I truly was in shock. There was confusion and missing that went beyond what I would ever have thought possible. My only child died! His future was gone, and my future was changed forever. Those frightening, uncontrollable thoughts were always hitting me with gusts of tears and sadness.

Within all this chaos was the fact that I had been married to my second husband for only nine months, and he had two children. He was still a dad, and I couldn't feel like a mom any more. This created more chaos, grief, and enormous anger...and yet I loved him so much. I was lost. I knew no one who had lost a child. I felt totally alone.

I had support from my family, who were all heartbroken too. They tried, but no one knew what to do to help me. My friends were there too, bringing me books and sharing what little they knew of death and grief and, most important, sharing their memories of Scott with me too. I was so grateful for their love. Scott's friends were incredible in their need to spend time with me and to help themselves, as they were grieving so deeply as well. I loved spending time with those amazing and courageous kids. They were my link to Scott. As they shared previously untold stories of Scott and their experiences with him, we would laugh and cry and laugh some more. It was such a welcome relief from the reality that existed in all our hearts.

But I had to find more help. I went to counseling. So desperate and needing someone to talk with, I found in counseling much needed support and answers to what grief was, is, what it might create within me, or for my family. I listened. I worked. I mostly wanted to die. Early on, much of this was a struggle to find reasons to go on. I went to counseling religiously. Desperation and pain were big teachers for me. They shoved me around and I fought back, until I began to see more. More in the ways of Scott's life and my life being so important. He, of course, was my focus. I could not see the value in my life as others could, and I know now that is not unusual. I only wanted the pain to stop. I never took anti-depressants or any medication. No one ever suggested it to me, and I never pursued it. I was not a martyr or anything close to that, so it never really came up.

Seeking more support and not having any bereaved parent support groups in my area, I tried calling other moms as I read or heard about their children's deaths. Some of these calls filled my heart with friendship and understanding; others were more one-sided and left me depleted as I hung up. I had to try.

I also returned to work. Financially, I had to. My employer was understanding and gave me time off. I was extremely grateful for that caring gesture. My job no longer had the same meaning to me, and I struggled. But I had to go, I had to try. I tried my best...even with a heart full of pain and my mind in a state of chaos. I didn't want to live, but ironically...I wasn't giving up.

*

DENISE SHELTON
Denise's 22-year-old son Nicholas died in 2010
when he struck a steel cable while riding an ATV

How does anyone survive the loss of his or her child? It was sudden. It was unexpected. When we got the call, my husband was about 175 miles away from me, and my daughter was 1,200 miles away. The hospital wouldn't tell us anything. Nicholas' friend said something about a fence. I couldn't picture what they were talking about. I couldn't understand what anyone was saying. There were about forty people in the ICU waiting room. We were supposed to have four to six. Were they being so nice because the hospital personnel knew something we didn't? To this day, I don't understand why no one told us that Nicholas was dead. We knew he was very ill, but thought that once the brain swelling went down he would start breathing on his own. He didn't, and we never got to find out, because the hospital said they needed the bed. Unbelievable in so many ways.

By the time word got out, his friends, our friends, my daughter's friends, neighbors and coworkers were at our house, bringing food and pictures of our son. They sat with us. We laughed and talked. It seemed like he must be in the other room. Someone would ask me, "When was the last time you ate?" I had no idea. I had no idea if I ate or if I never stopped eating. I remember wondering why all these people were at our house, because nothing seemed real. At times it was like I was watching a movie. I felt quite removed from all the loving chaos. As I watched, I realized why everyone was there. I felt so sorry for the family. They lost their son. Our son. My son. I felt the blood drain from my face. I felt weak. I felt faint. I could hear my heart beating loudly, feel my breathing speed up. Yet I felt numb. It was so surreal. I couldn't hear individual voices...just a faraway sound of many voices blended together.

I'm going to die. I wanted to be alone. Who cares if we have too much chicken or if so-and-so's daughter just got engaged? Why were they talking like nothing has happened? Didn't they realize my Nicholas wasn't here? Someone would ask, "When is the last time you got some rest?" I had no idea of the day or the time. Someone would take charge and clear the place out so I could get some sleep. If only I could. It was then that I screamed "No! NO! God, please!" and endless sobbing until utter exhaustion took us, one by one, to fitful sleep with moaning sobs.

After the work of planning the funeral, shopping for something to wear, buying a funeral plot, getting the minister, picking out a casket and getting through the next several days, you feel some relief. It's an unsettling kind of relief. But it's over. The people are gone and you are left with more leftovers than you could ever eat. Then what? What just happened? It's literally like you can say out loud, "My son was killed," and you might as well be talking in a foreign language. I simply couldn't comprehend any of it.

I didn't remember when I bathed or ate, or brushed my teeth. There was no sleep at all. I would walk the halls waiting for him to come home. Waiting for someone to wake me up. Waiting for my baby to text me to tell me what he was up to. I called his phone. The scene of where the accident happened played over and over in my head. I saw his injuries and I saw him in the hospital, which haunted my every waking and sleeping moment.

No one really knew what happened. It became my mission to try to find out what happened to my son. Who killed him and what killed him. All this while I traveled three hours away to visit my sister, who was moving closer to death. Her three children were so lost. My daughter was getting married in less than two months. Should she call off the wedding or should they continue with their plans? One month after Nick's accident, my sister died. One month after that, my daughter got married. She was beautiful. The wedding was beautiful. But her brother and aunt, to whom she was very close, were not there. I felt so removed...not at all like a mother should feel on her daughter's wedding day. I couldn't mingle and face all the people I had just seen at the funerals of my son and of my sister. I knew I would never make it through if stopped. I wish with all my heart I could do that day over.

*

No one can know how much I love you,
because you are the only one who knows
what my heart sounds like from the inside.
UNKNOWN

*

CHAPTER THREE

THE FUNERAL

Grievers use a very simple calendar. Before and after. -LYNDA CHELDELIN FELL

For many the funeral represents the end while for others it marks the beginning of something eternal. Regardless of whether we mourn the absence of our child's physical body or celebrate the spirit that continues on, planning the funeral or memorial service presents emotionally-laden challenges shared by many.

*

ERICA GALE BELTZ
Erica's 5-year-old son Luke Jordan died in 2005
from a fallen banister in his aunt's driveway

Just before I watched my son's life leave this earth the nurses asked if there was anyone they should call. Yes, my mom. They said she was on her way. I called my father in Texas; I will never forget the call. Donna answered. I said, "I need my dad to come to Georgia right away. There had been a horrible accident." My dad was on the line now and I said, "Dad, Luke might not make it!" He asked to speak to the nurse, and she delivered the truth to my dad. My fears left me as quickly as they had come. My son dying was not an option. I said to call my brother, Bill, and brother-in-law, Shannon.

Luke's dad, Steve, was in Jackson State Penitentiary in diagnostics. I said, "Call Uncle Tim and Aunt Sandra, tell them to please reach Steve." They rushed to the hospital, unware of the tragedy inside.

Within fifteen minutes after losing Luke, the ER nurses asked me what funeral home I would be using. The medical examiner needed to take Luke, but as soon as he was finished he would take Luke to the funeral home. We could then be with Luke again. It felt barbaric and too soon. There was no reason to stay at the hospital; we should go home to be with family.

Southern Illinois was our home. My mom's voice was so soft; she said they could call home and have my grandparents start the arrangements at the Herrin Funeral Home. I had been through two burials of friends recently at a peaceful little cemetery in the country. God must have spoken through me, because I said, "I want him buried there." Thirty minutes after Luke died, we were in my mom's living room. I asked Aunt Pam to ask her dad, the Rev. Halbert Jenkins, if he could do the service. Aunt Pam had the voice of an angel, so I asked her to sing. The Jenkins had spent their lives serving the Lord and it would be a gift to have them do the service.

The next morning we went to the funeral home as a family. My father had arrived. We were all seated around a large rectangular table. It reminded me of the table from The Last Supper. We spoke in faint whispers. Glen, the funeral home director, was so affected by the loss that he had to leave the room several times. I had no insurance and no savings. Glen asked where we wanted Luke to be buried. I described the cemetery I had been to. He told me it was Meadow Brooks, he knew it well. They owned a few plots there and wanted Luke to have one. The family broke down, we were so touched by such a random act of kindness.

We needed about one hundred pictures, three songs, and had to decide what Luke would wear. We discussed a casket; no one could imagine having to choose one but Glen said we wouldn't have to endure that. Luke was forty-two inches tall, and Glen knew of the perfect one. It was forty-eight inches long, and he donated it free of charge. My mom and Pastor Gwen, the female pastor at the Church of the Nazarene, worked on Luke's obituary. Gwen stayed and supported us until the end. Glen brought in the financial agreement once he was sure we had chosen everything we wanted. He then told us they had decided to cut the expenses in half. My father said his sister, Pam, would arrive the next day with a check.

Rev. Jenkins was in the beginning stages of dementia. They made a family decision that he wasn't well enough to go forward with the service. Our pastor had left two days earlier. We called Josh Smith and prayed that he could return from the seminary to do the service, but it wasn't possible. His brother Jarod called Bill Wininger, a friend. Pastor Wininger offered to preach the service. He had lost his daughter Stacey a few years earlier.

Tim and Sandra went to work to get Luke's dad, Steve, home. He was allowed to come to the viewing for three hours. We all went to work gathering what we needed. Shirley Rawlins, a friend's mom, called and offered to play the piano. No one would accept payment or gratuities for their services that day.

The funeral was on Friday. We buried Luke in his cousin Dylan's suit. Pastor Wininger delivered a message of hope and love. Heather Jones, one of Luke's teachers, spoke and captured Luke's spirit perfectly. We knew instantly that she was one of God's angels. When Aunt Pam sang, I could feel God's presence. The pastor said that twenty-two people gave their lives to Christ that day. It was standing room only.

It started to rain heavily on the way to the cemetery.....

*

STACY BERNDTSON
Stacy's daughter Cori Joy died in 2003, the day before her
fourth birthday, from an undiagnosed genetic disorder

The following day we went to my sister's home. Because my sister is older than me, her oldest daughter and I are the same age. My niece and her husband are pastors of a church about an hour or so south of us. They were both there the next day, as well as my sister's oldest son and his wife. My niece and her husband were at the hospital the day Cori died, and we had talked and prayed with him more than anyone else that day. I think it went without saying that he would do Cori's service.

At the time, because of Cori's disabilities we did not attend a church. When my dad died there was a memorial service for him at a local cemetery. I think it went well, and we didn't have any reason to not use them again. So it was determined that we would have a memorial service for Cori at the same location. To be completely honest, I don't really remember picking out a casket or those kinds of details. I know I was there, I know I must have had the final say, but I don't remember it. I do remember that we wanted Cori buried in her favorite pajamas. And it was VERY important to me that she be placed within the casket lying on her side, the same way she slept nearly every night of her life. She had special little stuffed animals that she slept with. She had one stuffy we put under her arm; it kept that arm from falling forward when she slept. I wanted everything to be exactly like it was that last night of her life.

We chose an open casket, but in the years since Cori's death I have spoken to many moms and it seems that grieving parents fall very much into one of two categories. Either there was NO WAY they would have their child cremated, or there was NO WAY they could put their child "in a box." I've not yet run across someone who didn't care one way or the other. I obviously fell into the first category. I could not have Cori cremated. It had nothing to do with my faith or religious belief. If I'm being honest, it was because I still truly believed that perhaps God would bring her back to me. In the Bible there is more than one story of Jesus raising someone from death to life. Before they took Cori to the cemetery that day we asked to go in one last time before the casket was sealed. In those moments I cried aloud to God to raise Cori like He raised Lazarus. We BELIEVE in Jesus. We BELIEVE the Bible is true. And so I believed that God could bring her back and that in doing so, the impact of that miracle would be far spreading, so much farther than her three years and 364 days. But that was not His will, and we had to let her go.

During her service we played a video showing pictures of Cori along with all her favorite songs. One of the things she loved to watch was bubbles. So we passed out bubbles to everyone, and at the end we all blew them in her honor and memory. I don't remember who was there, but there were a few people who I'll always remember were there. Two girlfriends from California were there. One of them could not fly, so she took Amtrak, traveling something like three days to get here, just to be with me and attend Cori's service. A mom we met one time at Children's Hospital had two very sick kids who required twenty-four-hour care. She found nurses and caretakers for them, and drove over an hour to be at Cori's service. Those selfless acts will be with me always.

Finally we all drove out to where Cori is buried, a beautiful cemetery across from a grazing field for cows. One of Cori's most loved books was called *And the Cow Said Moo*. The day we picked out her spot, there were two cows standing at the fence watching us. We knew that this was the right place.

*

KARI BROWN
Kari's 2-year-old daughter Dominique (Deedee)
died in 2014 from obstructive sleep apnea

Brandon and I were in so much shock that it was difficult to determine the first step and how to go about planning a funeral, because we never thought we would have to plan a funeral for our child. We were not supposed to; our daughter was supposed to bury us. A good friend reached out to a few funeral homes and shared her findings with us. Brandon and I agreed on one funeral home. Brandon wanted to bury Dominique, but I wanted to cremate her because we loved to travel and we moved around a lot. I did not want to leave her behind. Eventually Brandon agreed to have Dominique cremated and, to this day, he is still grateful we made that decision. Wherever we travel, we take her urn with us as a physical reminder that she is always with us. Once we arrived at the funeral home, however, the assistant explained that it would be costly to order a coffin in her size and then cremate her. Brandon came up with the idea of using Dominique's crib instead of a coffin, and then she would be cremated without additional cost. It was difficult picking out an urn, because we were still in a state of shock. Family members helped set up the crib along with Dominique's body surrounded by her favorite toys. During the wake, I felt somewhat relieved that she was laid to rest in her crib and not in a coffin, because she looked like she was sleeping. During the wake we held her hand and I started to feel warmth in her hand, like she was coming back to me. I prayed and prayed she would just wake up. But that didn't happen; the heat from my hand warmed up hers. I begged and begged for her to wake up, to come back to us. But that didn't happen.

We wrote the eulogy, however as I read it today, I am a little dissatisfied. It seemed unorganized and a bit rushed. We know what Dominique means to us, what she means to other people, and how much love she brought into our lives.

The day she was scheduled to be cremated, it was an ugly day; it was gloomy and cloudy. When Brandon and I walked to the front of the building where cremations took place, a ray of sunlight shone on my feet and then faded away. I cried, knowing it was a sign: Dominique was telling us that it was okay. She was placed in a small pink urn with three white doves etched in it. It's a simple but beautiful place for her remains to be in.

*

TANISHA CALDWELL
Tanisha's 23-year-old son Tariq (Jay)
died in a car accident in 2015

The planning all seemed so surreal. When I saw my son's name on the board at the funeral home, it was heartbreaking. Jay, as we called him, was buried and we did have a funeral. The funeral home personnel were very helpful and supportive. They guided me every step of the way. The planning went very smoothly. I had some family members with me to make arrangements.

*

LYNDA CHELDELIN FELL
Lynda's 15-year-old daughter Aly
died in a car accident in 2009

I was in such a state of shock that I remember very little from that time. I instinctively knew that Aly would have wanted to be cremated. She hated anything artificial and would have hated being preserved. We donated what viable organs we could while at the hospital, and then had her cremated. Shortly before cremation, we had a viewing for family only, but it was absolutely terrible. Aly's leg bones were harvested for donation, and the sheet just sort of dropped off where the amputations were. Even worse was that Aly wasn't cleaned up. A large white cloth laid across her forehead, and blood-covered hair strands stuck out from underneath the cloth. It was just horrific. I remember repeating, "That isn't Aly. That isn't Aly." Her hands were so tiny, folded across her chest. I still don't understand why she was presented for her final viewing in such a fashion. I didn't think the rest of the family should view her in that condition, but they did. It was just awful.

I'm not entirely sure who planned the funeral, I was in such fog. I think my sisters did most of it. I remember them guiding me to the computer and helping me pick out photos, but I could hardly comprehend or focus on anything. Aly had created a fun

PowerPoint slide show for her beloved swim team just weeks before the accident, and I wanted that to be played at the service because I knew her team would be there.

Although much of it is still foggy, I remember my large family assembled in a private room in the church while waiting for the service to start. I wore a long formal gown in Aly's favorite color. I'm sure I must have looked pretty silly, but at the time it represented all the fun Aly and I had with her teammates and friends in the formal shop we owned. I remember taking the stage wearing that long blue formal and looking out on the audience of people wearing blue. I don't remember requesting to take the stage; I just did. I remember addressing Aly's teammates, telling them they could achieve anything they set their minds to, encouraging them to "swim Felly fierce" in remembrance of their fallen teammate.

When Aly's PowerPoint slide show was played, someone had replaced all of Aly's upbeat songs with downbeat songs. I always wondered who did that, who switched her music, because it didn't go with the fun-filled slides. I felt like the audience was robbed of one last gift from Aly. Those are all the memories I have from that time; the rest is just a fog. Someone videotaped the service, but six years later it remains unwatched.

*

JACQUELYN CRUZ
Jacquelyn's 24-year-old daughter Jenna
died in 2012 from pulmonary edema

The funeral was planned by myself, my husband, my son Danny, and my husband's two oldest children. My daughter Jenna and I were very close, we talked about everything. In one of our conversations we talked about what happens to us after we die. Jenna was very spiritual and believed in heaven and worried about being forgiven for her sins. I always assured her she would be welcomed into heaven with open arms. She told me she wanted to be cremated and have a closed coffin. I know this sounds strange to talk about with a young girl; that's why I think she knew somehow that she would go before I did. I picked out her clothes, and made sure they knew how her hair should look and absolutely no makeup, she hated it! I wrote the eulogy one morning after waking up with a start. The words just flowed. I wrote everything I wished I had told her. My husband read it at the mass. I really don't remember much about that day.

*

MICHELLE DETWILER
Michelle's 19-year-old daughter Emily
died in 2014 due to congenital complications

My husband and I both planned the funeral. I had thought about planning a funeral in the months before, knowing how medically fragile our daughter was. Once it came down to it though, my brain just couldn't think. Planning the video or photo slide show was just beyond me. We had thousands of pictures of our beautiful girl, but how could I go through all of those? I copied all the pictures from Emily's life and gave them to my sister to work on the slide show. She put it together with some of Emily's favorite music and it turned out beautiful.

Our daughter had loved trucks, the big kind. Every afternoon the large trucks from the trucking company down the road would pass our home. We would say, "Emily, your trucks are coming!" And she would smile or start laughing until the last truck passed her bedroom window. On the day of the funeral we were told to go outside to meet our daughter as she arrived at the church. As we waited, I saw her funeral coach coming down the road. In front of her was a huge truck and behind her coach was another huge truck! When I saw the trucks on the road with her I started crying. In my heart I was thanking the Lord for being so nice as to have trucks around her on the road as she was arriving for her service. Little did we know that our funeral home director had planned this surprise for us! He had asked the trucking company that was close to our home, the same trucks that drove down our road every day, to escort Emily to her service. What a huge gift of love! The owner of the trucking company was one of the drivers. We were able to meet him and tell him how much our daughter had loved his trucks driving past her bedroom each afternoon. This was such a lovely and unique gift for her last party.

When I had to think about the order of the service, the pastor asked me what music and songs I would like. My brain was a blank. I asked my husband and he thought of a couple of songs he wanted to play in Emily's memory. How could I know what I wanted to use for her final party music? All I could think about was how she loved the Hokey Pokey. In the past we had to take her little disabled arms and dance them all around as we would sing and dance the Hokey Pokey with her. What a great song to play at her last party! I asked the pastor if it would be okay to play the Hokey Pokey; I didn't want to be sacrilegious or do anything wrong in a church. He was a little shocked I think, expecting something a little more reverent. But he was wonderful about my request, telling me that we could do the Hokey Pokey if we wanted to. So the last thing we did at the end of the funeral service was the Hokey Pokey. Standing in front of her coffin, we danced and laughed and shook it all about. I know she would have had a great time. What a fun memory for everyone to have, thinking about our beautiful daughter in heaven, now able to do the Hokey Pokey on her own!

*

ANNAH ELIZABETH
Annah's son Gavin Michael aspirated on his meconium
during the delivery and died 26 minutes following his birth

I spent nearly a week in the hospital following the emergency Cesarean section that brought my son into this world. Those days are really a blur, a combination of the shock and the drugs used to help keep me as calm as possible so I wouldn't damage my incision.

My husband made most of the funeral arrangements, like talking with the people at the funeral home, choosing a casket, listening to the steps we needed to take, making preparations for a burial plot, gathering information that he could bring back to me at the hospital. Together we chose the headstone.

One of the documents someone gave us in the first few days after Gavin died suggested that we write farewell letters to our child. So we did. Warren and I also wrote personal letters to our boy. Always a writer at heart, I also penned a poem that the minister included in the burial service, along with my goodbye letter that was written more as a we'll-see-you-later send-off-letter than a goodbye.

The only reason I recollect any of this that I made photocopies of everything and placed them in the box with the few mementoes the hospital had collected for us: baby's first blanket…Baby Boy Fleming's bassinet card…his little knitted cap and the paper tape measure they used to record his birth statistics…articles that serve as living testimony of our experiences, both good and bad…

We held the service in a small chapel attached to our church. Warren and I arrived early to spend our last minutes with our boy before his burial, and then gave anyone who wanted to pay their respects in private an opportunity to do so. We placed a few photos, toys, and a baby book in his casket before taking our places in the pews.

The skies wept hard as we arrived at the cemetery. Making the trek up the hillside was difficult for me, so we sat in our car and watched our son's body being lowered into the ground. I remember thinking how fitting the rain was in light of the tears shed that day.

*

WENDY EVANS
Wendy's 21-year-old son Kyle died in 2009
from diabetes when his insulin pump malfunctioned

My husband, mother, daughter and brothers were very instrumental in organizing what had to be done for the funeral. My responsibility was dealing with the police and the coroner's office. I remember little about the service, except that Kyle's friends presented my husband and me with a skateboard that was signed by all of them along with a statement about their friend Kyle.

I had to leave the funeral home at that time because it was overwhelming. Driving home, we noticed skateboards nailed to telephone poles around our neighborhood, with notes written on them by Kyle's friends. Although I expected there to be some friction with Kyle's father, it did not happen. Kyle and his father had not seen each other in many years.

*

BONNIE FORSHEY
Bonnie's 16-year-old son Billy died in 1993
from an overdose of prescription drugs

Billy's stepfather and I planned the service, although I don't remember much. I do remember Billy's friends standing in line waiting to get in. I heard so many positive things from them and their parents. They called Billy "The Peacemaker," because he wore a white T-shirt with no color. I saw members of two gangs, the Bloods and the Crips, come together that evening. They took off their colors (bandanas) and placed them in the coffin with Billy. Each one kissed his finger and touched it to his heart, and they told me how much they loved him. Many of them gave up their gang affiliation that night. They brought guitars and sang songs, and told stories of how Billy had impacted their lives. It was a beautiful service, but the shock prevented me from remembering a lot of it. Billy had more friends than he realized. I will cherish the memories.

82

*

TALIA GATO
Talia's 8-year-old daughter Poppy
died in 2009 in a car accident

My church planned the memorial. I had two key family friends who put things together exactly the way we wanted. My husband spent hours on music choices, who was going to speak and share. We picked music that wasn't really church-like but as a family we loved listening to a wide range of music. We had a video of pictures that were really beautiful. The funeral was huge. We both grew up here, and I think that when the loss is a child, more people come. Looking back, I think it was well planned and beautifully done. What I find ironic is that there was one time I told my husband that when I die, play this song at my funeral. How surreal that it was played for my daughter.

*

KORBY HAVE
Korby's 17-year-old daughter Taylor (Tayla)
died in 2013 in a car accident

My family helped me plan my daughter's funeral, and I invited her dad to be a part of the process as well. During the planning meeting there was fighting between my family and Taylor's father because he didn't feel like he needed to contribute financially. I remember sitting on the couch and thinking that this couldn't be happening. I couldn't be sitting here trying to plan my daughter's funeral. I think I emotionally detached myself from the situation and just made decisions based on what I could afford instead of what I would have liked. What other choice did I have? I was not financially prepared to bury my child; it was really something I had never thought of.

We picked out a plot close to a tree, and I made sure Taylor's headstone reflected her personality by splurging to have her pictures engraved on it. It all just felt like a dream. We held her funeral at our church and invited friends to speak. A friend posted a song online about seeing her again, and it was so moving that we ended up playing it at her funeral. At Tayla's grave site we released balloons with messages to her and dropped her favorite flowers onto her casket. Her best friends, her boyfriend and her brothers threw dirt onto the casket, and we all stood by and watched her be lowered into the ground. I remember thinking again that this couldn't be happening and that I would wake up from this nightmare at any second.

*

DEANA MARTIN
Deana's only two children, 25-year-old Amanda
and 21-year-old Logan, died in a car accident in 2011

I planned the funeral, or I suppose you could say the viewing. I had my children cremated and a large urn buried in a family cemetery in West Newton, Indiana. The viewing was for family, because I hate the concept, but it had been tradition in our Midwestern family and I knew nothing else. The mortician is a family friend and he had buried many of my family through the years. My mother went to high school with him, so by the time I reached Indiana he had already retrieved my children's bodies from the county coroner. By the time I landed in Indiana, a meeting with the mortician had been arranged for the next day. My father and my sister accompanied me to the funeral home where we flipped through catalogs of caskets and discussed prices. I remember thinking that only my family could be offered BOGO deals on funeral costs. My father was huge into sales and coupons, so it was rather ironic.

At one point we were discussing the fact that we would have to go with a custom casket for my son because he was such a big boy at twenty-one years old. The mortician said, "Let me go see." He disappeared through a door at the back of what was a break room of sorts or lounge where we were doing all the planning, so he could measure Logan's shoulder width. He was gone only for a second, and I remember asking him upon his return through the mysterious door, "Are they back there?" He said yes. I felt overwhelmed with guilt that I was not immediately on my feet and running through the door to be next to my babies' bodies. I was so scared of what I would find, for it had taken the emergency team six hours to cut them out of the vehicle, and the mortuary had to do a lot of reconstruction to allow for an open casket viewing. If I had known how my daughter looked beforehand, the open casket decision would not have been made! I was simply following directions, and I believed the professionals when they said that an open casket was possible. I regret not inquiring more, because that was not my daughter I saw, and it was the last time I ever saw her. She was rather unrecognizable to everyone but her three-year-old daughter, who immediately knew it was her mommy sleeping in that box.

I had much help with planning the service. It was a creation from the collaborative minds of my brother-in-law and myself. I did not want the typical clergy-led ceremony, rather I wanted something Amanda and Logan would have wanted, something more fitting for young adults. My brother-in-law is a wonderful public speaker and they loved him greatly. I asked him to officiate the service. My best friends, a husband and wife, are very much into their faith so they led prayers for us. My cousin played "Stairway to Heaven" on his guitar and then we opened up the mic to allow anyone to speak who wanted to, which several did. My sister shopped for clothes for my children to wear at the showing, for I could not face it.

The hall was used behind the funeral home because the rooms within the building would not be big enough for the hundreds of people who would attend. I saw people I had not seen in fifteen years, since we moved away from Indiana when my children were very small. Both my ex-husband and I have very large families, and each of them were in attendance, plus some others. There was a great deal of media attention and estates to be established for my children, attorneys to consult. The days before and after the funeral seemed to go on forever.

Even when I returned to Georgia, I could not return to my home. Once my daughter died, nobody had custody of my granddaughter due to the fact that she was not married when she gave birth. This is a very long story, but I knew the father would try to take her from me if he knew where I was. Until we could get legal papers in place giving me temporary custody, I had to take refuge in a friend's home for four to five days. Once home, it was even more surreal. My home was empty and quiet, where it had once bustled with endless activity and young adults or big kids. I was scared to be home, because I was frightened of my granddaughter's father. As time went on the fear began to subside. Eventually I obtained full legal custody of my last living heir.

*

MONICA MIRKES
Monica's 30-year-old daughter Marisa
died in 2013 due to Cesarean complications

Thank God for good friends. I had just lost a piece of my soul. I am holding her hand knowing I have to let go of it, of her. How do you do that? I looked up because someone had come to the door. We made eye contact and she asked, "Who do you want us to call?" I don't know about anyone else, but in my address book I do have a list of "just in case" numbers. Funeral homes? No. The woman starts to hand me a sheet of paper when it's intercepted by my girlfriend. We locked eyes, we said nothing, but I can tell you we had some form of mental conversation. She turned to the nurse and told her she would be making the arrangements. I do know that she called everyone on that list. She came back in and said, "This is the one we're using."

We agreed on cremation. We held a memorial service. Did the planning go smoothly? In hindsight I would have done things differently. How do you make decisions that will later be re-run in your mind over and over again? You have a very small window to make these decisions. How do you write an obituary for someone you dearly loved? How can you put into words what you would like other people to know about your child? What you and the world have lost?

*

DENISE PURCELL
Denise's 27-year-old daughter Megan died
in 2011 from an accidental overdose

My son-in-law planned everything. We had a viewing of Megan after waiting over a week for her to be shipped back after the autopsy. Then she was cremated and I was given half of her ashes in a plastic Tupperware container.

*

MARILYN ROLLINS
Marilyn's 37-year-old son Randy and 16-year-old granddaughter Sara
died in a car accident in 2006 during a family camping trip

Since my son Randy was married, his wife handled all the funeral arrangements for him and Sara. She did ask me to go to the funeral home with her and her mother to help with the arrangements. She did a wonderful job on everything, so I just sat quietly. The funeral was held a full week after the accident, because the rest of the family was still in the hospital. Since there were two people, we chose to have the wake in a large church, not far from their home. There were so many people there. Randy was with the fire department, so there were many firemen there, plus all the people he had worked with. Sara, of course, had all her high school friends. I was so surprised at how many came alone. I remember one teen who came to the front, but wouldn't walk up to the casket. I went and took her hand and asked how she knew Sara. She said she knew her from school. She walked with me to the casket as she shook and cried. I reached out and stroked Sara's beautiful long hair and heard a sharp intake of breath from her friend. "You can touch her?" she asked. I told her she could, but that Sara would feel very cold to the touch. She very gingerly touched Sara's hand. She was sobbing so hard. I wished her mother was there to talk to her.

There were two long lines of people, one line coming by my husband and me and the other by my daughter-in-law and her family. My brother-in-law said he counted close to a thousand people coming through the church on the day of the wake. There was an honor guard of firemen there, and I found out much later that they never left the bodies. They stood there for twenty-four hours, changing shifts every few hours. I can remember my husband saying over and over to people, "You're not supposed to bury your children." I methodically took people's hands and thanked them for coming. Many months after the funeral, I ran into a friend and said to her, "You know that Randy and his daughter were killed in an accident, don't you?" She said, "I know, I was there, at the church." I apologized for not remembering. At some point, my sister-in-law came and got me and took me to a back room where there were tables of donated food. I ate because I needed energy to get through the day.

The firemen that Randy and Sara (she was a junior firefighter) worked with actually modified two of the firetrucks so they could secure the caskets to the top for the trip to the cemetery. The day of the funeral was a beautiful, warm day. It was at the end of September. There was standing room only in the church, with firemen and police officers lining the walls, from front to back. Young people from Sara's school filled the church. After the memorial service the caskets were wheeled out, moved to a lift and raised to the top of the firetrucks and secured. The procession detoured past the firehouse where more firemen stood at attention and saluted as the trucks drove slowly by. As we came to the last turn before the cemetery, I turned to look and there were cars behind us as far as I could see. People in the small community stood in their front yards and bowed their heads as we passed by. At the turn there were two more firetrucks with ladders raised, and a large U.S. flag hanging between them, across the road. Again firemen stood on the road and saluted as we passed.

It took some time for all the cars to get into the cemetery and park. The caskets were lowered from the trucks and carried over to the gravesite. Bagpipes played "Amazing Grace" as they were being carried. After the minister said a few words, I heard the tones go off on the fire radio followed by an announcement, "Last call for Lieutenant Randy Rollins." One of Randy's friends took Randy's helmet off the casket and presented it to my grandson, Adam. Then he gave Sara's helmet to her sister, Emily. The flag that had draped Randy's casket was presented to my daughter-in-law. Then people filed by, leaving single roses on the silver and pink caskets, some kissing their fingers and touching the top. I could barely walk back to the car after the family said their goodbyes. I still have a hard time going out to the cemetery.

*

SARA RUBLE
Sara's 19-year-old son Scott died in 1994 from a
combination of a seizure disorder, Strep throat and dehydration

Scott died in 1994, so at that time we did what was expected and needed for Scott's dad and me to feel we had loved Scott into heaven. We planned Scott's funeral together, even though we had divorced a couple of years earlier. We set aside any hard feelings between us to bring our love to Scott, to work together...and we did it well. I felt his pain and he felt mine. We both loved Scott so deeply, and that was most important to us. My ex-husband lovingly insisted that I stand between him and my new husband at calling hours. They also walked on either side of me as we entered the church behind Scott's casket. I felt supported in a most unlikely setting. So hard, and yet so important.

Challenges did arise from my ex-husband's family, as they had not seen me for two years. I had wanted the divorce, and they were supporting him. I understood and either stayed away from some of them, or tried to embrace others. It was what it was. My grief for Scott was far too great to do much more than that.

One of the unique moments of Scott's funeral was being able to walk across the street from the church to the cemetery. Respectfully, the police stopped traffic as we followed the hearse and hundreds of family members and friends followed, walking through the cemetery to Scott's grave. It was beautiful, tear-filled and solemn, as everyone moved silently down the tree-lined road. It was breathtaking…and unforgettable.

*

DENISE SHELTON
Denise's 22-year-old son Nicholas died in 2010
when he struck a steel cable while riding an ATV

My husband and I mostly planned the funeral. We live in a small community and happened to know the family that owned the funeral parlor. We trusted them, so that helped, if anything can help when planning your child's funeral. It's funny how we discussed things we thought our son would like. "I think he'd like that casket better, or maybe this one." We talked about the details of the casket with the same care we had taken when buying Nick's mountain bike for his birthday. How strange. Even the concept of having to go shopping for clothes for the wake and funeral was strange. I didn't know how to answer the clerk when asked if I was looking for something special. My daughter, her fiancé, my husband and I all went shopping together. We went from laughing to crying in seconds. It didn't seem real that I was shopping for clothes because my son was killed. I mean, clothes shopping was not exactly the first thing that came to mind when I found out Nick had been killed. Picking a plot went along the same way as the conversation about the casket. Nicholas loved to sit in our tree or on the roof, even in his twenties. He loved the mountains more than the beach. He loved cars. So we wanted a plot that was near a big tree, not in a lot of sun, and near the road. My prerequisite was that it didn't flood. I don't know why. It makes me physically sick to think of his plot flooding. I know he's not really there, but I can't help it.

My daughter and Nick's girlfriend spent hours making picture boards to hang around the room at the funeral. Thank goodness for them; I never could have done it. I couldn't look at the pictures. Our daughter took care of so many things for us. I know she was hurting, yet she did it. I know I mentioned a few songs for the music, which was easy, as Nicholas loved all kinds of music. The rest of the music got picked and put on CDs. It was perfect. I don't remember who took care of following through on this. My husband called a restaurant for after the funeral. We went with the restaurant that we used for my mom's funeral dinner. Some of Nick's friends signed a soccer ball to put in the casket, as my son loved and played soccer. A few of his friends wrote beautiful tributes to him that were read. The American Legion put a flag in Nick's coffin, as he had been playing on their baseball team.

It's so strange the way your mind works. These people touched my heart with these items and their stories of my son, and in the back of my mind I'm wondering if it will be too crowded in the casket for him. He loved wearing suits or suit jackets, and when he was about sixteen he once said he wanted to work in a big city and wear a suit to work every day. So picking out his clothes was easy, and I use that term "easy" loosely. Actually, there is not another moment in the rest of your life that is easy once you lose your child. Nick loved the Chicago White Sox, so he wore his suit with his White Sox tie and the wingtip shoes he had worn to his prom.

As I mentioned, we knew the funeral director and he was very helpful. After all, I never thought I would be planning my child's funeral. Neither I nor my husband had any idea. Nothing prepared me for it. It's unnatural. It's not supposed to happen like this. I'm sure people thought I was perfectly okay with my son being gone as I stood and talked and laughed with the endless line of family and friends who came through at the wake. I heard myself say, "It doesn't even feel like I'm here. It's like I have no idea who that guy is," as I motioned to my son in the casket. By the time of the funeral, we had some information from the officer who investigated Nick's four-wheeler accident. It was Lake Central School's property, even though it was not marked in any way. There was a half-inch steel cable and a chain strung across the road between two pieces of wood. The officer said there was no way Nick could have seen them, and that Nick was going 10 to 15 mph. He wasn't speeding. For some reason, I wanted to tell everyone this story.

*

CHAPTER FOUR

THE TRANSITION

The bereaved need more than just the space to grieve the loss. They also need the space to grieve the transition.   -LYNDA CHELDELIN FELL

As we begin the transition of facing life without our child, some find comfort by immediately returning to a familiar routine, while others find solitude a safe haven. Sometimes our own circumstances don't allow choices to ponder, and we simply follow where the path leads. But the one commonality we're all faced with is the starting point that marks the transition from our old life to the new.

*

ERICA GALE BELTZ
Erica's 5-year-old son Luke Jordan died in 2005
from a fallen banister in his aunt's driveway

I hadn't been in the same room with Steve, Luke's father, since he attacked me at his parents' house two years earlier. I had a restraining order against him, and he had a bond condition prior to going to prison. In the final moments of Luke's life, I started the process to get Steve home. He was housed in Georgia Diagnostic & Classification State Prison in Jackson. He was the barber on duty when told to report to the chaplain. The chaplain asked Steve three questions: Did he have a TV in his pod? Did he watch TV? Did he have children? When Steve confirmed that he had two children, he was then informed that his son had died. He was granted fifteen minutes for phone time. I remember I was prepared for him to scream, cuss, and blame me. But he didn't. He simply said, "Erica! Oh, my god! What happened to our baby?" Regardless of the past, we were Luke's mom and dad. Steve was shattered.

At the funeral, there were concerns about Steve's family members who had been abusive to us in the past. Steve's great-grandmother, Mawmaw, asked if Steve's family could come. Mawmaw had buried a son too, and I trusted her. My answer was, "Yes." Anyone who had loved Luke was welcome to attend.

Both the viewing and funeral were filled to capacity, and both days had only minor glitches. Steve was transferred from Jackson to the county prison. That warden agreed to let Steve attend for three hours but only on one day, not both. I will never forget the moment he was led through the back door: dressed in the white state uniform, Steve was shackled and handcuffed. It must have been so hard to walk through those doors.

In those three hours, Steve was shown a lot of love and support. When it was time for him to leave, our families, the kids, and the pastor gathered around to pray. Steve said his final goodbye, and was then escorted out. Little six-year-old Preston said, "Welp, back to jail!" Just like that, the room filled with laughter. That moment was lifting beyond measure by Preston's funny comment.

As I write this nearly eleven years later, I decided to call Steve and ask about his experience from that time. I also asked for permission to share about his being in prison at the time Luke died. I realized I had never asked the father of my son how he survived the remainder of his prison sentence. Steve said that all he remembers is how pitch black it was when they arrived back at the prison. Steve was checked in, and then escorted back to his cell.

Therapy was never offered, the chaplain didn't meet with him; he did not receive any bereavement books or brochures. To the prison staff, Steve was simply Inmate Jordan, and the death of his young son was never mentioned. He had no choice but to get up every morning as Inmate Jordan and just survive.

*

STACY BERNDTSON
Stacy's daughter Cori Joy died in 2003, the day before her
fourth birthday, from an undiagnosed genetic disorder

After the service the house was no longer full of people coming over. It ended rather abruptly, I seem to remember. I think everyone wanted to give Steve and me a chance to grieve together. That time is truly a blur for me. I believe Steve got two weeks off from work. His coworkers donated time so Steve could spend more time with me. I had been Cori's primary caregiver for the last two years, and when Steve went back to work, I felt truly lost. I said many times that I felt like I'd been fired from my job. My whole life had revolved around Cori's care twenty-four hours a day. Steve and I received respite for two days total between May 2001 and her death in November 2003. Except for those two days, I had literally been in Cori's presence for over 900 days straight. And then she was gone. I think I pretty much cried nonstop when Steve first went back to work. I cried when he left, I cried while he was gone, and I cried when he got home. I am sure it was difficult for him to go back to work, as if nothing had happened, but I felt that at least he had something to do. I remember thinking that at least PART of his life is the same, whereas ALL of my life was changed.

*

TANISHA CALDWELL
Tanisha's 23-year-old son Tariq (Jay)
died in a car accident in 2015

My husband and I returned to work a few weeks after everything was over. It happened in the summer, so school was already out. Returning to work felt weird, because I didn't know if I was actually ready. I just felt like maybe if I was busy then my mind wouldn't focus on my son being gone. I was wrong about that though. I had a lot of support when I returned to work.

*

LYNDA CHELDELIN FELL
Lynda's 15-year-old daughter Aly
died in a car accident in 2009

I owned a little second-hand formal shop, a little boutique right near the high school. Aly and I shared a love of formal gowns and jewelry, and she helped me buy the gowns and accessories. I don't remember when I returned to the shop, but I do remember that it became a wonderful, safe place for us. Aly's friends, her teammates, and their mothers would visit me there nearly every day. We would just sit, laugh and cry together while Aly's friends and teammates tried on gowns, something they had enjoyed frequently before the accident. For months after the accident that little shop became a safe haven for us all. And then when school let out the following June, I couldn't bear to face the quiet summer until school started again. I needed to take a step back and focus on my own healing, so I closed the business. I left everything inside for a year, visible through the windows but untouched. I hated going back there from that point forward. What once had been a safe little haven filled with love became too painful. One day I finally forced myself to clean it out and allow someone else to rent the space. What had once been a source of deep comfort, like a cocoon, became terribly painful and raw just to drive past. Grief is a strange world.

*

JACQUELYN CRUZ
Jacquelyn's 24-year-old daughter Jenna
died in 2012 from pulmonary edema

I went back to work as a paraprofessional for special education children three months after Jenna's passing. I love my job. I wanted to go back to some sort of normality. I couldn't lie on the couch any longer. I was working in a classroom with a team of very young teachers. If I wasn't going back to them, I don't think I would have ever gone back. They knew exactly what to say and do for me. I wanted to work and keep busy, and they were happy to have me back. I still remain very friendly with them and love them like my daughters. Another great supporter was my friend Marni, who kept in touch with me. She came to my home and asked what she could do to make my return to work easier. My fear was about crying in front of the kids and scaring them. I told her I did not want anyone coming over to me and hugging me and asking questions; that would open up the floodgates! I don't know what Marni did or said, but my return to work went smoothly.

The week before, my husband and I went to the school for a visit. I thought it would be better to get the initial appearance over with and with my husband by my side I felt strong. Don't get me wrong, there were days and still are days that I'm hanging on by a very short thread, but now I know it will pass shortly. Some days I couldn't make it to my car before the tears would stream down my face. Once I was in the safety of my car, I would then allow myself to sob. I would cry all the way home and sometimes have to pull over, and think it would be so much easier never leaving the house again. But I did. My husband is retired, so he didn't have to return to work. Danny and Chelsea returned to their jobs about two weeks after Jenna's passing.

*

MICHELLE DETWILER
Michelle's 19-year-old daughter Emily
died in 2014 due to congenital complications

Since I own my own business, I was able to work when I felt I could and then set aside the work when I just couldn't function. I had very few customers at that time of year, and being able to adjust my own time schedule was a relief. However, I had a huge embroidery job that I was going to start the next month. The job was to do the exact same thing for twelve weeks. The lack of variation meant that I could do what needed to be done, even if I couldn't think or if I was too depressed to function. I remember standing at my machine and often just crying my eyes out. There was no one in the office with me, so I could cry when the grief came over me. It was actually a good thing that I had that embroidery job. It gave me something to do each day. I think I would have felt like sinking into oblivion if I had nothing to do.

*

ANNAH ELIZABETH
Annah's son Gavin Michael aspirated on his meconium
during the delivery and died 26 minutes following his birth

Though the details look different on the various types of child loss, I do believe that grief from the death of a child occurs whether that child is eight weeks gestation, a full-term baby, or an eight-year-old when he or she expires.

Having experienced the death of a living child as well as two miscarriages, my experiences varied. I eased back into work following my son's death and went back full time when the doctor released me eight weeks after the emergency Cesarean section. If memory serves me right, I returned to work within a day or two following both miscarriages.

During my grief periods that followed the death of my son and both miscarriages, I was fortunate to be working for a small family-owned business. The family offered me a great deal of support, comfort and understanding. For me, work helped keep my mind focused on other things besides my loss. I didn't want to sit at home and wallow in self-pity, so having tasks to accomplish during the day helped to manage the time I spent grieving and provided me a sense of success.

I felt needed, valued, appreciated, competent and trusted at work, emotions that offset those feelings of inferiority and shame that came with my grief.

Don't get me wrong, I'm sure I had sad spells during the day — when a particular song came on, a pregnant woman came into the office, or a customer came in with a baby in hand, but in the bigger picture, my visible grief came outside of office hours, so to speak. For me, especially in the aftermath of my son's death, being able to return to work and have something to focus on helped me through my initial suffering.

Because of their empathy and understanding, my employers allowed me to perform a few simple paperwork tasks at home, even before I was released to go back to work after the emergency surgery that brought my eldest child into this world. This allowed me the freedom to grieve when I needed to while still affording me an opportunity to feel a sense of accomplishment. The interaction with others also helped stave off that overwhelming sense of isolation and aloneness that accompanies significant sorrow. I am eternally grateful for those transition and therapeutic pieces that I was afforded in my employment.

*

WENDY EVANS
Wendy's 21-year-old son Kyle died in 2009
from diabetes when his insulin pump malfunctioned

I returned to work three weeks following the funeral. My husband returned the week after and my daughter and stepson went back after one week as well. I was able to work for two months and then hit a wall around ninety days after Kyle's death. I took a leave of four additional weeks to spend more time with family and go to counseling every week. My employer was supportive.

*

TALIA GATO
Talia's 8-year-old daughter Poppy
died in 2009 in a car accident

We returned to school two weeks after the accident. My husband returned to work. I didn't drive at first, so I was driven to school and errands by relatives. We bought a different van. Our younger daughter Livia asked me how she was going to go to school without Poppy. It was a very difficult and painful question to answer. I think I was very lucky to not have worked. I had a summer job which was seasonal. I cried with every client, but after I got that out of the way with each one, I could go on normally each time I saw them after that. But I am so glad I didn't have a regular nine-to-five job, because I was such a broken soppy mess. My hat is off to the parents who have no choice, and have to return to work after their loss. They have to put the mask on, and that takes a special amount of inner strength. Actually, it takes super strength.

After a while I was home alone. Oh, I was so lonely! I still cleaned, and moved around but I lost my creative ambition. I had absolutely no interest in the things I used to do like baking, cooking, entertaining, parties. I just couldn't do it. I remember going throughout the store checkout one day and glancing at Gourmet magazine. I used to enjoy looking for new ideas, but this time I glanced at the magazine and felt dead inside. It took years for that creativity to come back, and even now I reserve my energy selectively.

I remember how I made breakfast for my daughters. Now I was making only one breakfast and preparing one lunchbox; it was so daunting. To this day I haven't made the things my Poppy loved, liked cinnamon oatmeal and pineapple. There are so many layers of losses one can't fathom, the simple things like never again cooking the things your loved one ate.

Some of my family thought that if I got a job it would help me get over my loss, or at least have a distraction. I even had people call, inviting me to work for them. I am glad I was there for my remaining daughter, and advocating for her. My youngest daughter didn't do well in school. She didn't want to go to school, and we would struggle with that. She was overwhelmed with school, she was overwhelmed by it all. She stopped going out to play, and instead would hide in empty classrooms and write on the chalkboards. She was grieving so much, it pains me even to remember it. The teachers told me way after the fact what Livia was doing. They didn't send anyone to hang out with her in the playground like an adult. When she was told to leave the classroom, she hung out in the bathroom.

After three years of spiraling downward, Livia almost failed in school. The teachers seemed mystified about what was wrong! After getting Livia tested, we were told she had ADD and ADHD. I did extensive reading about different learning styles and we moved Livia to another school that taught the same subjects but the teaching style was different. Maybe it was the change of scenery and complete anonymity that helped, because three years later Livia has no symptoms of ADD or ADHD and is now flourishing in her new school.

We didn't know the different ways children show, or don't show, grief and loss. In our case Livia regressed emotionally and physically and kept loss to herself. We took her to a child counselor for a year. We also went for child occupational therapy. Livia had stopped playing at home and didn't play outside, so she forgot the simplest things like skipping and cartwheels. After all, she had lost her bestie sister, the one who taught her everything. After about three years, Livia is now at par physically and doing well in school. We also go to a family support group for her so she can relate to other kids who have gone through the loss of a family member.

I really wish there were more information on sibling loss and grief behavior with children. I felt I was floundering and trying to solve a mystery and didn't have any answers.

*

DAPHNE GREER
Daphne's 5-year-old daughter Lydia died in 2008 in a
car accident during a routine morning commute

Returning to work was a challenging time for me. I didn't want to go back, and I was haunted subconsciously by a barrage of thoughts, counting down those days until I had to go back, incessantly in my mind. It had been a little over three months. I was grateful that my coworkers had donated time, allowing me to stay home this long. However my thoughts on my career in law enforcement had changed immensely. I was terrified and alone, having to plan a new route to take to work to avoid the stretch of highway where our tragic accident had occurred. It was unbearable.

The day had come. With my waterproof mascara firmly in place, I arrived in the parking lot outside my work, dreading that walk down the long hallway to my office. I entered the building and was flooded with memories of the last time I was there. Life was normal. Life was good. No major worries. Both my children were alive and healthy. I slowly walked down the hallway, slipped into my office and sat exhausted in my chair. As I looked around, I saw the artwork that my daughter had drawn for me placed all over the sage-green walls. The memories encompassed me. I tried to hold back the tears but was unsuccessful. A few of my coworkers greeted me in my office, hugging me as they showered me with comments like "I'm so glad you're back," and "How are you?", which caused my eyes to water and glisten in the overhead lights.

My first few days were rather unproductive as my mind fantasized about how life used to be and the horrible reality of what was. In those first weeks I felt amazingly supported by warmth and compassion, as many made a point to check in with me daily. However, after a short while, reality hit. With the exception of a couple of close friends, the rest had moved on. I was left to navigate these waters by myself and face the terrifying reality that I had forever changed. The pressure to be the same person I used to be before my daughter died was a heavy load to carry. I used to be the one who laughed, joked, and was full of spunk and life, eager to get to work, excited about what the day would bring. But I was not me anymore.

Generally speaking, my coworkers were as supportive as they could have been while not understanding the circumstances of having a child die. No one at my work had experienced such a tragedy. Their efforts were not in vain but were done with good intentions. However, their warmth and comfort dissipated as the weeks continued. I was not only struggling at home but at my job duties as well. It became challenging to meet with my clients at first, knowing that most of them probably had heard of our car accident due to the media coverage. I was nervous that someone would mention Lydia, and I would cry in front of them. I, the stoic, powerful authority figure whom they had to answer to, showing my emotions to clients was seldom. On a couple of occasions a tear would slip down as her name was mentioned. However, I became extremely talented in diverting and changing subjects rapidly.

As the months and years went on, I felt my support dwindle. People had moved on and were back in their normal routines. I often wondered if they had forgotten what had happened to me. I would leave work and go home to be reminded daily that my daughter was never coming back. I would sit in my same spot on the couch and avoid everyone and everything as I cried myself to sleep, thinking how life wasn't fair. It was so hard. I became less productive, distracted and uninterested in my job. I realized years later that it wasn't their fault. Those who have not walked in your shoes cannot comprehend the devastation and life-altering changes that come with burying your child. All we can do is be honest and open and educate others that there is no timeline for grieving.

*

BONNIE FORSHEY
Bonnie's 16-year-old son Billy died in 1993
from an overdose of prescription drugs

I had a hard time going back to work. Billy's high school was right beside the nursing center I worked at. I went back six months later but could not handle it. I found a different position in a different town. I just could not handle seeing all his friends every day. Too many ghosts.

*

KORBY HAVE
Korby's 17-year-old daughter Taylor (Tayla)
died in 2013 in a car accident

I returned to work three days after the funeral and a week after her death, because as a single mom, I didn't have a choice. I didn't have any vacation time left, and my company had only three days of bereavement pay. I have always been really shy, and never really made any friends at work, so my coworkers pretty much left me alone. I remember spending a lot of time quietly crying at my desk or in the bathroom, but I never allowed others to see me fall apart.

*

DEANA MARTIN
Deana's only two children, 25-year-old Amanda
and 21-year-old Logan, died in a car accident in 2011

I returned to work half days after two weeks. I went back full time after four weeks. My granddaughter returned to pre-kindergarten at the same time. I do not recall a great deal about my return to work. I remember thinking I did not know how I was going to do it, and that I did not want to go back so soon. All I wanted to do was sleep. I could have slept for a year, and to this day I could sleep all the time if allowed to.

I had a hard time with how my coworkers avoided me for the most part. The ones who went out of their way to welcome me back made up for the others somewhat. My granddaughter initially had problems with anger, mainly with outbursts and some behavior issues, but quickly adjusted back into routine. Fortunately, my daughter and my granddaughter had lived with me since my granddaughter was eight months old, so she knew no other environment and had no other primary caretaker besides her mother and me.

Previous to my children's death, I kept her a great deal because my daughter was in college full time and worked several jobs. The father of the baby would not help much. I was let go from my job after three years due to grief-related symptoms, mainly lack of concentration, inability to focus, excessive time away from the office, and I made mistake after mistake. I had become a liability to the company because of money lost due to mistakes and my lack of productivity. They were kind enough to not put this in my separation package, and they gave me six months of severance pay.

They never came right out and said that was what I was being let go for, only that my job was being eliminated. But I knew what the real issues were. I had suffered with chronic depression and anxiety disorder before the death of my children. In the years since, I have developed what they call complicated or prolonged grief syndrome. I can't function in a normal workplace with set hours and the stress of deadlines and objective setting.

I have established a nonprofit to help parents like myself who are experiencing this indescribable journey. I still suffer from severe insomnia, and it is not rare for me to go a week or more without sleep. When I do sleep, I never feel rested. I have very low energy and I find very little enjoyment in life besides caring for my granddaughter and speaking to other bereaved parents, and knowing I am making a difference in both. I also have frequent panic attacks, nightmares and suffer PTSD which comes and goes in severity.

I don't know if I will ever have the capabilities I once did. I have filed for disability due to the conditions described and the great panic I experience at the simple thought of returning to the workplace. I could sell myself and the skills I once had, but it would all be a lie, and once I started the job they would soon find out I am not what they thought I was. I would be compromising my own integrity if I was not honest with them.

Some days I still can't fully function at the capacity I did previous to my children's death. I still have anxiety attacks, horrible insomnia that won't allow me to work the next day, outbursts of sobbing, uncontrollable crying, and sometimes anger and depression that force me to seek the refuge of my bed. I have learned how to cope to the point where my condition has little to no impact on my ability as primary caretaker for my granddaughter, but that is my top priority and some days it's all I can accomplish with confidence and pride. I often long for who I was, and find the new me hard to adjust to.

I know I am where I am meant to be in life and that my experiences are more normal than not. My children were and are my life. My identity as a mother and a career woman disappeared. I struggle with the question, Who am I now? I know it will still take time to rebuild and sift through the rubble of my shattered life of twenty-five years.

In time I will build a new foundation and new coping skills. There is one thing I know without a doubt, and that is that I have to give of myself to society, for I have a heart and compassion for other hurting parents like me.

*

MONICA MIRKES
Monica's 30-year-old daughter Marisa
died in 2013 due to Cesarean complications

We were trying to keep some sense of normality for Marisa's two-year-old son, keep him on his regular schedule, trying to make sure his little world didn't explode. Yet the adults in his life were barely hanging on. I went back to work after a week. Everyone was caring and supportive. I was in a safe place. Home was where the landmines were.

*

DENISE PURCELL
Denise's 27-year-old daughter Megan died
in 2011 from an accidental overdose

I am on disability, so I didn't return to anything. I didn't care if the world crashed around me. I don't even remember breathing. I did what I had to do, then retreated to within my bedroom walls to cry myself to sleep. Nobody could talk about it. The girls lost a sibling, and I couldn't relate. I lost a child, and they couldn't relate.

Most nights I would stare at Megan's pictures like I had never seen her before. I sifted through her ashes with my hands, smelling them to see if I could smell her. I was searching to find any part of her that might be left.

Later, after my breakdown, I signed myself and my daughters up for grief counseling. Regular counseling, yet support wasn't really given. It seemed like it was just us and nobody wanted to deal with it.

Almost four years later, it isn't any easier. We might talk or kid around a little, though not much. It is still too soon.

*

MARILYN ROLLINS
Marilyn's 37-year-old son Randy and 16-year-old granddaughter Sara
died in a car accident in 2006 during a family camping trip

I worked in a physician's office, though the practice was owned by the hospital. I had been with Doc Mike for eighteen years, almost since he had begun his practice. I had seen many people come and go in the office, and had worked with several of them for years. We were given the standard three paid days off. Of course, I did take more than that, but still went back rather early, about a week after the funeral. At first they were all very sympathetic and helpful. I'm not sure when that started to change, but I noticed that gradually nobody was really talking to me. This became especially true if I mentioned Randy's or Sara's name. They would find an excuse to get away from me as quickly as possible. This was not everyone. Doc, his nurse practitioner and our secretary did not behave this way. I felt as if I was going crazy and then eventually like I had some disease. My son and granddaughter died and I felt as if I was being punished for it.

Some of my work was taken away from me, and that made me angry. I had developed a recall system for patients with high cholesterol, developed forms and kept track of bloodwork and such. I was still doing that and I know that nothing changed, I was doing a good job! No one ever told me why the other nurse took it over. Even going to Doc didn't change things. Now it wasn't just silent in the office, it was a bit hostile. I was delegated to filing dictation and doing pre-authorizations for tests and medications. I remember that one day my friend stopped by the office. Our x-ray tech pulled her aside and ask how I was doing. She was so startled that she said, "Why don't you ask her?" The tech told my friend, "Oh, we don't talk about it." I was alone in an office full of people!

My husband wasn't faring much better. He had worked for a construction company for almost forty years. The owner of the company had come to the hospital in South Bend after the accident.

At the time we thought that was a very nice gesture, since it was quite a drive for him. After he went back to work, the owner never spoke to him again! My husband had extra pain though, because he worked with Randy and had to face his son's desk every day. After a few months of that, he told them he was taking a vacation. While he was off, he took another job with a company that had been trying to get him to come to work for them. He never went back to his old job.

I continued to work thirteen months. The day came when I was just worn down by it all. Doc was leaving on vacation to spend the holidays in Hawaii. I walked into his office and handed him my two weeks' notice. He was surprised, to say the least. I did continue to see him as my physician, and I have to say that there were some apologies as time went on. One person told me that she didn't want to think about it, because if it could happen to me then it could happen to her, like it was something contagious! Another one lost her husband and told me that she had no idea what I had gone through. It was too bad that it took a tragedy for her to realize that. My husband worked about another year and then he too retired. We both took our retirement and started a whole new life.

*

KATIE ROUSH
Katie's 26-year-old daughter Krystle
died in 2013 of accidental alcohol poisoning

I tried to go to work but I could not focus. I cried too much at the strangest times. My job was at a mail-order pharmacy, ordering and coordinating the shipping of lifesaving medication. It was too much for me.

*

SARA RUBLE
Sara's 19-year-old son Scott died in 1994 from a
combination of a seizure disorder, Strep throat and dehydration

Almost immediately following Scott's death, a woman from the human resources department phoned me. It was a heartfelt personal message she was delivering: I could take as much time as I needed to return to work. In the chaotic world I was living in at that time, I was extremely grateful, but could not have known how very needed that time would be...and what a gift that call was. I worked for Maybelline Cosmetics as a sales representative and had been with Maybelline for eleven years. I stayed home for three weeks after Scott's funeral and, in all truth, I really did not know what to do with myself. For whatever reasons, thinking that maybe filling my day with other thoughts might be helpful, I went back to work. My choice. It did not take me long to realize that I was not at all ready to even think clearly, let alone drive to three or four accounts a day to sell the displays and products I was expected to. The accounts I called on were wonderful and I truly felt their compassion. My boss and other reps who had to fill in for me were very understanding. Even so, I took a month off. Oh, God...I was beginning to more fully realize the reality of the life I was facing. I was a tangled ball of emotions. That time off was a godsend. Throughout the first year, I took time off again whenever I arrived at that totally overwhelmed place. I was very careful to not abuse Maybelline's trust in me, but I desperately needed that respite time. I wish other companies would be as generous. I worked for two more years until our financial situation changed. I can honestly say that I know how important it was for me to have to work. Day after day it got me up and out of the house. I was forced to think about something other than Scott's death for eight straight hours a day. It was exhausting, yes, but I know it was beneficial to me as well. It showed me I was stronger than I thought, and even though time itself cannot heal us...the time I worked brought me greater balance in adjusting to the real world and my grief world at home.

CHAPTER FIVE

THE QUESTION

The song is ended, but the melody lingers on.
-IRVING BERLIN

One day we have a child. The next, that child is no longer living. So where does this leave us when, inevitably, others ask how many children we have? How do we answer a question that appears simple to everyone but us?

*

ERICA GALE BELTZ
Erica's 5-year-old son Luke Jordan died in 2005
from a fallen banister in his aunt's driveway

I was warned about this question, and offered a piece of advice: Sometimes it will be easier to only mention the children who are alive. I thought that would be worse than the truth, to pretend that Luke was never here. I did struggle with answering honestly, because it just hurt. I was the mother of two children and nothing could take that from me. The answer had power. I had two children, regardless of where Luke was; I would always be his mom!

In time I learned all the ways that caring question could knock the wind out of you. They were trying to protect me. When a random stranger or a new coworker asks, "How many children do you have?" you think you can get through this. "Yes, I have a little boy, Luke, who is five, and one daughter, Lakin, who is nine." You need to get ready, because people are interested in conversation. They will feel connected to you because of the love that sneaked out when you said your children's names.

You might hear, "Really? Where do they go to school?" Then, "Really? Mine too." They won't stop until you have to say, "My child died, I just didn't want to blow your doors off with my tragedy." They almost always follow with one of two things. First, "Was your son sick?" No, I would reply that he died from an accident in my sister's driveway. Usually they would continue and ask, "Was it a car, was he run over? Did your sister run over him with the car?" I truly felt blessed because their questions proved they recognized the value of Luke's life. But over the years I grew weary with all the questions. I wasn't comfortable with the guy behind me in the grocery line asking how my son died. I found myself reliving the detail of my nightmare.

My daughter Lakin has chronic health issues and suffered greatly from age thirteen through seventeen. One night they just couldn't seem to get her pain under control, and I was beside myself. The nurse came in and, just like so many times before, she asked my daughter if she had any siblings while she tried to distract Lakin as she started the IV. Lakin replied, "Yep, I have one brother." She looked over at me. This time the pain was bad and Lakin was exhausted. She looked at me and just shook her head, pleading with me to not say anything. The nurse said, "How old is he?" Lakin answered. Then the lady asked if her brother would like one of the cool Band-Aids she was getting. Lakin said she thought that Luke would. On this day my little girl, who truly has endured more than anyone should ever have to, taught me how to fight when you have nothing left.

One thing I know I need to share is this: When someone tells you that their child has died, there is nothing you need to say to show them you understand the loss. They would never in a million years want you to understand it, even though your intentions are with a pure heart. Almost everyone will say, "Wow, your strength is incredible. I would not survive." Some say they would kill themselves because the pain would be too much. This is a statement I have made many times when talking to others with the intention of offering comfort. EVEN WITH THE PURE INTENTION OF TRYING TO TELL THEM YOU UNDERSTAND, THAT THEY ARE STRONG, they hear something different. That the fact that they haven't taken their life (trust me, it's all they think about) means they couldn't care as much as you do. Please, just hug them. Tell them you hear their hurt. You are sorry for their loss and will be there if they need you.

*

STACY BERNDTSON
Stacy's daughter Cori Joy died in 2003, the day before her fourth birthday, from an undiagnosed genetic disorder

At the time of her death Cori was our only child. When she died, to the outside world we were a childless couple. When we would meet someone new, the question would come up and you knew that would be the last question they would ask. As soon as you said, "We have a daughter, but she went to heaven last year," they would feel SO bad and uncomfortable that the conversation would soon end. When we adopted Molly, she was mostly always with us, so the question changed to "Is Molly your only child?" I have always said "We have two daughters, but one of them lives in heaven," or something to that effect. I was pretty upset once when Steve answered the question "Only the one [child] then?" with a yes. He felt so bad, but at the time he said he just felt that it was the quickest answer and he didn't want the conversation to go "sad" the way it always did when we would clarify. That is understandable but I was still hurt by it.

I made Molly a small scrapbook/storybook that tells "her story," but her story for us actually begins with Cori's story. So Molly's story begins with "Once upon a time," and speaks of a lady and a man who wanted to be a mommy and daddy very much. After a long time, God gave them a beautiful baby girl...Cori Joy. It goes on to say in very simple terms that they were very happy but that one day Cori went to be with Jesus. And how sad Mommy and Daddy were because they loved being a mommy and daddy so much. After a time, God brought them another miracle and that miracle was Molly Faith. In the book it says that we believe maybe Cori helped God pick Molly out just for us.

With this book and pictures of Cori in the house, Molly has grown up knowing that she has a sister, but her sister lives in heaven. As an eight-year-old she understands or at least has been surrounded by more talk of heaven than most eight-year-olds.

Molly Faith freely talks about her sister, and answers that she does have a sister when new friends ask her if she has brothers or sisters. It has caused some confusion. Some children have even called Molly a liar because they don't understand how we speak of Cori as living in a real place, just not with us - which IS what we believe. But to their understanding, if you have a sibling who died, then you no longer have a sibling. This kind of interaction tends to make Molly sad, and then causes her to voice her wish and desire that Cori were still alive and how much she wishes she had a sister to play with. And of course because we cannot make that happen for her, it makes us very sad too.

*

KARI BROWN
Kari's 2-year-old daughter Dominique (Deedee)
died in 2014 from obstructive sleep apnea

I've always had difficulty answering the question about how many children I have. At this time I have my only daughter, Dominique, who's not here with me. However, the answer to the question varies based on who is asking, and where I am at the moment. Sometimes I talk about Dominique as if she were still alive. It also depends on the "vibe" I'm feeling from the person who is asking the question. If I feel confident and comfortable enough to explain about my daughter, I will. If I am having one of those hard days, I may say nothing at all. It also depends on my mindset when I wake up in the morning; I may bravely battle the emotions boiling up in me, or I may let my guard down and cry when asked. But I never fail to hesitate at answering such questions. No matter how prepared I may be, or how much I practice the answer in my mind, I always hesitate. I feel guilty if I don't honestly explain the situation. My daughter passed a year and a half ago. And I still hesitate at the same question.

*

TANISHA CALDWELL
Tanisha's 23-year-old son Tariq (Jay)
died in a car accident in 2015

I haven't had to answer that question. And if I do...I'll say three. Or maybe three but one has gone on before. Jay still is my child. Nothing changes that! Not even death!

*

LYNDA CHELDELIN FELL
Lynda's 15-year-old daughter Aly
died in a car accident in 2009

I always answer that I have four children, I don't even hesitate. If pressed for more details, I reply that I have two sons and two daughters. If asked their ages, I share the ages of my living children and end with the age Aly was when she went to heaven. I always end with her, because inevitably people are so shocked when I share that she passed away that the natural conversation usually comes to a halt at that point anyway. Once a grieving mother, always a grieving mother, and we learn to live with the shocked expressions and quick escapes. Once, someone I knew actually crossed the street to avoid crossing my path. Another time, someone mumbled they couldn't chat because they had to let their dog out. That's when you realize how truly lonely this journey is.

*

JACQUELYN CRUZ
Jacquelyn's 24-year-old daughter Jenna
died in 2012 from pulmonary edema

"How many children do you have?" Such a simple question, yet so gut-wrenching at the same time. I still struggle with this question. I change my answer depending on where I am and who is asking. I know all the books say "Always include the child who passed in the number of children you have," but sometimes it's just too damn hard. What's even more difficult is the guilt I feel afterward, thinking that I'm denying Jenna as one of my children. I think I have a good sense of judgment of people's character, and sometimes it just doesn't feel right to tell them my story. Maybe I'm afraid of questions they'll ask, or maybe I'm afraid I'll start crying.

I have since found "safe" people and "not safe" people to socialize with since Jenna's passing. Some of my "safe" people are a group of girls I've known since I was ten. I was honest with them early on, and asked them to never be afraid to say Jenna's name or ask me questions about her. I didn't want Jenna to be the elephant in the room; I didn't want the girls to be uncomfortable around me. They let me talk, cry, laugh and be angry when I needed to. They have been some of my strongest supporters.

When I do feel brave enough to answer, I say "I have three. Danny is twenty-four, Chelsea is twenty-two, and my daughter Jenna would have been twenty-seven.

*

MICHELLE DETWILER
Michelle's 19-year-old daughter Emily
died in 2014 due to congenital complications

When someone asks how many children I have, I always say I have four. "Our oldest boy lives about fifteen miles away. Two of our kids still live with us, and our oldest daughter moved to heaven a year ago. I really miss her, but I know I'll see her again." The last person I said that to marveled at my words and how open I could be about losing my child. In my heart that is really the only way to even out my grief over her departure. If I think of her moving away, then I can also think about seeing her again someday.

*

ANNAH ELIZABETH
Annah's son Gavin Michael aspirated on his meconium
during the delivery and died 26 minutes following his birth

This is a question that has many answers, each dependent on the situation. Though I'm not quick to reveal that I have experienced child loss in the forms of miscarriage and infant death, I don't withhold the information. In the earlier years I would most often respond that I had three children, sometimes saying "I have three living children." If I were in a passing conversation, one that I expected to pass quickly, I would speak the former. If, however, I were in a casual conversation or getting to know someone new, I would give the latter reply.

In the last ten years, since I began my work on healing grief, I have begun more often than not by replying that I have four children. If the conversation turns to "What do they do?" I start off with my youngest child, who just graduated high school, and then work my way up. When I get to the eldest, I usually say something like "My eldest died shortly after he was born, and lives with us in spirit." I remember once, when I met someone with whom I was joking about parenting hardships and someone I immediately

117

identified to have a great sense of humor, I replied, "My eldest is wreaking havoc in heaven." More often than not, the conversation will then turn to the subject of miscarriage and other forms of fertility topics. I am constantly amazed by how often the conversation comes up and I am equally inspired and pleasantly surprised by the number of people who will open up and share their experiences with me once I've opened up the discussion.

*

WENDY EVANS

Wendy's 21-year-old son Kyle died in 2009
from diabetes when his insulin pump malfunctioned

I have four children. Sometimes I feel compelled to elaborate when asked names/ages/residence. If I feel a connection to the person then I might say, "We lost one of our sons."

*

DAPHNE GREER

Daphne's 5-year-old daughter Lydia died in 2008 in a
car accident during a routine morning commute

Swallowing that enormous lump in your throat as you encounter a conversation with a stranger or new acquaintance. My mind wavers back and forth like a child torn between which candy to eat, as I anticipate the question that is about to emerge. Do I take the easy road and say four children and not mention Lydia? Or do I say five and include all of them and wait for the follow-up, as they ask how old each of them are? And when I mention only four ages, do I put myself through the torture and endure that awkward look that bubbles up, creating a moment of silence I was so eager to avoid? And then the proverbial fork in the road lands at your feet as your mind contemplates the question: Which is the path of least resistance? How dreadful for a parent to have to go through such turmoil and uneasiness at the prompting of a simple question. What most don't comprehend is that it's actually quite a complex and distraught question for those like us.

118

It's easy to withhold the truth and say four children, avoiding the uncomfortable situations, not having to delve into a plethora of crazy explanation. However if you do, you're forever haunted by the guilt of failing to acknowledge your child who died, accompanied by the piercing pain in your heart as you feel you have just committed the biggest act of disloyalty and shame toward your child. The sadness and heavy burden of grief we carry day in and day out will always serve as a reminder of what was, and what we will never have. And yet what lives in our hearts.

And so, after seven years, I am not proud to say that I have experienced both sides of the coin here, so to speak. What I have learned, despite the circumstances, and without hesitation as I proudly acknowledge my child, is that this is what is right for me. I smile when the conversation arises and I am able to mention my firstborn, my beautiful daughter. It is not my intent to make others uncomfortable, but to give her the respect and honor she deserves. Any chance I get to mention my child's name, I will take. When we tell the stories of our children it not only brings joy to our saddened hearts, but also provides others a brief lesson in love and loss, gratitude and grace.

It wasn't as if they never existed. They were here. Real. Their hearts bonded with our hearts, we felt them in our wombs, softened their cries, changed their diapers, attended their dance recitals, hosted their sleepovers, wiped their tears, showed them the magic of Santa Claus, shuttled them to school, and answered questions like "Why don't worms have ears?" and all the wonders of this earth.

Our children left enormous footprints larger than life on our hearts which have been shattered into pieces and broken beyond repair. We will never be whole again. Yet no matter what, our children will always be an indispensable part of us.

*

BONNIE FORSHEY
Bonnie's 16-year-old son Billy died in 1993
from an overdose of prescription drugs

It depends on who I am talking to. I lost a baby at almost full term. I also lost a sixteen-year-old. They were both hard, but losing my sixteen-year-old was the worst. We had more time together, and I adored him. Losing him literally tore out my heart. I still have a daughter, so I am fortunate. It is a difficult question to answer; it always brings my emotions to the surface.

*

TALIA GATO
Talia's 8-year-old daughter Poppy
died in 2009 in a car accident

When I share stories about my kids, I mention both girls very naturally. If people are strangers, they really don't delve into it much. But for some, if it is a more pointed question about how many kids I have, I say two and mention their ages. Sometimes I answer matter-of-factly that one died. Some people say they are sorry. A few ask how or why, then I use it as an opportunity to tell a small part of the story. The worst thing that can happen is if they say nothing, like I had said NOTHING. I said this recently at a party of girls the other day... and it was a "nothing" moment. This is an interesting observation about human nature and compassion, or not!

I never delve too much into my story, because death is sacred. I share the whole story only to those in my tribe of loss, those who have sadly earned free entry. Mostly I say it, even though it is uncomfortable, because my daughter mattered. Her life mattered, and made an impact on this world. Not mentioning Poppy would make me feel like she never was a part of my life. Maybe it is what I need for me.

*

KORBY HAVE
Korby's 17-year-old daughter Taylor (Tayla)
died in 2013 in a car accident

I always say I have three children. Whether I elaborate and let them know that I have two sons who are living and a daughter who passed away depends on the situation. It is always sad to let someone know that my daughter has passed away, and I hate how their reactions make me feel, like I did something wrong.

*

DEANA MARTIN
Deana's only two children, 25-year-old Amanda
and 21-year-old Logan, died in a car accident in 2011

It depends on the situation. When asked if I have kids, I will say yes. When asked how many, sometimes I will go into detail and share that I had two young adult children who were killed in a car accident, and now I raise my granddaughter.

Sometimes I just say "Two, and I raise my granddaughter." Other times, when I am feeling particularly strong I will say, "I have three children. My two oldest, Amanda is thirty and Logan twenty-six, now live in heaven. They left my granddaughter, who is now eight, here so we could care for each other in their absence."

Even though Amanda was twenty-five and Logan twenty-one when they died in 2011, I am not one of the parents who say they are forever twenty-five and twenty-one. I like to believe that my children still have birthdays. They may not get physically older in heaven, but I like to believe they are not forever the age they were when their physical bodies died.

I have been rather fortunate. In the almost five years since, I have only been asked maybe three or four times if I have children. Most of my interactions now are in the bereavement communities. There, we all know that each of us has lost someone, and we ask one another about our families with more compassion. In a group of people who have lost a child it will go something like this: "How old was your child when they died?" "What is their name?" "How long has it been since they died?" "Do you mind if I ask how they died?" And then, "Do you have any surviving children?"

In a group where the grief experiences might differ, people will often ask, "Who did you lose?" Then they know the right question to ask. Once they know it was not a child who died, they don't have to go through the above ritual to inquire if you have children. They know it is safe to say, as it is to most in society, "So, ya have any kids? How old are they? Boys or girls?"

I know this is a very difficult question for some people but, if the truth be told, it never was for me. I just answer what I am comfortable answering at the time.

*

MONICA MIRKES
Monica's 30-year-old daughter Marisa
died in 2013 due to Cesarean complications

I always answer four, two boys and two girls. I have never had a problem with this question. I know I did go through some doubt with how to answer. It's funny how sometimes others are thrown off balance by my answer.

*

DENISE PURCELL
Denise's 27-year-old daughter Megan died
in 2011 from an accidental overdose

I hesitate and say "Five, but one passed away." If I just say five, it implies they are all living. The word "have" is different than had."

*

MARILYN ROLLINS
Marilyn's 37-year-old son Randy and 16-year-old granddaughter Sara
died in a car accident in 2006 during a family camping trip

It really depends on my mood. My feeling is that if you are going to say it, be ready to explain it. For some reason, this question always catches me off guard. Then I stand there with a blank look on my face while I am deciding which way I will answer. While I am standing there looking like dumb and dumber, I am also sizing up the person who has just asked me the question. Will they drop their eyes, mumble an apology and move on quickly? Are they truly interested in my answer, or are they just being polite? Have they lost a child? If I feel like they don't really care how I answer, or if I'm in a hurry, I just say, "Two, I have two boys." If I feel like they care and really want to know then I say, "I have two boys, and my oldest is an angel." Sometimes, if they are receptive, I will go on to explain the accident and let them know how it has changed me. Most responses are kind, but occasionally there are looks of horror and a rush to get away. I had one saleslady at a pharmacy who came out from behind the counter to hug me. I started to cry. She told me that she didn't intend to make me cry. I let her know that I was crying because of her kindness, and with her hug she was acknowledging that my child existed and that she was sorry for my pain. I wish there were more people like her. I have definitely learned to read people, and am often surprised at how accurate I've become on how I think they will react.

*

KATIE ROUSH
Katie's 26-year-old daughter Krystle
died in 2013 of accidental alcohol poisoning

If I feel okay with that person then I'll say, "Three, and one is in heaven." If I don't feel okay with them, I just say three and then turn the question back onto them.

*

SARA RUBLE
Sara's 19-year-old son Scott died in 1994 from a
combination of a seizure disorder, Strep throat and dehydration

I think this question will always be somewhat of a challenge for me. My only child, Scott, died suddenly at age nineteen. I was forty-six, so motherhood as I knew it was over. Over. I even questioned for a while IF I could still call myself a mother. This was the hardest and the most dreaded question…it went to the core of my soul, the deepest part of who I am. It was so incredibly hard for me to answer.

Like all other moms and dads, I needed to share my painful grief story, yet the look on another person's face as I shared Scott's death was the next hardest part. I remember being so needy and wanting to speak of Scott…and this question could either end a conversation or begin one. I could never answer with anything but the truth I knew. "I have one child - my son, Scott, died." And I would wait for the reaction of the person facing me. Compassion, angst, fear…love…or "…get me out of here." And so I learned, each time, to add more or less. My husband of less than a year had two children. Sometimes I would share about Scott and quickly follow those words up with "Jay has two children," to soften the blow for the person I was talking to. That never really felt right. I was not particularly close to Jay's children, and so my answer was designed for those who asked me the question of how many children I have. If I was not ready to tell all, I would revert to this answer.

My coping mechanism worked to relieve the moment's uncomfortableness, until I realized I was compromising myself and my journey to answer this way. I knew I needed to say it as it truly was. And again, some of those who asked me were loving and compassionate while others were horrified and wished they had never asked me. I could never be prepared for who THEY would be. In time, I began being more bold and would just say the words. "My son Scott died. He was my only child." Whatever reaction

124

came…came. I could not worry about the reactions like I had before. I HAD to share about Scott. I had to be authentic. Whatever someone's reaction was, was theirs. I had to share my truth.

Another part of this evolved as well. Unknowingly, I first used the words "had" and "was." Scott was my child. I had one child. When I realized I was saying those words, I felt sick at heart. Oh, my God. It was an epiphany. I knew Scott was still around me, sending me incredible signs and the most real dreams I had ever had. We were still very much connected…and he was showing me. I brought him into the present. "I have one child. His name is Scott, he died at age nineteen. He is showing me so much about life and death and the other side." Saying these words helps me tremendously. I am a teacher, and I feel that each time I share Scott's death with someone, I am honoring him as well as teaching about a mother's grief.

*

The depth of the love of parents for their children
cannot be measured. It is like no other relationship.
It exceeds concern for life itself.
JAMES E. FAUST

*

CHAPTER SIX

THE DATES

No matter what anyone says about grief and about time healing all wounds, the truth is, there are certain sorrows that never fade away until the heart stops beating and the last breath is taken. -UNKNOWN

Our expectations and memories of balloons and cakes and presents are as regular as the rising sun. When our child passes, however, how do we celebrate the life that is no more? And how do we acknowledge the painful date that marks their death?

*

STACY BERNDTSON
Stacy's daughter Cori Joy died in 2003, the day before her fourth birthday, from an undiagnosed genetic disorder

We have done many different things over the last nearly twelve years. Since Cori's birthday and death anniversary are one day apart, it is a little different for us. Her birthday was the day after her death, and so I have often said that I believe this was a gift to us from God. The worst day is followed by the happiest day of our lives. And so as the years have passed we have spent more time, I think, celebrating her life.

On the first anniversary we sent out a letter to family and friends and we met at the cemetery. Cori died in November, so it is never warm, and the Pacific Northwest is rarely dry in November. I remember, however, that first year was dry as we gathered. A pastor from our church said a few words and led us in prayer. Then we all wrote with markers on balloons and released them at the same time. We bought a huge dragonfly balloon that we released with the others. Dragonflies have had a very special meaning to me since Cori died, so it was wonderful to see that big balloon traveling skyward to Cori Joy. I remember we played a song on a boom box that had very special meaning for us. It is called "You Live What I Believe," by Jana Alayra. It was a special day.

In subsequent years we did different things. We took out an ad in our local paper with Cori's picture and story. One year, along with some family members, we took money to several local coffee drive-thru stands along with a card and Cori's picture. We asked that they be given out along with a free drink so customers knew they were getting it free in honor of our beautiful girl. One year my husband created a beautiful YouTube tribute to her for us. After Cori died I went back to work at a company that makes custom chocolates. I had a Hershey-size candy bar made that had Cori's picture and told her story. We passed those out at coffee shops etc. After Molly arrived, our focus has been mostly on her and experiencing the joy that being parents and having a little family again has brought to us.

Not to say that we have forgotten or ever will, but we have chosen to celebrate Cori's life by spending the day doing fun family activities. We took Molly to Chuck E. Cheese one year. From perhaps her second year, we typically always go to the cemetery and we each eat a cupcake and sing "Happy Birthday" to Cori. Just for me, I bought a beautiful white "girly" piece of furniture, a cabinet. I put all the mementoes that I've kept of Cori in it. We have several pictures in our house, but I have been able to move on from having several glass cabinets with all her things displayed as I once did.

Now once a year, usually the week of our "two days," I sit by myself and go through Cori's things. I let the memories flood back and let the tears fall freely. For that one period of time I am back on that day in November 2003. And then I am able to kiss those things and place them back in the cabinet and lower the lid for another year. One thing that has always amazed me is how my body seems to KNOW when those dates are coming up. I won't consciously realize it but sometime from mid to late October to early November I will find myself really emotional, very sensitive to what other people say and do, and just basically sad. At some point it will dawn on me and then it all makes sense. Those two days being so close together, the best and the worst back to back, are literally ingrained into the fabric of my body, heart and soul.

*

KARI BROWN
Kari's 2-year-old daughter Dominique (Deedee)
died in 2014 from obstructive sleep apnea

The very first birthday Dominique was not here was heart-wrenching. I was overwhelmed and torn that she was not here for her third birthday. My mother-in-law purchased a ranch and wanted to bless it on Dominique's birthday. So we decorated the ranch in purple and white balloons, and put together a special cake with the number three on it. Later that evening, we took turns speaking about Dominique and the impact she had on each of us. We then released a bundle of balloons and watched as they floated away in the sunset; I wished I could have floated away to her too. For her first angelversary, my fiancé and I had mixed emotions about what we should do, or how we should celebrate it. We ended up doing a simple photoshoot with bluebonnets, a canvas print of Dominique, and her urn along with her favorite boots. I've always wanted to take pictures of Dominique in bluebonnets because it is the state flower of Texas, but I never got the opportunity. We felt that honoring her in a field of bluebonnets was a special way to remember her. I think our rituals will be different every year, depending on how we feel when the time comes around.

*

TANISHA CALDWELL
Tanisha's 23-year-old son Tariq (Jay)
died in a car accident in 2015

It has been only three and a half months since Jay has been gone. So I'm not sure what we will be doing, if anything. When I think about it, it gives me anxiety.

*

LYNDA CHELDELIN FELL
Lynda's 15-year-old daughter Aly
died in a car accident in 2009

The accident happened in August, and Aly's birthday is in February. I dread both dates. They are still so brutal that I feel utterly paralyzed on both dates. The first birthday after the accident was Aly's sweet sixteen. Some of her friends and teammates skipped school that day to make us a beautiful blue cake in the shape of a dolphin. We also filled 50 blue organza bags with an inspirational quote and chocolate kisses, and the girls gave them to strangers around town as a random act of kindness in memory of their fallen teammate. I was so grateful. On the first anniversary of the accident, my husband Jamie, our fourteen-year-old son, and I went out of town. One of my husband's colleagues offered to let us stay at his oceanfront cabin. We left our two adult children at home because they had jobs and couldn't go with us. But, at ages twenty and twenty-four, I underestimated their needs on that day, and I will forever regret that we left them to their own devices. Clearly, in my fog of grief, I wasn't thinking. It's been six years now, and we don't plan anything special for either day. It feels most comfortable to just hunker down, hibernate away from the world, and let the day pass quietly. We still receive heartfelt cards in the mail and messages on Facebook, which I'm grateful for. And I usually write a note on Aly's Facebook page to mark the accident date as well as her birthday. Sometimes I still tag her in new family photos, simply because it makes me feel better.

130

*

JACQUELYN CRUZ
Jacquelyn's 24-year-old daughter Jenna
died in 2012 from pulmonary edema

On the first anniversary of Jenna's passing my emotions were all over the place. I didn't know what to do. We are Catholic, so I knew I wanted a mass for her. I thought about all the kind people who supported my family during the most difficult time of our lives, and wanted to have a celebration of Jenna's life. Jenna loved my baking so I decided we would have all her favorite desserts and celebrate. I baked and baked! I made the homemade chocolate cake that she loved so much, her favorite très leches cake, flan, and cookies. I filled candy bowls with Jenna's favorite candy and placed them all over the house. I ordered her favorite hero sandwich and salads. I invited her friends and all her coworkers.

Jenna was a paraprofessional like me, for children with autism, and she was great at her job. Our home was filled with people who loved Jenna and showed their support throughout the year. Her friends brought balloons and we wrote messages on them to Jenna and released them up to the sky. I always let everyone know at this point how many lives Jenna helped by choosing to be an organ donor. The first year it was nine people, the second it was up to seventeen, and this year I'm proud to say Jenna has made the lives of twenty-seven people better! I plan on doing it again this year, and for as many years as I'm alive.

Her birthday has to be the hardest day for me. Even as I'm writing this the tears are flowing down my face. February 8, 1988, was the best day of my life; it was the day I learned unconditional love. I never knew you could love someone as much as I loved my new baby girl. I remember her first birthday without her here, I woke up early and just had to make her a très leches cake. The only problem was that there was a snowstorm and nobody could drive; the roads were covered with three feet of snow. I had to get to the store and get the ingredients I needed to make the cake, so I walked.

It wasn't easy, but I was successful! I don't even remember if we ate the cake. Maybe I was just determined to do something that day that kept my mind from not wanting to kill myself. Maybe it was Jenna telling me to get up and make the cake because Danny and Chelsea needed me to be here with them. I don't like to share her birthday with anyone; it was our day, I and her. Together, she and I got her into this world after pushing for two and half hours; we were a team. My husband will get birthday balloons and we will release them with the hope that Jenna sees them and knows how much she is still loved and still missed.

*

MICHELLE DETWILER
Michelle's 19-year-old daughter Emily
died in 2014 due to congenital complications

After our daughter died we created a memorial garden in our yard. There we could place little mementoes, flowers and plants, and most of all decorate it with love in memory of Emily. Friends came to help us dig up grass and spread white rock. As we filled the garden with memories of our girl, a healing process began. Although she is not in the garden, it is as if we are saying to the world, "She was important, she was here!"

Our daughter's birthday is on our wedding anniversary. We have always celebrated her birthday, and not so much our anniversary in the last twenty years. When we came to the first birthday without her we were lost. What do we do? Should we celebrate our anniversary? I ended up purchasing a couple of birthday balloons and putting them in the garden where we could see them. As they waved and bobbed in the wind, I cried. We celebrated our anniversary five months later.

Emily's death anniversary was more difficult to bear than her birthday had been. In that first year coming up to the date, it seemed that I relived each day of the "death week." I could hear and smell the things that had happened that week. The detail of each conversation seemed to come flooding into my thoughts. When I drove past the funeral home, the tears that I had been trying to hold back rushed out like a flood. How could I bear living through that date again? But when the day finally arrived we received such support from friends and family, and again they held us up. What would we do without their loving support? I've come to realize that her death date was really just her moving date. I know where Emily is, and she's having the time of her life.

*

ANNAH ELIZABETH
Annah's son Gavin Michael aspirated on his meconium
during the delivery and died 26 minutes following his birth

Gavin died twenty-six minutes following his birth, so both of these events fall on the same day. We always buy a few balloons and some special spring decorations, since his special day falls on the heels of winter's end. We pull unwanted weeds from around his grave marker, we pad the empty space with pine needles, and set out the gifts we brought. Since he was born so close to Mother's Day, I decided to have each of my other children baptized on Mother's Day. It was a way for me to celebrate each new life while honoring the memory of another. On his twenty-first birthday we went to a special restaurant we'd never visited before and I had a chocolate raspberry martini in his honor. I commissioned a painting in honor of Gavin's twenty-fifth birthday; a creative work that captured one of the conversations we had during an earlier birthday visit to Gavin's grave. One of my most special traditions, though, is how we form a circle around his gravestone. Hands held, we wonder aloud about things Gavin might be doing in heaven, what toys he would have been playing with, or when he became of driving age, what kind of car he'd be driving. We take turns sending Gavin a special message. I've always believed that Gavin's spirit is with us, so visiting the cemetery is more of a formality for us, but it is the tradition that my three living children have always known and it is one they have always remembered.

*

WENDY EVANS
Wendy's 21-year-old son Kyle died in 2009
from diabetes when his insulin pump malfunctioned

The birthday is usually recognized by Facebook posts and phone calls from family. The death anniversary (I call it the Sadaversary) is acknowledged through phone calls, Facebook posts, and we have done a butterfly release and balloon release. The first two years were very emotional, especially the days leading up to the actual date of the Sadaversary.

*

TALIA GATO
Talia's 8-year-old daughter Poppy
died in 2009 in a car accident

Every year it is different. The first year we had a family gathering. It was okay until my sister-in-law told me to move on as I tearfully thanked them all for coming. The second year, and each year since, there are no calls, no emails, no texts, except maybe just one. No acknowledgment that I did have a daughter, and that I did survive a very horrid and violent accident; that's what hurts the most. The ones from whom I thought I would get a hug or word of support, I get nothing. I think that's why we changed celebrating Poppy's birthday. We go out of town so we are not confronted with the absence of her, or the pain from no support or weird support, if at all. We are still figuring out how to honor the day peacefully. Maybe a bonfire with my support group? They understand completely.

*

DAPHNE GREER
Daphne's 5-year-old daughter Lydia died in 2008 in a
car accident during a routine morning commute

To celebrate, remember, recognize or simply ignore? Shortly after Lydia died, my husband and I had joined a support group for parents whose children had died. It was uncomfortable at first. As twenty-five grieving adults sat around the table, I listened to stories of many who tackled and shared this topic, how to acknowledge the birthdays and anniversaries of their children. They exchanged accounts of baking birthday cakes for their children who had passed, purchasing small gifts for their child or others, among other ways of celebrating them and reminiscing as their birthdays arrived. For several months I had a difficult time processing this and thought them to be loony. What could they really have to celebrate? Are they crazy? What is wrong with these people? Are they deranged? These thoughts, among many more, raced through my clouded mind like a thoroughbred.

And then when Lydia's first birthday in heaven came around, four months after she died and no one acknowledged it, not even my family, I was devastated. She was the first grandchild, the first granddaughter, and everyone welcomed her, eager for her arrival at birth. It was Thanksgiving 2008, my daughter's birthday, and her first one in heaven. Our extended family had a gathering as usual for the holiday. Grandparents, cousins, aunts, uncles, brothers and sisters. With twenty-plus people, we were all there except Lydia.

In years past, it would include cake and gifts and a celebration of Lydia, since her birthday would occasionally fall on Thanksgiving Day itself. But this year was different. It was her sixth birthday, her first in heaven and no one said a word. My heart was broken and a sense of betrayal came over me. Again. I felt pain on an entirely new level. The void was already there. Lydia was gone, and it was as if they pushed the knife in farther, adding pressure and a slight twist. Didn't they get it? Didn't they have a clue? Did they remember? Were they just uncomfortable? Well, what about me? What about Lydia?

That empty chair at the table, that prolific elephant in the room lurked like a predator in the wild. There was an unspoken silence, an uneasy feeling among the people at the party. Everyone knew, but no one muttered those words or even mentioned her name.

It was then that I understood what my fellow grieving parents were talking about. They are our children. They didn't just vanish, they weren't a figment of our imagination. They were here and they matter. Real, living, breathing souls full of life and love. Every year since then, my husband and I make sure to honor our little princess by writing messages to her on balloons and releasing them, soaring into the blue sky as the tears silently fall down our sorrowful faces. With our other four children, we sit and stare until we cannot see them any longer, watching in wonder as they disappear into the clouds, pondering life outside this world while remembering our girl.

Her anniversary date falls in midsummer. A day of immense grief and painful memories, but one that cannot go without recognition. A day that I will never work on again. On July 16, you will find us gathered at the cemetery, consumed with bittersweet sadness, wearing pink and purple flowers for Lydia. We are riddled with sorrow, yet see a glimmer of hope as we picnic at her graveside with her favorite lunch of chicken strips, french fries and ranch dressing. We proudly celebrate her life, acknowledging the joy and love she brought to each of our lives. Forever in our hearts.

*

BONNIE FORSHEY
Bonnie's 16-year-old son Billy died in 1993
from an overdose of prescription drugs

I always post an online tribute for birthdays, anniversary date, Christmas, Easter, and all holidays. I take flowers to the cemetery, but I go alone. It is too painful for my daughter. We all handle our grief in different ways.

*

KORBY HAVE
Korby's 17-year-old daughter Taylor (Tayla)
died in 2013 in a car accident

In order to help keep my daughter's memory alive, we decided early on to always remember her birthday and death date in a special way. For her birthday, we get together with family and her friends and boyfriend and go out to dinner at Tayla's favorite restaurant. After dinner we go to her gravesite where we release balloons with messages and spend time chatting, getting caught up on everyone's lives. On her death date we all get together again at her gravesite where we light sky lanterns and again spend time getting caught up on everyone's lives. It is a mixture of emotions, because I am happy that her friends want to remember Tayla and it's always good to hear about what they are up to. But on the other hand, it reminds me of what Tayla will never get to do.

*

DEANA MARTIN
Deana's only two children, 25-year-old Amanda
and 21-year-old Logan, died in a car accident in 2011

On Amanda and Logan's birthday, it's not as much as it was when they were here. Logan's birthday is usually over Memorial Day weekend, so we will often go to the beach or Florida. One year we went on a Disney cruise for his birthday. We try to do something he would love! This year we had plans to go to Florida a few weeks after Logan's birthday, so we had a casual birthday celebration at home. We cooked his favorite, Mom's meatloaf with tomato gravy, and of course his cake must be the richest chocolate cake we can find because that is what he would want. We will often send balloons to heaven with "happy birthday" notes tied to the bundle, or we will release mylar balloons that say "happy birthday" on them. I sometimes buy something I would normally have bought him, like his favorite cologne, boxer shorts and T-shirts with goofy sayings, etc. One year I even bought a karaoke machine and gave it to his girlfriend, because they met over karaoke. Whatever I buy, I then give it to someone Logan loved, and this warms my heart and the hearts of his friends and family.

For Amanda's birthday we usually go to hibachi, because that is what we normally did on her birthday. Because Amanda's birthday is in December, going out to dinner with family was common instead of outdoor parties with ponies and clowns like we did for Logan. When we go to hibachi, Amanda's daughter Armaya tells people that it is her mommy's birthday. They will bring Armaya the drums and the fruit boat with sparklers, and we all sing "Happy birthday" to Amanda in heaven. We usually have balloons, and I encourage Armaya to write her mommy a letter so we can attach it to the balloons to send it to heaven. I try to buy something on Amanda's birthday that she would have wanted at Armaya's age, and I give it to Armaya. She LOVES this, needless to say.

If we stay at home, which is not common, we have Amanda's favorite steak and lobster. She preferred tiramisu or cheesecake over regular cake, so we usually make sure we have one or the other for dessert. We often invite some of their friends to join us for our celebrations, and often one or two will come. It is always a nice time and yet bittersweet. Armaya loves celebrating their birthdays, and I suppose that is why I do it. I am the walking memory of her mother and uncle, because she was only three when they died.

We often take time on her mother's birthday to go through the chest of Amanda's belongings I kept for Armaya. I take each item out and tell stories about each thing or about the last time Amanda wore a particular dress. Armaya really enjoys this activity. It is very painful for me at times, but I know how much it means to her. And I know Amanda is watching and is so proud and happy that I make every effort and occasion to teach her daughter about her, and that I work diligently to keep Amanda very alive in her daughter's life. Is so many ways, Amanda and Logan are still a huge part of our daily lives.

*

MONICA MIRKES
Monica's 30-year-old daughter Marisa
died in 2013 due to Cesarean complications

I do like the way The Compassionate Friends address this as her "angel date." What is hard for me is that Marisa died the day after her son's birthday. Difficult for me to split my feelings. I don't want Connor to think his birthday is bad, but on the other hand I really am not in a place where I want to party and be around a lot of people. This year I felt relieved to give him a "half birthday" that he celebrated with his classmates.

What is difficult for me, the one thing I have not yet been able to address is that as a Montessori teacher, I was able to have Connor in my classroom since he was an infant. He goes to school with me. Normal birthday celebrations usually have a poster with a picture of the child and the family. A picture for each succeeding year, with a brief discussion. Not wanting to open a can of worms, I have avoided this but I know time is not on my side. Marisa's birthday and angel date are both celebrated with a family dinner and shared memories. I am sad that not all of my family are here. Close friends will send notes. It will be sad for me as Marisa starts to fade from their memories.

*

DENISE PURCELL
Denise's 27-year-old daughter Megan died
in 2011 from an accidental overdose

On Megan's birthday I pull out the CD of songs she made me and I go through her box I've kept since she was little. I will smile, cry, write, look at pictures and make her favorite dinner. Her picture follows me. Then I post it to her Facebook timeline. It's still there, and some days I'm grateful and some days I'm not. It's a bittersweet sadness. I always feel like she's there with me.

*

MARILYN ROLLINS
Marilyn's 37-year-old son Randy and 16-year-old granddaughter Sara
died in a car accident in 2006 during a family camping trip

On Randy's birthday, we get up in the morning and go out to the cemetery. I usually buy a balloon and some flowers to put on his grave. In the early years after his death, this was a very difficult day for me. I would drift back to the day he was born, and remember the feel and smell of him as I held him against me. I would struggle to remember every birthday we had celebrated together, and of course I couldn't remember them all, so I would drag out the pictures.

Now, after nine years, we try to have a special dinner and make a toast to him. We go around the table and everyone tells a "Randy story." We usually end up laughing at something we remember him doing. We also release a sky lantern as soon as it gets dark. I softly sing "Happy Birthday," as I watch it sail toward the heavens. When I can't see it any more, I think to myself, "He grabbed it." Only then I can go in and sleep.

The death anniversary is different. There is absolutely nothing to celebrate about that day. The clock becomes my enemy. As the hands move, I think to myself, "This is when we got the phone call, this is when we got to the hospital, this is when they told me Randy and Sara were gone..." One year I went through the house covering all the clocks; it didn't really help.

Sometimes we leave town and go visit family. That is a little easier for me. It still remains the most dreaded day of the year, though. A few years after their deaths, I wrote the following:

Until September.

I can't very well ignore it. My birthday falls in it. Labor Day falls in it. Autumn starts in it. There is no way to get around it, I must go through the ninth month of the year. I've heard it said about grief that you must go through it, you can't go around it. I've heard so many things the last few years, so many clichés. Time will heal, you've got to remember the good times, you'll get through this, you'll find your new normal, etc.

For the most part, I guess some of these are true. It does get easier, if not better, and I try to remember the good times. I have faced it head-on, and I have gone through it. Time has indeed helped with the pain, but I don't know if I've found my "new normal" yet. Yes, I guess these things ring true.

Until September.

That is when my old normal ended, and I lost both my son Randy and my 16-year-old granddaughter Sara in an auto accident. As the month of September comes around, the grief becomes unbearable. As the 21st approaches, I realize that in 2006 it was the last normal day in my life. On the 22nd, the clock betrays me. As I watch it, the day begins playing like a DVD in my head, until every nightmarish detail has been remembered. I push STOP to no avail. It continues to play. The tears come again, the pain comes again, my heart breaks a little more.

Eventually I fall into an exhausted sleep, the memories stop and I wake to a new day. Now I have a new lease: September is almost over. Of course, we have birthdays, holidays, anniversaries and other special days coming up, but we include Randy and Sara in our celebrations. So I manage with a few tears to get through those days. In fact, I come close to thinking that maybe I'm getting close to my "new normal."

Until September.

*

KATIE ROUSH
Katie's 26-year-old daughter Krystle
died in 2013 of accidental alcohol poisoning

On Krystle's Angelversary, I spend it at home with her sister, my grandson and my husband. We have Krystle's favorite dinner and I make a pineapple upside-down cake. At night we release sky lanterns and send wishes to heaven in her name.

On her birthday, I usually spend that day by myself. I relive some of my favorite memories with my daughter, and I do things she and I used to do together, like thrift store shopping, baking, or just watching some movies.

*

SARA RUBLE
Sara's 19-year-old son Scott died in 1994 from a
combination of a seizure disorder, Strep throat and dehydration

As Scott's birthday approached, the first one after his death, I was dreading each day that brought it closer. It had been a day of great celebration for nineteen years. Now I was so heartsick…and yet something kept telling me to order the birthday cake. Scott and I loved chocolate birthday cake with scrumptious white buttercream icing, covered with as many flowers as possible. We were very particular about our cakes, and they always came from our favorite bakery. The anticipation of a birthday coming meant the cake was coming too! But this birthday could never be like before. Those words, and the feeling that I needed to order this cake were insistent. Was it Scott? It had to be. I would trust that deep feeling of it being him…and so I ordered the cake.

When the day came, Scott's birthday, I could hardly get out of the car to walk into the bakery. I was certain this was a horrible idea and I felt sick to my stomach. But then the words I had heard came rushing back to me. Did he want this cake for me? Could I do it for Scott? Honestly, somehow, I knew he was pushing me to follow through. I took the cake home. In the midst of my tears and the deep, deep need to celebrate Scott on his day, I placed only one candle on the beautiful cake. I lit it and immediately felt that the flickering flame was a sign of Scott's spirit. That one bright sparkling light! It was extraordinary, and brought him closer than I could have imagined. My husband and I, with Scott's smiling photo next to his cake, were able to celebrate his birth and the tremendous joy Scott had brought in life...knowing that this birthday cake was meant to be. The cakes have become our tradition for the last twenty-one years. Whether it is just Jay and I, or celebrating with friends and family...that one single candle is always a symbol for Scott's bright spirit. And I know he is happy that I am still eating chocolate birthday cake with him...

The anniversary of Scott's death has been different for me every year for twenty-one years. Emotionally I never knew where I would be. I could never have known grief could be so debilitating. The first year, I took the day off from work, not knowing what it would bring because the anticipation of May 20 was absolutely agonizing. I tried to have a plan of sorts, which I knew was important. Scott loved nature, so I had a flowering pear tree planted at the cemetery next to his headstone as a tribute to him. I tied a black satin bow around it to express my grief. I had to show it outwardly somehow, and that's how I felt. A sadness beyond anything I'd ever known. It helped me to see how many friends and family left flowers at the cemetery too. It's always about the love, I've learned. I received many cards and remembrances from friends and family. I was so, so grateful they remembered, and I felt a little less alone.

Those first years, as that May 20 date rolled around, were grueling, but I always tried to bring something into the day to help others in Scott's memory...through a donation or sharing it with his friends or my family, doing random acts of kindness. In time, I knew he was reaching out through a song or a sign to show me he was still very much with me. That was the greatest help I could have ever received as he continued to show me he was not "gone."

It's okay to cry.
Giving in to the tears is terrifying,
like freefalling to earth without a parachute.
But it's vital to our wellbeing as we process the deep anguish.
LYNDA CHELDELIN FELL

*

CHAPTER SEVEN

THE HOLIDAYS

The only predictable thing about grief is that it's unpredictable. LYNDA CHELDELIN FELL

The holiday season comes around like clockwork, and for those in mourning, this time of year brings a kaleidoscope of emotions. If the grief is still fresh, the holidays can be downright raw. How do we navigate the invitations, decorations, and festivities without our precious child?

*

ERICA GALE BELTZ
Erica's 5-year-old son Luke Jordan died in 2005
from a fallen banister in his aunt's driveway

Luke died nine days after Christmas and three days after the new year. His stocking was still half full and his toys still had pieces of wrapping paper on them or needed batteries. We all truly loved the holidays. We had already lost the excitement of Christmas after going through hell in 2002.

Journal entry from 02/02/02: *My mom has never left my side. She had to guide my path because of the poor decisions I had made. She took on my responsibilities as a parent when she felt I wasn't making the best choices. She was firm and gave me direction until I was back on track.*

One night, two years before Luke's accident, my mom held my hand and gently wiped my tears away at the hospital and sat silent as I relived the details of a physical assault I had just been through. She let me talk because I was still fighting to be heard. When no one assured our safety after the attack, my mom alone marched in to the police department and demanded to see Sheriff Miller. With our full medical report in her hands, an investigation began and an arrest was soon made. My mom arranged the financial opportunity for me and my two kids to relocate to a safe place. She never let me see her pain or hear about her sleepless nights until it was over.

We came home on Christmas Eve, a poor choice on my part but it was Christmas. When my mom's car pulled into the cul-de-sac, the police were waiting; waiting to take my kids away. Mom walked straight up to the officers, determined to keep the kids out of harm's way. When honesty, restraining orders, arrest warrants, bond conditions from the same county against the people who had hurt us were not enough, my mom begged the officers not to do this. But they took my children away and placed them into the very harm we had escaped. Fear is learned and for the first time in my life I truly feared for my safety. It came with its own level of psychosis.

The depth of the planning and the people hired to execute it all was thick as thieves. Mom knew of one attorney who still stood behind the justice system and would always err in favor of the law. We hired that attorney and sat on his sofa while his family opened presents in the next room. Mom sat beside me on the bed until I cried myself to sleep. She was still there when she woke me up to take Sheriff Miller's call. She was carving the turkey as I took his call in the kitchen. My hope turned into despair when he told me that the order stood; court would open in five days and we could

146

file a motion then. For the first time I saw my mom brace herself on the stove. She composed herself, looked me straight in the eye and said with affirmation, "Erica, WE WILL GET THOSE BABIES BACK NO MATTER WHAT IT TAKES!" Her words alone gave me the strength to fight.

Christmas didn't exist that year, and we both knew it would never be the same for either of us.

Mom drove alone to Douglas General Hospital the night Luke died. When they told me he wasn't going to make it, I called for her. I was trembling and in disbelief. There she was, my Army of Angels, my rock and safe haven. I told my mom that Luke was gone. For the second time, I watched my mom brace herself, this time on the rails of Luke's hospital bed.

The holidays sucked for a really long time. We still suited up, we still gathered as a family and took it slow when we needed to. I trod very carefully through the stores and when I left the house. Halloween costumes, plastic Easter eggs, and Valentine cards could take me down for weeks. I stayed drunk, quite honestly.

One Easter we were at church, and I held it together pretty well. I had all the kids in their pretty Easter clothes and I told them to go stand beside my mom to take a picture. When I looked through the lens, I realized one was missing. I collapsed in the restroom. On my knees I prayed, "God, give me the strength to get back up." And He did. Mom cooked a huge dinner, and we took the kids to the cemetery to tell Luke about their baskets. It started pouring rain. The ground was a mess. Mom had her camera so he would still be in pictures. Everyone tried to help replace the flowers and make it right. We had mud on our faces and clothes. We attended candle lightings. We talked about Luke a lot, laughed a lot and loved on each other. Tears were always understood. One Halloween I bought five costumes in Luke's size and hid them in my trunk. After my nervous breakdown and I got sober, I was able to participate instead of just showing up for the holidays.

*

STACY BERNDTSON
Stacy's daughter Cori Joy died in 2003, the day before her
fourth birthday, from an undiagnosed genetic disorder

Because of Cori's disabilities we did not really have any traditions during the holidays. I just remember them as being a quiet time together, just the three of us. I think we did spend maybe one Christmas or Thanksgiving with extended family when Cori was out of the baby stage, but mostly during that time it was just us. She died just before the holidays, so I was in the very early stages of grief that first year and that time is somewhat blurry for me.

After Cori died, and with the holidays fast approaching, I began to see her middle name everywhere: Joy. And for several years after her death I collected anything and everything I could find with the word Joy on it. Joy ornaments and also angel ornaments began to multiply. One very odd thing we did, considering we had just lost our child, was that we watched the first episode of the series *Six Feet Under*. I am not sure why, but we both became a little obsessed by that show and as soon as we'd watched one DVD full we'd head to Blockbuster to rent the next one.

I believe it was the second Christmas after Cori's death that we bought a little live tree and took it to her cemetery spot. We put little ornaments on it that reminded us of her including Sponge Bob, angels, etc. That tree is planted in our yard to the right of our dining area and kitchen, so I have watched it grow from a little three-foot-tall bush into a fifteen-foot or taller evergreen. That is 'Cori's tree.'

The third year after she died we took a trip at Christmas to a cabin in Leavenworth, Washington, that we hoped would be snowy outside and warm inside, and would get us away to something different. I believe we left on Christmas Eve and got over there just in time to buy a tree before they closed up the tree farm for the season. We had brought only our Cori, Joy and Angel ornaments with us. We arrived to find that the cabin owners had decorated a fake tree in the living room. So I think we pulled that into one of the bedrooms and decorated our fresh-cut little tree.

As with her anniversary and birthday dates, once Molly was on the scene we believed the best way to honor Cori was to do with Molly all the things we would have loved to do with Cori too. Visits to Santa, horse-drawn carriage rides, cutting down our own Christmas tree each year, decorating our house with tons of lights and blowup decorations, and getting just as excited as Molly to see what Santa brings each year. I don't believe that any holiday will ever feel fully "right" until that day in which my little family will once again number four. It is my hope of heaven that often gets me through holidays and other difficult days.

*

TANISHA CALDWELL
Tanisha's 23-year-old son Tariq (Jay)
died in a car accident in 2015

The holidays are coming, and it will be our first without him. I am dreading the holidays. They won't be the same without him.

*

LYNDA CHELDELIN FELL
Lynda's 15-year-old daughter Aly
died in a car accident in 2009

For the first five years the holidays were almost unbearable. Aly and I loved decorating the house for the holidays and usually started in early October, sometimes even September. We just loved the whole autumn season that flowed into Halloween, Thanksgiving and Christmas. So this window of time spanning October through January became incredibly painful. If the truth be told, I desperately wanted to skip the entire holiday season. But I couldn't let my family down, so each year I went through the motions and prayed that my smile would hold.

Thanksgiving is the holiday when dinner is hosted at our house. Our immediate family is quite large, over twenty people, and the cousins have all been raised together, so they are more like brothers and sisters. Our large family enjoys being together, and Thanksgiving is a messy, memorable favorite. After dinner we have a long-standing tradition where the cousins divide into teams for a gingerbread house decorating contest. Each year I would buy the premade gingerbread house kits from the store and hot-glue them together the week prior. So after Thanksgiving dinner, the real fun would start. The teams remained the same every year, cousins partnering with the same cousins. But after the accident Aly's team had a hole that couldn't be filled. The tradition continues to this day, though it took a few years for it to become less raw. Instinctively, I feel it is important to continue making happy memories to balance out the sad ones our family has suffered the past few years.

I remember the dilemma that first Christmas over what to do with Aly's stocking. I simply couldn't bear the thought of her stocking not hanging alongside the others. Yet leaving it to hang empty alongside the stuffed stockings wasn't an option. Worried that our young grandson might ask questions, I had to figure out something. Aly loved cats and we had two new kittens, so that first Christmas after the accident I stuffed Aly's stocking with toys and treats for the pets. We continue to do that to this day.

This past year was our sixth without Aly and the rawness of the holiday season has finally begun to soften. As such, I now believe that each passing holiday will be a little more magical than the year prior. Grandchildren also help tremendously through the holiday season, so more grandchildren, grand-nieces and grand-nephews will always remain at the top of my Christmas list.

*

JACQUELYN CRUZ
Jacquelyn's 24-year-old daughter Jenna
died in 2012 from pulmonary edema

The last time I saw my mother alive was on Mother's Day 2010. Two days later she died unexpectedly from a brain bleed. The last words my father spoke to me were "I love you," and he died two days later on Christmas Day 2011. The Saturday before Thanksgiving 2012, my daughter Jenna went away with her girlfriend and never came back. So as you can see, the holidays are a painful reminder of what I've lost.

We still celebrate Christmas because I still have two living children; it would be unfair to them not to. But our rituals have changed; we no longer put up a Christmas tree or hang up their stockings. We go through the motions of exchanging gifts and pretending we're happy but inside we're screaming out in pain. Thanksgiving was Jenna's absolute favorite holiday! Her wake was the Wednesday before Thanksgiving. On Thanksgiving Day the funeral home was closed. Friday was the funeral and Jenna's cremation. So during Thanksgiving dinner my daughter was alone in the funeral home; that's all I could think about. The beautiful sight of colorful mums, pumpkins, apple pies and turkey dinners make my stomach turn. When I see these things, it's like my brain automatically knows something is wrong....she's not here.

*

MICHELLE DETWILER
Michelle's 19-year-old daughter Emily
died in 2014 due to congenital complications

Our daughter loved Christmas. As a matter of fact we listened to Christmas music all year long in our house. There was at least one Christmas movie playing each day, and talk of Santa and snowmen always brought a smile to her face. When we put up our Christmas tree each year Emily would sit in her wheelchair and

151

watch as each light was checked and each ornament placed just so. However, after the tree lighting she wouldn't see the decorations much. Her medical condition had limited her ability to be out and around most of the time.

One year I purchased a small pre-lit Christmas tree to put in her room. That way she could have the joy of the season to look at just as we were looking at the larger version in our living room. For several years a friend brought kids from school, from Scouts, or a youth group to decorate her little tree for her. Together they would sing Christmas carols and sometimes silly songs which brought out the laughter in everyone. It was all so magical! Her face would light up as soon as the little tree did.

The first Christmas after she died I didn't really feel like decorating or setting up the large tree. I didn't even care if I ever celebrated Christmas again. As I remembered Christmases past, ones celebrated around that little tree in Emily's room, I decided to make an arrangement in our living room with her little tree. But when I went to look for it I couldn't find it! I was frantic and began to tear apart each hiding place where I thought it might be. I called her two nurses and asked if I had given the tree to them. Suddenly that little tree became the most important thing in my life. How could I have given it away? My heart was sad. It was gone. Christmas was gone. My daughter was gone.

Then one day, when looking for something in my daughter's closet, I found it! I found that little tree stored safely in its little box with ornaments stashed around it! It was as if Christmas was reborn in me. The excitement of finding that treasured tree ushered me into the first Christmas season without her. Now I could put up a tree and I could make it through Christmas. With tears streaming down my face I thanked the Lord for that wonderful miracle of Christmas.

*

ANNAH ELIZABETH
Annah's son Gavin Michael aspirated on his meconium
during the delivery and died 26 minutes following his birth

The earliest holidays were the hardest...several Mother's Days and Father's Days without a child. Halloween. Christmas. Valentine's Day. Easter. No silly costumes. No child for Santa's lap, no cheesy photo ops, and no little one's stocking to hang...

Warren bought me one of those mechanical bunnies around the first Easter. I remember bawling because it reminded me of what I was missing. When Fave came along, I felt a little bit of initial guilt at being happy, but the presence of this child seemed to dull the pain of missing the first.

A year or two after we buried Gavin, Warren and I made seasonal wooden decorations to put on his grave. I created the stencils, transferred them to wood, and then painted them after Warren carved them out. We had an Easter bunny reading a book, several Easter eggs, some spring flowers, a couple of Christmas stockings, and a Santa Claus. We keep all these items in an oversized boot box that has its own place on a shelf in our closet.

For Gavin's birthday, we always buy a few balloons and some special spring decorations, since his special day falls on the heels of winter's end. We pull unwanted weeds from around his grave marker, pad the empty space with pine needles, and set out the gifts we brought.

On his twenty-first birthday we went to a special restaurant we'd never visited before, and I had a chocolate raspberry martini in his honor. We've participated in an Easter sunrise pageant for the last fourteen years. We come home to find the treasure the Easter bunny left behind, have breakfast, and then head to the cemetery before returning home for a nap or a rousing video game found in one of the baskets.

Visiting Gavin is as much a part of our holiday traditions as the homemade pumpkin, apple, and pecan pies that grace our buffet, a staple in our family's celebrations. If Warren and I fail to mention that part of our day, one of the children will inevitably ask when we're going. One of my most special traditions, though, is how we form a circle around Gavin's stone. Hands held, we wonder aloud about things he might be doing in heaven, what toys he would have been playing with or, when he became of driving age, what kind of car he'd be driving. We take turns sending Gavin a special message. I've always believed that Gavin's spirit is with us wherever we are, so visiting the cemetery is more of a formality for us, but it is the tradition that my three living children have always known and one they have always remembered.

A few blocks from the cemetery there's a little store that sells the best locally made ice cream and eggnog. They are always open Christmas Day. As my children grew older, we would stop to buy several half gallons of the frozen treats to top our after-dinner pie. While there, we'd also pick up a few lottery tickets for everyone to scratch off. When they were younger the kids knew they couldn't cash them in, but, oh, the delight once they became of age!

The other special part of these events is that we are creating memories with our loved one, even when he is not in this physical plane. Gavin has always been and will always be a part of these stories. It is a relationship that we have continued to develop, even in his absence. That is one of the most beautiful things I learned in my healing, that we can create new memories and carry on relationships with our loved ones after they are gone. It's just that those things are different; they exist in ways we never expected or envisioned.

*

WENDY EVANS
Wendy's 21-year-old son Kyle died in 2009
from diabetes when his insulin pump malfunctioned

The first year was incredibly difficult for Christmas and Thanksgiving. In 2009, I only knew I could not be home for either holiday. Too painful. I randomly selected a town to visit based on where we could rent a large enough house for the family. Thanksgiving was spent in New Orleans and Christmas was spent in Florida with our daughter. No holiday decorations since 2009. I still can't bring myself to decorate. That process always involved everyone in the family. The absence was too obvious for the first four years. Last year was somewhat better; we joined our daughter and husband in Florida for Christmas. We left after Christmas to travel to Montana. Our first grandchild arrived on December 19, 2014. Holidays are starting to feel better now, but still sad.

*

BONNIE FORSHEY
Bonnie's 16-year-old son Billy died in 1993
from an overdose of prescription drugs

I hate holidays. We used to go all out, decorated for every holiday, inside and out. We enjoyed life. We had huge dinners. I don't celebrate anything now. It is too painful for me. I will go out to a restaurant to eat, I won't even accept an invitation to anyone's home. Too painful.

*

TALIA GATO
Talia's 8-year-old daughter Poppy
died in 2009 in a car accident

Holidays are difficult. They don't hold the joy they once did. I still decorate and do everything I must do because I have another child to raise and I want her to have joy. Have you ever had to fake joy? I hope I do a good job at that.

155

We have the major holidays with my in-laws, the big meal with special china and all the dishes nicely prepared. They are a religious family, quiet-spoken. Lots of presents. But not a word spoken of my daughter or how I am doing or even what I am doing. Just small talk and pass the sweet potatoes. Lots of TV watching.

It feels lonely when there is no space for sharing how you really feel. I just swallow it even though it feels empty. Now we just go to half of the holidays and start to create new memories with our daughter, like making meals and doing things I want my daughter to learn. What helps is special holiday special music or to go on a small trip somewhere else, go to a special service. Eat different foods or make the foods from my own childhood.

In some ways I feel as if I am starting my life over again and doing it my way….what works for us, what is healthy for us as a family. And if sometimes we have to say sorry to our families for the big holiday dinners or gatherings? We do.

*

KORBY HAVE
Korby's 17-year-old daughter Taylor (Tayla)
died in 2013 in a car accident

I think I still just go through the holidays on autopilot. If it weren't for my sons I think I would just skip the holidays but because they deserve to be happy, I just go through the motions. My daughter loved Halloween, Thanksgiving and Christmas, so October through December are especially hard. I only do the bare minimum of what needs to be done, and I don't go all out like I used to before her death.

*

DEANA MARTIN
Deana's only two children, 25-year-old Amanda
and 21-year-old Logan, died in a car accident in 2011

The holidays have basically remained the same for us, keeping old family traditions alive for my granddaughter. This has been difficult for me, and if it was just me I would more than likely travel over the holidays or do something totally different than what we did as a family. At Halloween we still decorate the house with a truckload of scary decorations in Logan's honor, because he always decorated the house when he was here and did such a good job! The first year after their death we threw a huge Halloween party in their honor. Logan's fraternity came out and helped me run kid games in a carnival theme during the day, and helped me construct a haunted trail complete with Bigfoot in the woods behind our house. We had so much fun. Thanksgiving is hard because my daughter helped me cook for years, and I miss having her by my side in the kitchen. If family comes to visit, we go around the dinner table and tell funny stories about both Amanda and Logan. We laugh about silly times when Amanda, Logan and I would dress up as pilgrims and Indians on Thanksgiving, and other crazy stories.

The hardest tradition is that I still put my tree up the day after Thanksgiving. Getting out the boxes and opening the ornaments that remind me of all our Christmases together usually causes me to cry. Amanda usually helped me decorate the tree or did it with her brother. It always turned out beautifully when she did it. Everything she touched turned out beautifully. I taught Amanda's daughter Armaya all about the parades, and we watch them as long as I can before I have to get into the kitchen. I usually light a candle in front of their picture the day of the holiday and keep it lit all day. The Christmas without them was so very hard.

Family members turned against me for the manner in which I chose to grieve, which was watching Amanda's and Logan's Facebook pages for merry Christmas messages from their friends, and listening to songs about Christmas in heaven that I found on the internet. I wanted so badly to share these songs and Facebook messages with my family, but they felt my actions were inappropriate around my granddaughter, who was outside in the pool with her aunt at the time. Anyway, it caused huge problems at a very highly emotionally charged time. I so needed my family's understanding that my deep grief on this holiday was normal. I needed them to acknowledge my pain and support me in whatever way I chose to deal with my sorrow during this time. But that did not happen, and I ended up staying in my room most of the rest of the trip because my feelings were hurt and my heart crushed when they said I was "doing it wrong."

Like I do for Amanda and Logan's birthdays, for Christmas I usually shop for them like I always would and I give their gifts to people they loved, rotating people each year. It's not much, just typical articles I would get Amanda and Logan at Christmas. I lead a support group and we will often paint ornaments in honor of our loved ones at Christmas, and giving to others in need during this time seems to soften my heart a bit and ease the pain just a bit. I now collect angels since the kids have died, and I have some new angel ornaments for the tree.

New Year's remains the same. I usually toast a cheer to heaven and say I wish they were here, and to have a beautiful New Year's in heaven. Sometimes I write when the holidays have me down. I either write letters to them or poems about my feelings on passing another holiday without them. But again if I could choose, the holidays would be totally different and involve travel. But it is one of the most important things in my life to teach Armaya about her mother and uncle, and to pass down to her the traditions her mother and uncle would have if they were here.

*
MONICA MIRKES
Monica's 30-year-old daughter Marisa
died in 2013 due to Cesarean complications

Again I fall down the rabbit hole. We have Marisa's toddler to think about. Wanting him to have good memories, I force myself to decorate the house. Marisa was hospitalized the last year of her life. She always hoped to be out for Halloween, which is a family favorite. And then Christmas came and went. Marisa had been planning her son's second birthday, looking forward to that. Making and buying things online. My heart aches for all that she lost. I am in the Twilight Zone of emotions, knowing what I should do, what I want to do, and being so very tired of having some family members tell me that I have to move on.

*
DENISE PURCELL
Denise's 27-year-old daughter Megan died
in 2011 from an accidental overdose

Megan died Thursday, November 24, Thanksgiving, so it's a double whammy. First the 24th is sad, and then Thanksgiving Day is when all those memories of that day flood back. I find myself looking at the clock. I still do the big dinner for the girls, because I am thankful for them.

*
MARILYN ROLLINS
Marilyn's 37-year-old son Randy and 16-year-old granddaughter Sara
died in a car accident in 2006 during a family camping trip

I mentioned in an earlier answer how I was a little crazy during the first Christmas after the accident. I bought a new Christmas tree and all new lights and ornaments. All presents had to be wrapped in red, green, or gold or they didn't go under the tree. Nine years later, I now laugh. I realize it was a control issue. My life was out of control, my normal gone, and yet this I had control of.

The year before the accident, I went to Kohl's department store right after Christmas and caught an unbelievable sale on village items. I bought several houses, stores, people, trees, etc., for the village I set up every year. I didn't set the village up for two years after the accident. The next time I set it up, my husband came down from the attic with all these new village pieces. I had no idea where they came from! I didn't remember buying them. Thank goodness a friend was with me when I bought them, or I might still be wondering where they came from.

Each holiday got a little easier as the years went by. We did make changes though. My daughter-in-law remarried a couple of years ago, and stopped coming to our house for the holidays. The children's gifts would sometimes sit here for months, until we finally would take them over. I miss seeing Randy's children so much. We recently renewed our relationship, and I hope they join us this year for the holidays.

At our Christmas party, we like to go around and have each member of the family tell a "Randy" or a "Sara" story. To this day, I will sometimes hear a new story, and it is such a gift. We still hang Sara's stocking at the top of our stocking tree, and the other grandchildren will write a note to put in her stocking with a little gift they made for her. At our holiday table, we always light two candles to represent their presence at the table. After Thanksgiving dinner, I'll look over at the recliner and envision Randy with his head back, softly snoring as he dozes from his turkey dinner stupor. I sit and look at the Christmas tree and picture Sara on her hands and knees crawling around, trying to see which presents are hers. A tear may fall, yes, but the memories are so wonderful. They help me survive.

*

KATIE ROUSH
Katie's 26-year-old daughter Krystle
died in 2013 of accidental alcohol poisoning

Halloween is very hard for me. That was my daughter's favorite holiday. We would put out tombstones and decorate the front porch and act crazy and laugh. She liked to pull a lot of pranks on me at this time, so I still put out the tombstones and all the decorations that she bought for me, or we bought together. For Thanksgiving we usually have dinner at my house. All the kids come, so now it's a little strange to see my daughter's chair empty. So we just do it very low-key now. We still go around and say what we're thankful for, but it's just not the same. At Christmas we still go to church on Christmas Eve, and I try to carry on traditions like I did when my daughter was alive.

*

Just as it is impossible to explain childbirth
to a woman who has never given birth,
it is impossible to explain child loss
to a person who has never lost a child.
LYNDA CHELDELIN FELL

*

CHAPTER EIGHT

THE BELONGINGS

Of all possessions, a friend is the most precious.
-HERODOTUS

Our child's belongings are a direct connection to what once was and what we desperately want back. They ARE what is left of our child until one day the smell has dissipated, the threads are bare, or we discover a need greater than our own. When does the time come to address the painful task of sorting our child's memory-laden belongings, and how does one begin?

*

ERICA GALE BELTZ
Erica's 5-year-old son Luke Jordan died in 2005
from a fallen banister in his aunt's driveway

Months before I lost Luke, I had to move back home in an effort to rebuild my life with my kids in tow. My room was next to Luke's bedroom; he chose the room I had before I left home. He loved his room, but he slept with me and it was no secret that my room was also his. His sister liked her independence and, I think, the safety of being next to Grandma.

Shortly after the funeral, a small fire started in the kitchen above Luke's room. When the insurance company came, they had to tear the ceiling down and replace the carpet in Luke's room. Everything had to be boxed up and placed in the garage so repairs could be made. I hated seeing his things in the garage. I hated the fact that Luke wasn't there. It wouldn't have mattered if his belongings had all been dipped in gold; it was still awful.

When the repairs were complete, my mom asked me what I wanted to do about Luke's belongings. I said I wanted them to go back just the way they were. She asked me to think about that, and I thought maybe it would be harder putting them back. I was so consumed with what I wanted and what I needed that I don't think I asked my mom what she thought would be best. I felt so ashamed of having to be back home and to depend on her. In the end I agreed that it wasn't a good idea. The days that followed were awful and no place felt right. My sister had lost her home and was moving, and she invited us to come and try to start over with her family. Within weeks Lakin and I moved from my mama's house to my sister's new home. It seemed like the right thing to do. Moving somewhere different had just the opposite effect. Taking Luke's things to a place he had never been was so painful. We tried to place his things everywhere, but his absence is what stays in my mind. I felt a strong need in those first few days to allow those closest to Luke to choose something of his to take home. I wanted everyone to stay close to him. I had no idea that the longer I went without him, the more I would long to have those things back.

I have moved many times in the years since Luke has been gone, and every one of his possessions go with me. Many people have suggested that I donate his toys or clothes to someone who could really benefit from them, but I just haven't been ready to do that. The truth is that I still need them. I still have the lunchbox Luke took to school that day. It still holds a couple of Oreos, and I love that time hasn't eroded them away. Recently I was able to throw out broken toy pieces if I couldn't remember what they went to.

Around six years out I decided to take Luke's favorite shirts and pajamas and have a quilt made. At first I was so sick after sending these items off, feeling like I was discarding his life and trying to sum it up in a blanket.

My knees buckled when the woman, Sandy, came to deliver the finished product. I was sweating and thought I had made a huge mistake. When I pulled out this blanket my heart literally sang with joy, and I held it to my face and wept. It was beautiful. It was wonderful to see these things in a beautiful blanket and to have them free from the boxes and crates that had kept them prisoner. I love it so much. Everyone who comes to my house uses it. It gets worn, washed and taken to the beach and the fireworks show. I have no idea how long I will keep his things, and everyone knows it's for this family to decide. Do not let anyone tell you what you should do with their things or make you think that you're doing something wrong because you're not ready. You will know when you are.

*

STACY BERNDTSON
Stacy's daughter Cori Joy died in 2003, the day before her
fourth birthday, from an undiagnosed genetic disorder

Because Cori was unable to walk and had medical issues, we had a fair amount of equipment that was not standard to a typical child. We donated some of the items and had small tags affixed that said "Donated in memory of Corinne Joy Berndtson," and because we had significant expenses after her death we sold several of the items as well.

Over the course of Cori's short life she was given many, many soft stuffed toys and animals. After her death we let each child in the family go into Cori's room and select a stuffed toy that would remind them of Cori Joy. Cori had many blankets as well. We had "In Memory of Cori Joy" embroidered on the blankets. We donated these along with a letter I wrote to young moms who were living at a pregnancy home. In the letter I told them how precious my child's life was to me and that by simply allowing their child to be born-whether they chose to raise that child or to place the child in the loving arms of another couple, they were heroes in my book. We donated all but a few of Cori's favorite books to our local library with "In Memory of" labels inside.

Before Cori was born I had purchased several crib-size checkered sheets with matching soft blankets in pastel colors. After her death I had these made into a quilt that we will always keep. Someone from my niece's church made a small fleece blanket for Cori with a crochet edge around it and gave it to us during one of Cori's hospital stays. To this day I sleep with that little blanket at the head of the bed. We have a chest in which we store mementoes of Cori. Inside are pictures and various remembrance items we were given after her death. We kept a few clothing items: the clothing Cori wore on her last day, she loved her special ducky jammies so we had two pairs which are also inside. Cori was buried in one pair and we kept the other with us. We also kept a little pair of tennis shoes that Cori wore though she never walked in them.

*

KARI BROWN
Kari's 2-year-old daughter Dominique (Deedee)
died in 2014 from obstructive sleep apnea

Handling Dominique's belongings was hard, but we had to move three months after she passed. We packed everything else first, and let her room for last. It was extremely difficult, and I could not get through even one hour of packing without crying. It felt as if I was packing her memories away. We were moving in with Brandon's step-brother, so we could not bring much and had to keep most of our belongings in storage. I hated the idea of leaving Dominique's things in storage; it felt like they should be with us, in the open.

A lot of emotions came up: anger, bitterness, heartbreak and especially sadness. We packed things that she loved or never had a chance to wear. A few things were picked out that we could bring with us: a couple of her favorite clothing items she loved to wear, and a couple of favorite toys that we wanted to keep close to us. After we moved into our own apartment, we unpacked some of her belongings such as a few toys and more clothing items that we could hang next to ours. We moved into a one-bedroom apartment so we didn't have space for her crib or other large furniture. But having her items around the apartment like her beanbag, feeding utensils (bowls, bottles, silverware) and her trunk of toys helped to ease our ache of her absence. We have always talked about moving into a house and setting up her room the way it was before. It may sound crazy, but it reminds us that we are still parents.

*

TANISHA CALDWELL
Tanisha's 23-year-old son Tariq (Jay)
died in a car accident in 2015

A few days after Jay's death I went to get his belongings from his roommate's house. I was overtaken by sadness; it just didn't seem right. I still have everything. My youngest son has most of Jay's clothing. My daughter has a few things as well. I might give some of Jay's hats away, and I will be giving his shoes away because no one can fit them. I just look at his stuff and shake my head in disbelief. I often grab a shirt and sniff it for his scent. We plan to get pillows or something made with some of his clothes.

*

LYNDA CHELDELIN FELL
Lynda's 15-year-old daughter Aly
died in a car accident in 2009

It's been six years, and Aly's bedroom remains untouched. The hardest part was that family needed to grieve, and they naturally migrated toward Aly's room, yet I didn't want anyone to touch her stuff. I didn't mind people being in her room, I just didn't want *anything* touched. Maybe I was afraid that their fingerprints would somehow erase Aly's energy.

My husband and I still find comfort in her room. I love seeing her bed, her letterman's jacket hanging under the window, her stuffed animals, her medals. I love seeing her nail polish and jewelry and cellphone on her nightstand. Her room brings us comfort. The thought of using her bedroom for something different just feels wrong. The first grief counselor we saw asked why we hadn't changed Aly's room, implying that there was something wrong with our decision. We don't need the space, so why should we change it? Maybe one day we will, but for now it feels comforting to leave it untouched.

A few well-meaning individuals have suggested making a quilt from Aly's clothing. The idea of cutting up her clothing remains horrifying to me, even six years later. I have memories of Aly wearing her clothes and how she painstakingly paired her accessories with each outfit. I won't have memories of her wearing a quilt.

*

JACQUELYN CRUZ
Jacquelyn's 24-year-old daughter Jenna
died in 2012 from pulmonary edema

My husband packed up Jenna's things days after her passing. I think he thought he was doing me a favor, saving me from having to do it. I wished he hadn't. Months later I went through the boxes of clothes, desperately hoping to catch Jenna's scent. She loved her T-shirts and sneakers, and of course they always had to match. I plan on making a quilt from all her favorite shirts and her sneakers, which are still in a box. I cannot bear the thought of getting rid of anything of hers now, but maybe one day.

*

MICHELLE DETWILER
Michelle's 19-year-old daughter Emily
died in 2014 due to congenital complications

Emily died at home. After she died I left the room and then walked back into it a thousand times. She was just there, just an hour ago, just a day ago, just a week ago. I had seen it on TV and in the movies, parents not wanting to sort out and remove their child's things. It was real. This was not a movie, this was my child. Things that had once given her such joy still lined the shelves and were scattered about the room. But there were also the things that reminded us of pain and suffering. The medical equipment and the wheelchair were a burden that needed to be relieved.

The wheelchair was the first thing to go. No need to think of Emily sitting in that chair as she had done for most of her life. She was free now, in heaven, with new arms and legs that worked! It was so easy to get rid of that chair. It was gone in the first week.

It was much more difficult to go through the other things, her personal things. It took months. I couldn't open her closet. Then there was Emily's bed, her source of comfort, the other place she had been for most of her life. It was next to go. But I wanted it. I wanted to keep it in the room because it had been hers! But there was someone else who needed it. And so I called.

After the bed left, I cried. The room was so empty. My heart was so empty. Why did I wash the pillowcase? I wanted to smell her, to feel her, to hug her.

Deciding to give away the communication device was next, and the most difficult of all to share. It was part of her, her voice, and now I was giving it to someone else. I knew I was helping, and in a way Emily was helping someone else by my giving it up. But it was like cutting an appendage off. Would the new owners ever know how much it had meant? Would it mean something to them? After it left the house I had a mini crisis and I couldn't stop crying.

My life was so different. How could I ever live again? How could I ever be a mom and love again? I have people here who love me and need me, and I cried, "God, please help me. I don't have the strength!" My life is gone. How can I live in this different life?

Another week passes, and then another. After rearranging Emily's clothing in her drawers I made a decision to hold onto them. No one needed her clothing that badly except me. But when I looked at it all I would just cry. I told myself I was going to make a quilt from some of her garments, and I nearly did. I met some ladies through a friend of mine. They were going to help me do this. We talked on the phone a couple of times, and then they disappeared. I never did hear from them again. Oh, well. I didn't think I was ready to start cutting up these woven treasures so soon. Maybe it was God's grace. So I put them back in the drawers.

This year was easier. A friend's little girls wanted some new play dresses. They wanted to dress up and play princess. Emily's closet held the bulk of their desire. In it were a number of Disney princess dresses from a few years ago. They were nicely made and still in wonderful shape. The dresses had been among her favorites. I hugged and smelled each one... a last goodbye to her fairytales. My heart sank, and I cried as I sent them on their way. And that opened up the door to sorting out and cleaning the closet. It's only halfway sorted now, but it's a door that's finally open.

*

ANNAH ELIZABETH
Annah's son Gavin Michael aspirated on his meconium
during the delivery and died 26 minutes following his birth

I'm not sure where it came from, but while I was in the hospital following Gavin's death someone brought me a large box. One of my strongest memories is of me holding that square clothing container on my lap as the staff person wheeled me to the front door of the hospital, where my husband waited with the car, the one with the baby carrier we'd painstakingly secured in the backseat well in advance of our baby's arrival. My son's entire life seemed to be packed into a piece of mass-produced cardboard...his hospital blanket and hand-knitted hat...the paper measuring tape that recorded his birth statistics...the bassinet card...the many condolences and the two Mother's Day cards that friends and family sent...

I later added copies of the love letters and the farewell letters Warren and I wrote before Gavin's funeral...the floral tags...the VCR tape of his only ultrasound...the few photos his nurses took of him...the funeral guest registry...the funeral bulletin...the scraps of paper I'd recorded my contractions on...the photos Warren and I took with him at the funeral home...

Twenty-five years after his birth, those treasures are preserved in that same box, which I now keep in a fireproof safe.

I had so many items that I ended up filling a large shopping bag with his other belongings: photos from my pregnancy, special items from my baby shower, another baby book, the many other condolence cards and special notes we received from family, friends, and even a few strangers...the baptismal jacket I hadn't put on him because I chose to send him off in the crocheted sweater my mother-in-law had made especially for him. My boss and I were pregnant at the same time, our boys born two weeks apart. We shared McDonald's buttered biscuits in the mornings, chocolate confections whenever the urge struck, as well as our hopes and fears. And we, along with our husbands, finished out our pregnancies in the same Lamaze group. It was in one of our final birthing classes that our instructor ended the session with a task none of us expected.

"I know you're all in happy places with happy times ahead," she began, "but I would like you to ponder something—what you would do if something happened to the baby? I know it's not anything you want to think about, but you should really spend a minute or two discussing it."

"What would you do if something happened to the baby?" I asked Warren on the way home. "I don't know," he replied. "You?" "I don't know either," I said. We didn't talk about it again. Until we had to.

Like all the other pregnancy-related matters my pregnant pal and I shared, we shared our experiences around that topic. She told me that she and her husband had also considered that question on their drive home. "I told him if something happened I didn't want him to do anything with the nursery; I would want to come home to it just the way I've prepared it," she said.

I was grateful to have that foresight and equally thankful to have the freshly washed bedding to cuddle with and the mobile's music to listen to as I grieved, dreamed, and sometimes fell asleep in the antique rocker at the foot of Gavin's crib. I ended up using the nursery items for each of my three children to come. Like life, the threads and fibers of those belongings bear the marks of good and bad, happy and sad, laughter and tears. For me, all these years later, they are more like symbols, little tangible objects that show Gavin lived.

Those things, however, are nothing more than fabricated products. One of the truths I've always told my children and my students is that material possessions come and go; they are expendable, but our relationships are forever. The bond I have with my son is eternal. Nothing can take that away.

Even though I occasionally have fleeting moments of longing—like when Gavin's would-be playmate proposed to his girlfriend, when I watched those two stand at the altar and exchange their vows, and when I helped them welcome their own first child—I am now able to celebrate the life I had with my son and the one I continue to have with him. It is a connection independent of stuff; one that is filled to brimming in a form that is far different from that which I'd ever expected, envisioned and imagined.

*

WENDY EVANS
Wendy's 21-year-old son Kyle died in 2009
from diabetes when his insulin pump malfunctioned

I still have not handled my child's belongings. After Kyle's funeral, his apartment had to be cleaned out. My mother, brothers, daughter and sons packed up all of Kyle's belongings and moved his furniture into a storage unit. It is now six years after his death, and I have not unpacked or gone through the boxes of his things. In 2012 we donated his furniture and kitchen items to a young mother of five children who lost the contents of their home in a flood.

*

DAPHNE GREER
Daphne's 5-year-old daughter Lydia died in 2008 in a
car accident during a routine morning commute

The issues of my daughter's belongings was one that brought with it profound fear and much trepidation. It terrified me. It posed a devilish portrayal of something much larger than me with the potential to unravel the pent-up guilt and regret. Lydia's door to her bedroom had remained closed since shortly after the accident. What lay behind it after all these years remained a familiar mystery.

This was a monstrous task to tackle. Insurmountable, it seemed. Really? Why must I do this? I thought. There were so many nudges and pushes and expectations from close friends and relatives and outside sources, as they cast preconceived judgments from a distance. Some pushed, saying it should have been done a long time ago. Others said I was avoiding it and not dealing with her "things." Well, they weren't just "things." It was all I had left of my little girl. That and a thousand memories that I feared I would forget.

However, as time continued I learned that they had no idea. Not a clue as to the giant uphill battle I was facing. And so, as chance would have it, a job opportunity for my husband came our way. Our need to relocate across the state left me no choice but to confront that colossal monster.

The day had come, and it was time. Nervously I faced the blue puppy sticker that decorated the outside of Lydia's door as a rush of anxiety swept over me. As I walked into her room, sat on the cream carpet colored in pink glitter from her hours of art projects she would do in there, I could feel the energy. I felt Lydia everywhere. The bittersweet moment consumed me. It was terrifying, horrifying, to think about opening that scar that had nearly five years of healing on it. The scab was there. It protected me from the pain and injury that lay just beneath. I don't want to deal with it. Don't want to. I can't. I cannot go back there. I have worked so hard just to be able to survive. One day at a time. Going back to the place where my emotions set sail, leaving me helpless and gasping to catch my breath, fills my entire being with fear. A place where the storm rages, leaving behind a pillage of tattered and torn scraps, exposing a raw, painful and seeping love. So scary.

But the time was right and I was so glad I did. Love poured into my soul like I had never felt. Meanwhile, my eyes purged rivers of tears that expressed a lifetime of love. It felt like a dream, but it was too real. Slowly I made piles of Lydia's clothes, taking them out piece by piece from her wooden dresser. One pile for her favorites that I would keep (I have always wanted to get a memory bear). One pile to save just in case I had another daughter some day, and a pile of clothes Lydia never wore and didn't like. These I would donate and give away.

I kept all her trinkets, stuffed animals, hats, and jewelry. I carefully packed up her pink and blue polka dot bedspread and neatly folded it, putting it as well as her other belongings in a pink tote. Her Barbies, baby dolls, books, and purses inhabited another tote. I gracefully labeled them with her name.

174

This process of going through Lydia's possessions took several days. I could do only about thirty to forty-five minutes at a time, as it was a highly emotional process, leaving me physically and mentally exhausted. The giant monster I feared turned out to be a soul-cleansing, sentimental encounter that reminded me of how deeply we can love.

At our new home, Lydia's artwork, photos, and belongings are sprinkled throughout every room, allowing her spirit to remain with us. My advice for others facing this arduous task is to be patient. There is no "right" time, and you must do what is best for you. This could be going through your child's belongings shortly after they pass away, or years later. There is no magic answer or timeframe. When the day comes, take your time and make sure to savor every moment.

*

BONNIE FORSHEY
Bonnie's 16-year-old son Billy died in 1993
from an overdose of prescription drugs

My son was always giving his things to others who were less fortunate, so after his death I gave all his clothing to one of his friends. His mother was a single parent and also disabled, so I knew that Billy's friend would really be able to make use of the clothing. I also gave Billy's bedroom furniture to someone who really needed it, and his basketball outfit to a boy down the street. I know that my son would have wanted it this way.

*

TALIA GATO
Talia's 8-year-old daughter Poppy
died in 2009 in a car accident

I saved a lot of Poppy's things for her sister, who now wears them so I got to see them again. There is one special outfit, a dress I sewed and saved; it is still in Poppy's closet. Her room has stayed the same for the most part. Every year I ask Poppy's sister if she wants to change it. "No" is always her answer. Even the poster that Poppy drew is still up.

I read what people say in books, that you can't have a shrine. How judgmental. I don't give tours. It's what I like, and my family is okay with it. Even though I did keep a lot of Poppy's artwork and writing, I wished I had kept more of it. They are treasures to my heart. Sometimes I will even find a note here and there, and when I find them my heart swells and it makes me happy.

I remember that not long after Poppy died I scoured the house to look for anything she had left behind. I knew I also dumped things at our local recycling outlet, so I even called the recycling place asking if they would let me crawl into the huge container to find anything of Poppy's. I think there is a law against doing that, but I so badly wanted to. My brother stopped my insanity. That's the thing about grief: it's how it makes us feel insane. But now I know it's normal; it's what we do for love.

I still have a lot of Poppy's things hung up, her artwork and what she wrote to us. She was a very loving kind of kid. My plan is to rotate it out, and this year put a huge poster of her in our house. We are fine with it as a family, and that is all that matters.

*

KORBY HAVE
Korby's 17-year-old daughter Taylor (Tayla)
died in 2013 in a car accident

I was living on autopilot for much of the first year after Tayla's passing, so I invited her best friends to come over and go through her things and take what they wanted. The rest I split with my sister and mom. I think if I had to do it over, I would have waited a while and then slowly gone through Tayla's things and kept more to remember her by. But Tayla loved to share her things with her friends, and I knew she would have wanted them to have them.

176

*

DEANA MARTIN
Deana's only two children, 25-year-old Amanda
and 21-year-old Logan, died in a car accident in 2011

A wonderful group of friends came into my home to do what was needed while I was out of town. My daughter Amanda and her three-year-old were the only ones living with me. When I returned home, Amanda's room was freshly painted and clean. It was like coming home to a whole new place. I was so glad, because it would have been harder if her room had been a complete disaster the way she usually left it.

It was a few weeks to a month after the funeral when I asked a dear friend from Indiana to come be with me. I wasn't doing well at all. It was during this time that I was able to go through my daughter's things and decide what to keep and what would go. I wish now that I had waited, because later I had a quilt made of her clothes and I didn't have much left of her that I had not given away. I was pretty numb going through her things; I just remember making piles of "to keep" and "to go." My friend Valencia kept Amanda's scrubs because she finds them comfy. Amanda was going to school to be a physician assistant and had to wear scrubs to school. I am not even sure if I cried as we went through my daughter's things; my memory is so bad from around the time of their deaths. I have a vague recollection of picking something up and sobbing, and then putting it down and going on about the task at hand.

My daughter's fiancé, who was also killed in the car accident, lived with us at the time. I believe that the army of angels who did so much for me while I was gone packed up his things for me before I got home. He was a clothes hound and had so much, and I don't remember having to deal with all of that. I remember keeping one set of my daughter's bras and panties and someone said, "Why do you want that?" I said that someday Armaya might want to see what kind of bras and panties her mom wore. Amanda did not have a lot of belongings. She had been in a very abusive relationship before moving back home, and he did not allow her to take much. She was lucky to get out with what she had.

Logan's things, on the other hand, were much harder. He was away at college and I just could not face going to his dorm and packing up his things. He was so happy there; it just would have been too painful. The dean of the school kept Logan's room locked until his girlfriend and her mom offered to pack his things up for me and take them to the mother's home across town. It sat there for months. I brought them home when I needed to get a few things to set out at the memorial service that we held for their friends in Georgia. Again, I could not face going to get them, so a friend of mine offered to drive the two hours over to where they were and bring them to me. As soon as they arrived, it was almost by impulse that I opened the first box so I could smell my son. I could actually smell him the minute the boxes came into the garage. My son had a very distinctive strong body odor, not always bad, just strong. Luckily, the items I wanted for the memorial were on top, so I left the rest of the boxes until I had the strength to go through them. When I did, it was very hard. I was holding and looking and smelling the items I had bought Logan, like his school jerseys. They brought back such vivid memories. I found a little pillow that Logan called his horsey pillow. He had taken it from his nephew years before and took it everywhere with him. He slept on it every night and everywhere he went. The smell of Logan's hair was so prevalent on that little pillow. I held it tight to my chest and cried and cried. To this day I have it wrapped in two Ziploc bags so it won't lose its smell.

I gave some of Amanda's and Logan's things to their family and friends. I had teddy bears made from their robes, and quilts made from their shirts and other clothing. I recently bought a huge cedar chest, thinking I would put it all in there for Armaya, Amanda's daughter. It is almost full, and I still have five tubs plus a trunk in the garage. Something tells me I might have to purge again...no, not again!

*

MONICA MIRKES
Monica's 30-year-old daughter Marisa
died in 2013 due to Cesarean complications

When Marisa died I wanted to get her things immediately, put them in a box and save them for Connor, her son. I envisioned us both going through them so I could tell him how much his mom liked certain things. Toe rings, she loved toe rings. I have held back getting her things, waiting for her husband to give me a signal.

I have been to her house only once since she died, that was to get diapers for the baby. The house felt so empty. I found myself in her closet touching her clothes, trying desperately to catch her scent, sitting there in the dark crying. Finally, having to get up for a tissue, I turned on the light and looked down at her shoes. Recognizing a few of mine, and thinking to myself "that little brat!" I just started laughing and crying at the same time. It was so like her to go shopping in my closet. I felt like she was there giving me that look kids give you when they know you're going to give in.

It has been two years, and I haven't been back. Her husband has started to date, so I feel it's time to go and get her things. I want to have those special baby things from Connor that I know she saved. His homecoming outfit, his christening gown. Things that held her dreams. Her last Christmas tree, the one she had in the hospital. These things that can make me smile while the tears are falling.

*

DENISE PURCELL
Denise's 27-year-old daughter Megan died
in 2011 from an accidental overdose

Since Megan was living in a different state, which belongings we received were chosen by her soon-to-be ex. So it was sporadic that first year. Each time we received some of Megan's belongings reopened the wound for Megan's sisters, which remains still raw.

They all grabbed clothing and shoes, anything that could give meaning to the madness. I, on the other hand, found myself feeling and smelling each object. Her smell was still the same, and I wished I could preserve it. I ended up taking a few sweatshirts that I knew Megan liked, but it was like reliving the reality of her death again. I swallowed hard and pushed it deep inside, afraid that if I let it out I might not survive.

It's now been almost four years, and I recently had to return to the storage unit to clean it out. I hadn't touched anything of Megan's or even mine that I had around the time of her passing, like plates and decorations. I was anxious, angry, and hesitant but I knew it had to be done. Three days of sifting and sorting, baby pictures, memories and gifts. I was able to get rid of a lot, maybe the things I didn't care about anymore that weren't important. Sorting through Megan's pictures was the hardest. I did it, but not without some bleeding from my heart. But I survived. I knew Megan was happy. I moved forward to some degree.

*

MARILYN ROLLINS
Marilyn's 37-year-old son Randy and 16-year-old granddaughter Sara died in a car accident in 2006 during a family camping trip

Because my son was married and lived in his own home, this is something that I really didn't have to deal with. I did have something from his childhood. It was an old Winnie the Pooh bear that my husband had won at the fair for Randy when he was just a baby. I dug it out of the closet before the funeral. It was so tattered. It had been sewn many times and stuffed on more than one occasion. It was a much loved little bear. I made the decision before the funeral to put it in the coffin with Randy, and his wife agreed that it would be okay.

I will say this now, nine years later: If you ever have to deal with this, think carefully. I wish now that I had not done that. I have so little of Randy, a few Christmas ornaments and crafts that he made in school. I would love to have that tattered little bear back, but I know Randy is happy that I sent his Winnie with him. Later, I did find a jacket that had belonged to Randy, and even now I will sometimes put it on and wrap up in it.

It's funny how we covet the smallest things. I looked above my cupboard one day, and among the other knickknacks sat a paper coffee cup, the kind you get from a gas station. I turned to my husband and said, "Why do we have a cardboard coffee cup sitting on top of the cupboard?" With a tear in his eye, he said, "It was Randy's cup, from the coffee he had on our way to work on the morning that he died." It still sits there, nine years later.

*

KATIE ROUSH
Katie's 26-year-old daughter Krystle
died in 2013 of accidental alcohol poisoning

Krystle did not have much. My daughter was a recovering addict who died from accidental alcohol poisoning. I made sure I went through her things first so her two sisters would not see anything related to that. Krystle died in the apartment she shared with her boyfriend. He was a bit wishy-washy about when I could come get Krystle's things. When we did, they were all packed up. His mom even tossed in a few empty bottles of vodka for good measure. I don't know why, but she did. So after I went through Krystle's things at my house, I repacked everything that I thought was precious and put it into a red plastic bin. Her clothes were put into a huge suitcase.

*

WHAT KIND OF MOTHER HAS NO CHILD?
ANNAH ELIZABETH

There are so, so many of us who have lived this truth,
this nagging question.
This is the kind of mother I was and am,
that you and our other grieving mothers are:
We are the women who longed for a child since we were young ourselves;
We are the women who swore we wanted no part of parenting and somehow
found ourselves with child;
some of us embraced this new life while others of us lament...something...
We are the women whose bodies bulged early or late,
whose breasts swelled and ached in preparation and then spilled over
when there was no mouth to release the stored up nourishment.
We are the women who laughed when we saw our friend's infant smile as he
passed gas and we dreamed when we spotted a toddler taking her first steps.
Some of us plotted and planned a nursery while others plugged away,
bellies bulging, in the day-to-day grind.
We are the women whose children left their physical,
earthly form far earlier than we expected
...the humans who plead with gods to reveal the why's even after we realize
that sometimes the only explanation is simply Because it is...
...the beings who beg for forgiveness even when there is nothing to forgive...
...and the souls who love, as I used to say to my three living children:
"Always, forever, and no matter what."
We love, Journeyer; we love so fully our bodies split with
pride and shame and joy and fear and hope...
Split wide open, sometimes...
Where this is great pain there is an even greater love.

*

CHAPTER NINE

THE DARKNESS

Walking with a friend in the dark is better than walking alone in the light. -HELEN KELLER

Suicidal thoughts occur for many in the immediate aftermath of profound loss, yet few readily admit it for fear of being judged or condemned. While there would be no rainbow without the rain, where do we find the energy to fight the storm?

*

ERICA GALE BELTZ
Erica's 5-year-old son Luke Jordan died in 2005
from a fallen banister in his aunt's driveway

From the moment your child dies, it's as if a bomb has gone off. You literally feel like you have been shot in the chest. I had that physical pain; I held my hands over my heart because I thought it would burst out of me. I begged for God to take my life instead. I would not take my life, but it would be perfectly fine if God came for us all. Then we would be with Luke.

Every day someone asked how I was. I was as good as could be expected. But if it was a stranger at the gas pump I would say,

"I'm good." Each morning the hell started all over. You can't say what you're thinking, that earlier you thought about dropping the toaster in the bathtub. They can't handle hearing that you are thinking about driving your car into a tree. They admired my strength and how I was so much stronger than them.

Eventually I realized that physically I would survive. It was also then that I found myself with no will to do that. I started making plans. Make sure my son will always be remembered, make sure I would leave Lakin in good hands. It wasn't something I could ever do, because I knew I would not be able to be with my children.

Six months out, a videotape started playing in my head around 10 p.m. at night. When I closed my eyes, I could clearly see the day Luke passed. I replayed pulling up to my sister's house, the silence as Adam and I drove to the hospital, Luke lying there on the table, the chest compressions being performed, and the tears of everyone in the room. I could see myself standing there speechless. I could feel the cold of Luke's little hand and face when I kissed him in the casket. I remember how his hair felt soft and normal, so I kissed him there instead. The smell of embalming fluids still haunt me. I opened my eyes to make the nightmare. Was I losing my mind? How could this happen?

Things became dark. I was miserable to be around. I tried to tell a friend about the pain I was experiencing, but I couldn't explain it. I made him promise me that if he didn't hear from me first thing the next morning, he would come get me and have me admitted to a psych ward. When I opened the door the next morning, my friend handed me twenty dollars and said I might need some toiletries. I drove myself to the doctor's office and I told the doctor I no longer wanted to live. I stayed six days in a psych hospital. Admission took thirty-six to forty-eight hours. My only requirement was that I be allowed to smoke. When I got there, they let me know it was a nonsmoking hospital; it didn't matter.

I was evaluated the next morning. The doctor asked if I ever heard voices. I said no, and told him I thought that was a scary question. That night my mind snapped, and I became very suspicious. I thought my elderly roommate who had also lost her will to live because of a loss, was actually there to observe me. I thought the janitor was purposely dressed to try to scare me. I heard the footsteps of the police as they asked where I was, because I was being charged for the death of my son. Behind him stood an angry crowd. I was defeated. I couldn't move; a force was restraining me. I tried to scream, but I had no voice. After hours of trying, I finally broke free by barrel-rolling onto the floor. Everything was normal in my room; it was just a nightmare. Thank God.

I went to the window and saw a van pull up. Luke's dad along with Jeremiah, Adam, and every male friend I had were standing around spitting on the front steps. They were so angry at me, and would find joy in my suffering.

I saw the doctor again the next morning. He asked if I heard voices. My answer was yes.

*

STACY BERNDTSON
Stacy's daughter Cori Joy died in 2003, the day before her
fourth birthday, from an undiagnosed genetic disorder

Though there were times, especially in the very early hours and days of our loss, I felt like dying and I prayed to be taken to where Cori was, I am thankful that I have never been plagued with thoughts of taking my own life.

*

KARI BROWN
Kari's 2-year-old daughter Dominique (Deedee)
died in 2014 from obstructive sleep apnea

I have had thoughts of suicide when my daughter passed, but I couldn't do that to my mother. She had already lost her husband

and an infant years before, and now a granddaughter. I mentioned my thoughts of suicide to a couple of very close friends, but had no intention of following through with it. I just wanted to die so that I could be with Dominique again. I wanted to die so that I wouldn't have to feel this daily heartbreak, and the occasional bitterness I feel when seeing other parents with their children.

But instead of thinking more about suicide, I thought about what I could do. I could help by sharing my story with others and offering advice when asked. I found that by sharing my experience, I pass on Dominique's light and love to new people who have never met her. So I feel proud to be able to turn pain into something positive, and help others by sharing what Dominique taught me.

*

TANISHA CALDWELL
Tanisha's 23-year-old son Tariq (Jay)
died in a car accident in 2015

I have not had thoughts of hurting myself.

*

LYNDA CHELDELIN FELL
Lynda's 15-year-old daughter Aly
died in a car accident in 2009

I often thought of suicide in the beginning. The pain was just so horrific and unbearable. I was sure it would crush me; I was positive that it was simply not survivable. Yet other mothers before me HAD survived it. This kept me going. Everyone reminded me that at least I had other children and a grandchild who needed me. That wasn't helpful and, in fact, made the heartbreak worse because not only was I hurting for myself and my husband, but I was also hurting for my whole family. The sorrow was truly crushing.

My maternal grandmother lost a six-month-old infant. A few years later, while pregnant with her fifth child, she lost her husband. This was back in the 1930s, so imagine my grandmother's journey of being a widow with five young children. In her later years she lost two adult sons. One died from cancer, leaving behind a wife and four teenagers. Knowing what my grandmother and then my aunt and cousins had gone through gave me hope that I, too, might survive. So I held on for dear life, and eventually the strong need to go be with Aly lessened.

Now active in the bereavement field, I've become acquainted with many bereaved mothers through Facebook. One mother, Rhonda, had written a book about losing her daughter to suicide. But her family's pain was too great to bear, and last year Rhonda took her own life. That hit me really hard. I understood Rhonda's pain all too well, but we need to reassure each other that it does subside with time. It really does; one just has to hang on until then.

*

JACQUELYN CRUZ
Jacquelyn's 24-year-old daughter Jenna
died in 2012 from pulmonary edema

In the days and weeks following Jenna's passing I definitely had thoughts of suicide. I begged my husband for his sleeping pills, but through his tears he pleaded with me to stop asking. He never left my side, always afraid of what I would do. I quietly thought out my plan. After Jenna's service I would wait a few days and take all the Xanax that was prescribed for me. My husband must have sensed something, because the bottle was nowhere to be found. When my sobs became too much for me and him to bear, he would place a Xanax in my mouth and make me drink water to swallow it.

As the days slowly passed and the outbursts lessened, so did the Xanax. I started taking an antidepressant, Zoloft. It helped with the crying and cleared my head so I was less dopey. But the thought

187

of being with Jenna still was my goal. I thought of my other two children, Danny and Chelsea, and how hurt they would be if I died by suicide, choosing to leave them. How would they feel? Would they think I loved Jenna more than them? So suicide wasn't the answer. Maybe, just maybe, if I got into a terrible car accident that was out of my control, right? I began to drive recklessly, hoping that this would bring me to my Jenna. I wished for a fatal disease, anything that was out of my control, so Danny and Chelsea couldn't say that I left because they weren't loved enough by me.

A few months later I woke up during the night with numbness in my arms and horrible pain in my chest. I woke my husband and he brought me to the hospital. The doctors ran a battery of tests and nothing was found. They kept me for twenty-four hours for watchful waiting, then decided it must be just stress. The following week I was telling my therapist, Dr. Connie, what had happened. She sat listening quietly with a smile on her face. I asked her why she was smiling, and she replied, "Best story I've heard in a while." Somewhat confused that she would find my trip to the hospital amusing, I asked her why. She said, "Because you now want to live. If you really wanted to die, you would never have awakened your husband or gone to the hospital."

Dr. Connie was instrumental in getting me on the path to healing. When I think back to our first few visits when I couldn't even speak, she was patient and kind. She wanted to know all about Jenna, and assured me that Jenna was with God and at peace. During one of our sessions I was asking why, why would God do this to me? Every single day I would pray for Jenna, the same prayer every day and every night. Why didn't he listen to me? Dr. Connie asked me what the prayer sounded like. I asked God to protect Jenna, let her know how much she's loved, let her know how great she is, let her be free from all her suffering, and continue to guide her in helping the handicapped children.

Dr. Connie's response was, "I guess your prayers were answered."

*

MICHELLE DETWILER
Michelle's 19-year-old daughter Emily
died in 2014 due to congenital complications

I cannot say I ever thought of suicide after Emily died. But there were so many times I wanted to run away to heaven and not be here anymore. Could I just go to sleep and not wake up? My life is different now, so different. Emily was our third child, disabled and full of medical challenges. Our lives centered around her needs. There was nothing normal about our home, our routines or our family. We lived on the edge daily. Medical surprise, mystery and disappointment waited for us at every turn. For nearly twenty years we lived like this. We laughed and cried and we were a family.

Because of Emily, our community was enclosed and involved. There were special doctors, special therapies, and special teachers at school. Nursing care and medical supply agencies walked through our revolving door. We were open for the world to dissect, and yet we were a family. When Emily died, all of that disappeared. No school, no doctors, no nurses in our home. No phone calls, no appointments. Everything was gone. My world was gone. How could I live in this new world where I had no friends?

No, I didn't think about suicide, but I thought a lot about where Emily is, in heaven. I want to go! God, why don't you take me!!! Some days I would yell at Him. I know He hears me. He hears my sorrow.

I joined a group for grieving mothers. I don't really want to be there, but I know I need to be. I need someone who knows how I'm hurting. When I go to the group, they are laughing as they talk. I'm thinking I'll never go again. How can they laugh? I'm crying on the outside and on the inside. They hug me and love on me. They understand where I'm at and they know what it feels like. So on the days I want to run away to heaven, even though I can't, I contact one of these new friends and I ask her to pray. My life is in a whirlwind; I can't see where I'm going. And they pray. Life is one day at a time for me now. The next day isn't always better, but I have to trust that God is on the throne. He knows what my sorrows are and He is in charge. And one day all my tears will be wiped away and replaced with something better, because I know for sure that He cares for me.

*

ANNAH ELIZABETH
Annah's son Gavin Michael aspirated on his meconium
during the delivery and died 26 minutes following his birth

This is a simple, yet equally complicated question. The simple answer is yes, I thought about suicide after my son's death.

The more complicated answer is that I had also been dealing with a long, undiagnosed depression that had also contributed to suicidal thoughts I'd had in my teen years. In the five-year span following Gavin's death I also experienced two miscarriages and two more complicated pregnancies that ended in successful births.

My husband and I were young parents who were each grieving and celebrating differently. We were trying to navigate a family business and realizing the differences in our thought processes about most everything, including parenting, business practices, and the roles other relationships should play in our own little family.

My body was tired, stretched out and stressed beyond recognition. On one particularly grueling night it all came to a head. Alcohol and I had always had a tenuous time of it; sometimes I'd be the life of a party after a few drinks and other times my mood swings would turn the merriment into a nightmare. Not knowing about the depression, I figured the alcohol was fully responsible for the outbursts, and I had chosen to either abstain from legal beverages or to limit my consumption to the occasional one or two beers.

I began writing in a journal on May 30, 1995, a few days following one of the last times I'd ever fall into that state of suicidal drunkenness again. I found a compatible therapist and began the grueling task of tapping into my long-standing depression and undoing the many forms of dysfunctional thinking it had caused. Frequent thoughts of suicide had become one of those side effects. I remember telling my therapist that I'd figured out a way to take my life but make it look like an accident, an important detail because I didn't want my living children to have to face the stigma.

Counselor Hank responded with this pearl of wisdom: "If you really wanted to be dead, Annah, you'd be dead by now." He couldn't have been any closer to the truth, for what I really wanted was for the pain to go away so that I could truly live.

There was a point in all of this when I realized that I couldn't take my own life, so I switched from plotting to pleading with God. This was one of my prayers: "God, please take me tonight. I can't endure the pain. Everyone says You aren't a cruel God. They say You don't give us more than we can handle. You must know my agony; I can't bear any more. You know I can't bring myself to end my own life. Please, God, have mercy. End my suffering."

I distinctly remember that day. Gavin came to me that night. He was dressed in white shorts with suspenders and a white top, a sort of baptismal outfit. "I'm okay, Mommy," he said. "You need to stay there; my brother and sister need you." That event created a turning point for me, a foundation that I've continued to build on. It gave me something to hold on to, something to help me get through each day. It gave me hope, it helped me consider my son's spirit in a whole new light, and it provided me a different sort of promise.

*

WENDY EVANS
Wendy's 21-year-old son Kyle died in 2009
from diabetes when his insulin pump malfunctioned

I feel like I did have thoughts of dying. There were times when I felt like I would die and I was okay with it. I remember only once having a thought that I would take my life.

*

BONNIE FORSHEY
Bonnie's 16-year-old son Billy died in 1993
from an overdose of prescription drugs

When my son died, a part of me died. I did try to commit suicide multiple times, but always woke up. I guess it wasn't my time to go.

*

TALIA GATO
Talia's 8-year-old daughter Poppy
died in 2009 in a car accident

I didn't feel like dying, but a part of me felt dead for a long time. I just existed, and felt like I was floating around and motionless. I kept moving, though. I felt like half of me died when Poppy died, half of my dreams and her future wedding, graduation, grandchildren, and what would have been. She had a good future ahead of her. That's what I think her life would have been. But I know she is in heaven and I will see her again.

*

KORBY HAVE
Korby's 17-year-old daughter Taylor (Tayla)
died in 2013 in a car accident

I honestly believe that if I didn't have two other kids at home I wouldn't be here today. I could never put them through losing a parent after losing their sister, so that keeps me from taking my life. But there have been many times that I wished I could join my daughter. I never share this with anyone because I don't want to burden others, so I just keep everything bottled up until I am alone. I spend a lot of nights crying quietly in my room.

*

DEANA MARTIN
Deana's only two children, 25-year-old Amanda
and 21-year-old Logan, died in a car accident in 2011

I have had nonstop suicidal ideation since the passing of my children. "Ideation" is a word I learned in an inpatient mental facility the third summer after they died. I had been in a custody battle to keep my granddaughter for the first two years, so that gave me something to fight for. Not that I didn't think about it those first two years; I did all the time. Once the court hearing was finally over and I had won custody, I then lacked purpose and my identity had been stripped from me.

I have suffered from chronic depression since my early twenties, and the grief from my children's death was more than I could handle. I managed to care for my granddaughter and keep up around the house, but my job suffered. I had no short-term memory, focus or concentration. I knew Armaya needed me and I could not go, but that wasn't enough at the time. I would think about turning the wheel of my vehicle and intentionally being run over by a semi, the way my children had died. I also thought about running into trees or light posts. All I wanted to do was to be with them! One morning I was suffering horrible chest pain and my mother called 911. We knew it was not my gallbladder, because that had already been removed. I told my mother that I was pretty sure I was not dying because I did not see Amanda and Logan appear to take me home with them.

Year three, when I ended up in the mental health facility, the suicidal thoughts were impossible to stop. I became scared, so I finally sought help. I spent one week as an inpatient and an additional five weeks in outpatient therapy. I can't say it did a lot of good, but it did allow for a very structured environment and the much needed rest I had been lacking. I underwent EMDR (eye movement desensitization and reprocessing) treatments with my therapist, and that seemed to help the posttraumatic stress disorder and the suicidal ideation to some degree.

When I was weak, sick or tired, when my resistance was down, suicide was the first place my mind went. I lost my job three years after my children died, so not only had I lost my identity as a mother, but I also lost my identity of a career woman with twenty-five years in the pharmaceutical industry. I was so lost, and had to rebuild from the very core of my being, for I had no identity left.

I had been doing some work with bereaved parents leading a support group and I had been asked by a dear friend to staff a weekend workshop for bereaved military (Gold Star) families. It was through this work and through learning how to be a mother again, through my care for Armaya that I started to heal. I read every book I could get my hands on and sought out every resource there was on the loss of a child and on grief. Some of it made sense and I absorbed it, some of it didn't and I let it go. I never wanted this experience to define who I am, and it has to some degree.

I have chosen along the way to allow the love for my children on the other side, and my desire to serve people engulfed by the worst pain they will ever face, to define me. Still, when very sick, overly tired or run down, I think about suicide.

I had a bad episode about a month ago that I believe was the shift for the thoughts of suicide. While lying in bed, I thought about what I would write in the goodbye letters. I knew my limited friends and family would understand and in a way be surprised that I had made it this long. In a way I felt they could justify it, but when I got to the goodbye letter to my granddaughter, my mind went blank and I stumbled over things to say. It was then when I realized there were no words that could justify my leaving her, that this choice would destroy her life beyond repair forever. Losing two mommies in eight years was more than any child could handle, for she was older now and would no doubt blame herself. She would never be convinced that it wasn't her fault, that somehow she caused this. It was right then and there that I knew I could never hurt my baby that way; I could never leave her until my time.

So far since then I have had no thought of joining Amanda and Logan. I truly hope that was the turning point. I am tired!

*

MONICA MIRKES
Monica's 30-year-old daughter Marisa
died in 2013 due to Cesarean complications

I have most definitely thought about suicide. There are times when I just don't want to think, feel or hurt anymore. Then the heavy dose of guilt comes. I would never want anyone to feel that they could have or should have done something to prevent it.

At one time I felt I owed it to my husband, children, parents, and brothers to write them letters and tell them the "why." So I sat down to write. After about the fourth letter, I was drained completely. I sat there looking at the letters I had finished and the ones I needed to write and thought, "Oh, the hell with this. It would be easier to just live." I told a close friend and gave her the letters. She would take them only if I promised to put her on the list. I love her for that. No judgment, no lecture. We cried, and then burned the letters.

*

DENISE PURCELL
Denise's 27-year-old daughter Megan died
in 2011 from an accidental overdose

The days and months passed by in a blur. I did what I had to do and then retreated to my room to be alone, waiting for the next day to come. Nothing mattered. I wanted to die, to be with Megan. All that pent-up emotion festered for two full years before finally bringing my life to a screeching halt. I was on a road to self-destruction that led to a mental breakdown, a rest in the mental ward. I didn't attempt suicide, because I already felt dead. But everything shut down and I had to deal with it. From then on I started therapy and grief classes and made a promise to myself that I wouldn't give up. My other children needed me.

*

MARILYN ROLLINS
Marilyn's 37-year-old son Randy and 16-year-old granddaughter Sara
died in a car accident in 2006 during a family camping trip

I would be lying if I said that I didn't think about suicide. I think most parents would. The first few days after the accident, I felt such a strong sense of my child around me. I just wanted to go be with him. I wanted to talk to him one more time. I wanted to tell Randy how much I loved him. Common sense, however, told me that I couldn't do that. I couldn't put my family through that much more pain. The other reason that I would never commit suicide is my religion. I now have to work extra hard to get to heaven, because my son is there waiting for me.

*

KATIE ROUSH
Katie's 26-year-old daughter Krystle
died in 2013 of accidental alcohol poisoning

I had one brief moment, four days after Krystle died. I went to visit a friend, and she talked only about herself. Krystle's death was merely glanced over. I had so much to say, but it was squashed by what was going on in my friend's life. I left, and cried all the way home. I thought of just jerking the wheel of my car so I could end up with my child. It was a brief second, but it passed.

*

SARA RUBLE
Sara's 19-year-old son Scott died in 1994 from a
combination of a seizure disorder, Strep throat and dehydration

I did have suicidal thoughts after Scott's death. For the first time in my life I did not want to live. The pain was so great, and I wanted out. Out of life, out of pain. Out. I had never ever felt such pain. The immense feelings of love and missing were more than I thought I could endure. I did not share these thoughts with anyone for a while, as I contemplated how this could happen. I did not want to scare my husband or family. No, the invasive pain that overwhelmed me was too deep to even explain, and I did not want to try to express it. Too deep…too painful…too private. But I envisioned my car speeding into a large bridge abutment. Fast, easy, over with. Just me, no one else hurt or involved. My earlier thoughts, or really hopes, that a large semi would run into my car were changed when I realized the truck driver would be left with that agonizing horrific experience forever. I did not want that to happen to another human being…not ever. But I just wanted it to happen…

And then I worried that my husband and family would never get over my death. Could I do that to them? I did not want anyone to ever experience what I was experiencing with Scott's death, especially those I love. But how could I live without my only child? My heart and soul…crushed. I so desperately wanted out of the pain…and yet I did not want to create pain for others. So many mixed-up feelings and emotions, so deep and constantly running through my mind. I felt very, very alone. I was waging a war between excruciating pain and love…

I was also fearful that if I took my own life I might not ever see Scott again, and that was one big thing that was keeping me alive. Yes, seeing Scott in heaven. The old belief that if one dies by suicide they might not make it into heaven, or go somewhere else, really scared me.

One night when all the darkness of grief and pain was caving in on me, and my husband was out visiting with his two children (which created more pain than I could endure), I had the strongest moment of totally giving in to the suicidal thoughts. As I literally exhausted myself with sobbing and the agony of Scott's death, I was taken to a place of just giving into the grief. "I can't fight you anymore. I don't have the energy to do anything. It's all too much…" I was pretty much immobilized. Then I fell asleep right there on the bedroom floor.

The next day, still so drained from the emotional and physical night before, I went to my grief counselor and shared it all. She asked me why I did not call my sister and talk with her about my suicidal feelings. "I don't want her to know. It's too private," I told her. "I don't want to scare her." The counselor took me by surprise by saying, "You are needed here, Sara. Scott said you are needed here. You cannot leave." I now know those were Scott's words coming through her…but I did not get it then. Even so, I trusted her and began to see my life more joined with Scott than ever before. I had received signs from him, dreams too. I knew there was a connection, but had not thought of our journeys continuing as they have. We do work together spiritually…we did then and we do now.

This awareness brought me to a place I needed to be in order to leave the suicidal thoughts behind. I continued to grieve deeply and miss Scott, but sometimes if we have something so important to hang onto…we can.

So much to learn and grow from too. What I must share is that today I know for certain that we all go to heaven. After the death of our human bodies, the spiritual journey takes us back to Spirit…God…One….Love.

*

It is not until you become a mother
that your judgment slowly turns to
compassion and understanding.
ERMA BOMBECK

*

CHAPTER TEN

THE FRIENDS

Remember, you don't need a certain number of
friends, just a number of friends you can be certain
of. -UNKNOWN

When we are mourning, some of our friendships undergo
transitions. Some bonds remain steady, dependable and faithful.
Some we sever by choice. And, perhaps unexpectedly, new friends
enter our life, bringing renewed hope rich with possibilities. But
what about your children's friends? Do you keep in touch with
them?

*

ERICA GALE BELTZ
Erica's 5-year-old son Luke Jordan died in 2005
from a fallen banister in his aunt's driveway

Luke built relationships. He was many things to many people
in his life. If he was your friend, he had your back and would give
you anything he had. If he was your cousin, well the adventures
and tales to this day will fill your heart with so much joy that one
might forget for a moment that he is gone. If Luke was your Sunday
School student, you had an extra skip in your step the rest of the
week, and you can guarantee that he did too. He loved Ms. Rebecca

and the Church of the Nazarene. If you were his bus driver, you always kept your eye on him, and he knew just how much you cared for him. This didn't go unnoticed, and Luke valued the partnership.

If Luke was your next-door neighbor, your days were filled with adventure and laughter when he walked through your door as if he lived there. He sure did love it over at Gay's house and the Dubrocks. He truly valued their friendship and loved them so much. Luke always knew who had the kind hearts.

Luke made relationships with people he had only met for a moment, and I could tell that he really respected them. He told me he had a girlfriend named Peyton and that he kissed her on the bus. He quickly followed it days later with "But I'm not gonna marry her, Mama."

Not long after, his accident happened. The school and parents of the students in his class were so incredible. They did so many things that were so thoughtful. They will always hold a special place in my soul. Imagine the horror of trying to explain to your five-year-old child about death because of one of their classmates, why their friend wouldn't being coming back to school. Then have to come to the funeral home and see this tiny boy, in his tiny casket and move through those motions. I know how haunting this is. I will always remember the hugs and love extended to my family. Thank you.

Luke was five, way too young to die. I honestly thought his friends and classmates would fill the funeral home and be there to lay him to rest. In my mind it was the only thing that made sense. I realize now why they weren't there, and that each parent did what he or she felt was best for their own child.

Peyton's mom and I had been pregnant together, and had even been coworkers in the past. We lost touch and were not close friends. So when Mike and Beverly came to the funeral home with little Peyton in their arms, it brought me to my knees. The three of them hugged me so tight, and I'll never forget the love they poured into my heart that night.

When Luke's class graduated from kindergarten, I was invited as a guest of honor to join in the celebration and in memory of Luke. I was thrilled and couldn't wait. As the day drew near, fear filled every ounce of me. I waited until the end of the day, before the class was dismissed, to finally walk into his classroom. Peyton's mom had made the class DVD and dedicated it to Luke. It really meant so much, and I was so ashamed for missing the celebration and not being strong enough for their children that day.

It was years before I saw Peyton again, but always listened for updates. My sister started working in the town we were from, and started seeing Peyton around. She shared that when her class graduated the fifth grade that she led the announcements and included Luke. How one little girl who was only five when she lost her buddy could still have awareness of my son's life here on this earth really spoke to me.

It came to those who knew Luke best that he loved with his whole heart. This little girl, however, had kept a piece of Luke alive, and it made me so proud. Then, when she was fourteen, her fathered died suddenly in a home accident. I was horrified, but knew that we would rally around them as they had us. Peyton called us almost immediately after the accident, and wanted us close to her. My whole experience with Peyton and her parents is spiritual, and I will always treasure it.

*

STACY BERNDTSON
Stacy's daughter Cori Joy died in 2003, the day before her
fourth birthday, from an undiagnosed genetic disorder

There were a few children whom we met through a support group for parents of children with special needs. The children did not really play together as such. I remember seeing one at a street fair after Cori died and having emotions wash over me. Any time I see a girl, especially one in a wheelchair or assisted chair, I am drawn to her and feel the urge to just hug her. Often that would not be appropriate for a stranger, so smiles have to do.

There was another couple whose daughter was near Cori's age. She had an identified condition, but it left her in a condition similar to Cori Joy's. At the time, she too was an only child. When Cori Joy died, we did not hear from them. We did not hold this against them, but when their daughter passed away about three months later, I felt it was important to go to her memorial service. It was even held at the same place. I remember we sat at the very back in case I could not make it through the service. In the end I was able to endure it. Approximately another year or two later I happened to run into the mom in town. She apologized profusely that they were not at Cori's memorial, saying it just hit too close to home at the time, which of course I understood. We all do what we can, when we can, and none of us can predict our responses to things that are so foreign such as the death of our own child or the death of another child.

Because I was born late in life to my parents, I gave birth to Cori the same year that my niece as well as my nephew and their respective spouses also had babies. When Cori was alive there was little comparison. We were busy with all that comes with a special needs child, and the joy that Cori brought to our home filled our lives.
But after she died, when it was my great-niece's birthday I would reflect on Brooke turning six, so Cori would be six too. Brooke is ten years old, and so would Cori have been.

Brooke has grown into a beautiful, kind and loving teenager, and I can't help but wonder about the "what ifs." What if Cori had been born healthy? What if she was turning sweet sixteen this year, like Brooke did? The "what ifs" are futile, yet in a way, something about being able to see firsthand how Brooke has changed with each passing year has given me comfort. It is a comfort I cannot explain, but it is one nonetheless.

*

TANISHA CALDWELL
Tanisha's 23-year-old son Tariq (Jay)
died in a car accident in 2015

Many of Jay's friends reach out to me on social media. The only interaction I've had is with his girlfriend Megan, who was also in the accident. We talk often and we've seen each other once. It's hard to see her, because she was always with Jay. And that hurts. Sometimes jealousy creeps in, because as I see Jay's friends going on, doing their own thing, I think Jay should be right here doing the same thing.

*

LYNDA CHELDELIN FELL
Lynda's 15-year-old daughter Aly
died in a car accident in 2009

Aly was a member of a large swim team, so immediately after the accident we were surrounded by her friends and teammates, and even their parents. They kept us close to their hearts for a very long time, and many still check in with me on occasion. They became lifelong friends, and that warms my heart. But at some point the interaction with Aly's team became too painful. Heck, interaction with the *world* became too painful. So I began hibernating at home to lick my wounds in private. I wanted Aly's friends to go on with life, do all the wonderful things that Aly couldn't do, and leave me behind to carry the sorrow. While it made me happy when the time came for them to navigate their senior year and start applying to colleges, it also made me very sad. I was happy that they had found solid footing in the aftermath of a team tragedy, but it was also a kick in the gut.

When it came time for Aly's class to graduate from high school, I learned after the fact that her classmates had remembered her with an empty chair with her name on it. I would like to have seen that, but I didn't know until someone told me a few months later.

Now, six years later, I very much enjoy seeing Aly's friends. They have all moved on with their lives, and that makes me very happy. I love seeing what they are up to, who is graduating from college, who moved where, who is still swimming. I'm grateful they continue to hold Aly's memory close while enjoying all that life has to offer. And I'm thankful that they allow me to remain a part of their lives. We remain fond of the eighteen-year-old driver of the car, and keep in touch with him and his parents. The other passenger, a friend Aly loved dearly, doesn't stay in contact with us. We were once told that his family didn't feel he should be around us, that it was too painful for him to see us. This is hard to bear, as Aly adored her friend, so we did too. The driver, on the other hand, is a wonderful boy Aly really looked up to, another team leader, and his family keeps in close contact with us. They hold a special place in our hearts, and our lives will always be intertwined.

*

JACQUELYN CRUZ
Jacquelyn's 24-year-old daughter Jenna
died in 2012 from pulmonary edema

Jenna met her best friend, Kim, in the seventh grade. They were trouble together. Kim practically lived at our house until she went away to college. Jenna made other friends who were always here too. Jenna wasn't much for going out, she was a homebody so everyone always came to our house. I didn't mind at all. They were funny, smart, and they loved to see Jenna happy, and that made me happy. Afterward, Jenna's friends would text me or call for weeks, and then it tapered off, which was fine with me because it was just a reminder of terrible sadness. The girls came over a few times for dinner, but for days afterward I would be in bed crying. I decided I couldn't do it anymore; it's was just too sad. I truly miss them and their funny stories. I see them at Jenna's memorial service once a year, and I hope they never stop coming.

*

MICHELLE DETWILER
Michelle's 19-year-old daughter Emily
died in 2014 due to congenital complications

Emily didn't have friends in the traditional sense. Her medical issues created a barrier to her being at school for most of her high school years. Sometimes we would have a party at our house, and the kids whom Emily had gone to school with from her earliest preschool days would join us.

The school had a program called Connections. It was a volunteer program for the graduating seniors who wanted to work with people who had disabilities. This program allowed the volunteer students from school to come visit Emily each week, connecting her with what she was missing: her friends at school. They were wonderful kids, bringing with them surprises like fingernail polish and the latest news on the cute boys in class.

The year Emily died was the year she was supposed to graduate. However, her life was cut short before the cap and gown event. As the days leading up to the graduation approached, my stress and grief were magnified. Social media was abuzz with senior pictures and graduation parties. It seemed that everyone was happy, but my heart was broken. We were missing the final event, the big one. Tears dripped from my eyes as well as my heart that weekend. It felt as if our future was gone along with our daughter. I wanted to think about other things but it was difficult to do so. There were no friends, there was no school and it was over.

One of the things we had decided to do when school got out was to take a mini vacation. It had been only three months since Emily's death, and we needed to get away. So we left for a few days in the hope of rejuvenating any semblance of life left in our family.

When we returned a few days later, there was a package waiting for us. Inside, wrapped in love, was a maroon and gold graduation cap with the signatures of each of the students who had walked the aisle with Emily's graduating class. My heart soared within me, and we cried and cried as we hugged that graduation cap. She wasn't forgotten! She had been in their hearts all along, even as they took their first steps into the future. Her friends thought of her and sent the message to us. She would never be forgotten! We placed Emily's cap in an enclosed frame and hung it on the wall. And when I'm sad it reminds me that she had the ultimate graduation that day in February, when she moved to heaven.

*

ANNAH ELIZABETH
Annah's son Gavin Michael aspirated on his meconium
during the delivery and died 26 minutes following his birth

Given the fact that my son died twenty-six minutes following his birth, he didn't have the opportunity to meet and make friends. I have, however, stayed in touch with the one person with whom he likely would have been friends. You see, my boss and I were pregnant at the same time. Our boys were born two weeks apart. Though it's been more than a decade since I worked for her, we have reconnected from time to time. I've always seemed to know when there was something important happening in her life, and I happened to phone her the day her son proposed to his girlfriend. I rejoiced as they exchanged vows, bought a gift for their baby shower, congratulated them following their gender reveal party, and have recently delighted in seeing photos of their new baby.

Each of his milestones — from first teeth, to kindergarten, to sixteen and driving, to high school graduation, to proposals, to fatherhood — has brought about different emotions for me. The melancholy has been mild, even more so as the gap from funeral to function has grown bigger. The greater emotions for me, however, have been more related to those of wonder and longing...What would my boy have been doing at the time? What I've come to realize is that those things are limited only by my imagination. My emotions then follow whatever I allow my mind to construct.

208

*

WENDY EVANS
Wendy's 21-year-old son Kyle died in 2009
from diabetes when his insulin pump malfunctioned

I've had occasional interaction with some of Kyle's friends. I have gotten phone calls and text messages around holidays and the anniversary of Kyle's death. The interactions feel good. They remember Kyle and don't seem to feel awkward about mentioning him. The best interactions occur when one of them calls to tell me a funny story about something he or she remembered about Kyle.

*

BONNIE FORSHEY
Bonnie's 16-year-old son Billy died in 1993
from an overdose of prescription drugs

My son's friends still remain close to me. Although it is still difficult, I am happy that they care enough to stay in touch with me. They still email me and stop by to visit. They all have relationships, careers and children. I wish my son were here, and I wish he would have had the chance to have a family too.

*

TALIA GATO
Talia's 8-year-old daughter Poppy
died in 2009 in a car accident

This is a great question. As much as we wanted to follow through with playdates, it really didn't happen unless I initiated it. Friends in our circle quit coming over, even though some had kids the same age as ours. We didn't get invited to their birthdays after a while. That hurt. One mom even verbalized it: "We didn't come over because we didn't want you to be reminded of your loss." Really? You actually thought that out loud? Did that make me feel better? No. Did I not have a constant reminder each day to remind me that Poppy was gone? And was she speaking for the rest of my friends? Having playdates with my daughter would have helped so much. I can't tell you how lonely she was. So lonely. She did play with her neighbors, even though they were younger, which helped.

We changed schools, and when that happened, none of the families stayed in touch. Sometimes I see them and I wonder how tall or what my daughter would have been like. To this day, that is one of the things that the sibling left behind needs: having a buddy for a simple playdate. Livia lost her confidant and playmate.

It is strange how the pecking order and dynamic changes once one sibling is gone. The skills and adaptations that needed to happen so Livia could develop....I had to fill in, like running around and playing tag and dressing up for Halloween and games. I did this for her fulfillment and mine. Everything changes when a child dies.

*

KORBY HAVE
Korby's 17-year-old daughter Taylor (Tayla)
died in 2013 in a car accident

I have tried to maintain a relationship with many of Tayla's friends and am able to do so because of social media. It is still very hard to watch them go on with their lives when Tayla can't. I didn't attend their graduations, even though they all wanted me to because I couldn't bear the thought of watching them walk across the stage and not see Tayla there. It is so hard watching her friends get married and start families when I will never get the opportunity to experience that with Tayla.

*

DEANA MARTIN
Deana's only two children, 25-year-old Amanda
and 21-year-old Logan, died in a car accident in 2011

My children's friends and people in my life of similar age were such a comfort to me after the death of both Amanda and Logan. Logan's fraternity Phi Delta Music kept in close contact with me to ensure that I was okay, and that I knew if I needed anything I could call on the "brothers," which I still do. We recently held a fundraiser for Cry For Me, No More, my legacy project, to help other families in grief through the love I have for and from my children. We held the fundraiser in Carrollton, Georgia, where Logan went to college. My heart was so full to see so many of the "brothers" show up to help. Most of them had never met Logan, but it is a part of the program to get into the fraternity that a pledge must learn about Logan, his extremely high morals, values and integrity, and his contributions to not only Phi Delta Music, but the world through music! Logan started an a cappella group in high school named The Originals, and they still exist. Through Logan's high school choir teacher, I was able to invite present and past members of The Originals to sing at my children's memorial. It was such a blessing to have them there memorializing my son in music! Phi Delta Music also sang in Logan's honor. I know he was there and he was so proud and sad at the same time. Proud because he knew they would carry music to so many in his honor and his legacy would live on, but sad because he would no longer would be able to sing or teach music in this realm and fulfill his dreams. But Logan's friends and I know that he is directing the angel choir these days and singing in the bass section of the gathering of heavenly voices, and they raise their voices up to God and even send music down to Earth as a gift to be passed on through our musicians here.

Amanda did not have a lot of friends because of certain circumstances around a relationship that kept her very isolated. The few friends she did have checked on me often and let me know how much they missed her. They all tell me that Amanda's daughter Armaya looks so much like Amanda. It makes me feel good to know that Armaya is part of my daughter. My children's half-sister and my closest cousin's daughter have gone out of their way to make sure I still feel like a mom by sending me cards and gifts, and visiting me. I know that when I go to Indianapolis I can stay at either of their houses. They are special to me and have been crucial to my survival in ways they will never know. We employed a live-in nanny when we got back from the funeral. We have had a couple of young adult women who have helped us in our time of need, and these beautiful souls have filled an indescribable void in my soul, a void of young adult energy.

Recently the last couple who were Logan's friends who were staying with us had to move because we needed the space for my mother-in-law. God, how I miss them. I miss them all, I miss the young adult energy in my home. It is so depressing and not nearly as energetic. These young adults in my life have literally saved my life, and I have made sure they know how much that means to me. I also know that on any given day, if I needed anything, I could call them and someone would be here to help. I might have to call six to ten people, but eventually I would find someone. The entries on Facebook become less with each passing year but occasionally I will get a private message or text when one of my dear surrogate children is reaching out to tell me how much he or she misses my babies, and how he or she think of us often. They remind me of what a beautiful person I am to have raised such beautiful children. It is on these days that my heart soars and I sing praise the powers that be for sending me the sign that my children's memory does live on and hopefully will live on way past me through their generation. And maybe they will tell their children about this amazing brother and sister who left one snowy day in Indianapolis to go to heaven, but before they left they changed the world more than hundreds of people could have. I am universal NaNa to all the babies and Momma D to their generation, so I have no doubt I am still a mom.

*

MONICA MIRKES
Monica's 30-year-old daughter Marisa
died in 2013 due to Cesarean complications

Another loss. You spend time with your children's friends, you hear all about them from your child, some of them you love as if they were your own. I would get texts from them from time to time. The gaps became longer and then dropped off to none at all. I know they have their own lives. It hurts. Another chunk of your life drops off the chart. One of Marisa's friends gave me a beautiful locket with her name on it and charms of her favorite things. A friend of mine gave me a heart pendant. These are very precious to me. I make it a point now to do the same for my friends who have lost a loved one.

*

DENISE PURCELL
Denise's 27-year-old daughter Megan died
in 2011 from an accidental overdose

There are a few people, friends of Megan's, who keep in touch. Then there are the friends who remember Megan's birthday or the date of her passing. I don't like using the term "anniversary" because it's not a celebration. I did hear stories about Megan I never knew. She went down to Mexico to help build houses for Habitat for Humanity. She climbed mountains in Colorado. She helped people and influenced many. She was my gift, and presented herself to anyone in need.

*

KATIE ROUSH
Katie's 26-year-old daughter Krystle
died in 2013 of accidental alcohol poisoning

Just a few. They paid their respects. That's it. One still keeps in touch two years later. That is nice.

*

SARA RUBLE
Sara's 19-year-old son Scott died in 1994 from a
combination of a seizure disorder, Strep throat and dehydration

I have always been so grateful for Scott's friends. They were wonderful to Scott in life…and in his death, they helped me beyond words. None of us knew what we were doing as we tried to absorb the reality of Scott's sudden death. What I began to see was that they could feel comfortable reaching out to me as well as Scott's dad, with stories we had never heard before. They knew we desperately needed whatever support they could give us, and they were very willing to give. Such great love I experienced. These stories turned out to be the best gifts his friends could ever have given me. We would laugh sometimes hysterically, at times when laughter seemed totally impossible. We would cry and know we understood how much we missed Scotty. It was obvious that these courageous nineteen-year-old girls and boys, so shaken as well, needed me as much as I needed them. We all wanted to keep Scott close. We held on to one another in the ways we could. Emotionally, I was so grateful for their love and presence in my life. It wasn't always easy, but to not have them around to share with me would have been harder.

As the years flowed past college graduations, jobs, marriages and children, I tried to stay focused on their lives, not on what Scott was missing, and be there for them as Scott's mom. Not always easy for a now childless mother. Their love for Scott, and for me, was so important and so beautiful. I could not say "no," as they made every effort to include me in their lives. My tears flowed, but I had grown to love and admire every one of these now young adults and truly wanted the best for them. I knew Scott would want me to be there for them…I just knew that. In time, I began to understand more deeply the spiritual meaning of having these young people in my life. They did not stay away. They showed me unconditional love, as they had done with Scott. Because they missed Scott in many of the ways I did, we became kindred spirits. I could be open with them about my pain and grief, and they would share openly with me. We did not scare one another. We needed the bond, the connection. Life sometimes shows us so much more than we thought possible. My gratitude for Scott's friends will never end. He still lives within them as they continue to share stories about him twenty-one years later. And we smile.

*

An angel, in the Book of Life, wrote down my baby's birth.
Then whispered as he closed the book,
"Too beautiful for Earth."
UNKNOWN

*

CHAPTER ELEVEN

THE RELATIONSHIPS

I have found the paradox that if you love until it hurts,
there can be no more hurt, only more love.
-MOTHER TERESA

For many of us, familial relationships are the cornerstones that help us stay sane; they keep us laughing, learning, and loving. We speak one another's language and finish one another's sentences. Sometimes, however, loss touches us in different ways. What family relations, if any, were impacted by the loss of your child?

*

STACY BERNDTSON
Stacy's daughter Cori Joy died in 2003, the day before her fourth birthday, from an undiagnosed genetic disorder

I would say that my relationship with my husband has been the most impacted by our shared loss, but in a good way. Cori's death cemented our bond farther than it was to begin with, and I think we were pretty solid. I know that the death of a child destroys many marriages, and I am ever grateful that it did not go that way with us. My husband has been with me through the darkest days of my life. Grief is often filled with anger and bitterness which, of course, comes out full force onto those we love and feel safest with.

Steve has been a rock for me, and I am sure he has had to deal with his own grief, sometimes quietly, because being there for me was always his first priority.

I lost a lifetime friend as a result of circumstances surrounding Cori's death. I believe it could be best described as collateral damage. In 2003, when Cori died, not everyone had cellphones and it was long before texting was a way of life. A relative of mine offered to make the hard calls. One was to my friend, and my relative told my friend what had happened. The day after Cori died many people came to our home. It was Cori's birthday, and we asked those who were intending to come to still come. I remember spending time trying to be a hostess, but being told to sit down and basically just paced around my house. At times I would go into our bedroom and break down. At some point in that day my friend called, wanting to speak to me. Steve's recollection is that he told her I would want to talk to her, but not when the house was full of people. My friend did not come to Cori's service. She said no one told her what time the service was going to be. And she chose to be offended that Steve did not give me the phone that day. She wrote me a very long letter, sharing with me how badly her feelings were hurt that no one called back to tell her the time of the service. And, if they had, she said she would have been there. She mentioned that she didn't even know if I had been told she called, and she wanted to let me know that my husband was possibly keeping it from me. She told me that I simply did not know what it was like for her to watch her eighteen-year-old son walk away from home, knowing he might have a drug problem and not knowing if she would ever see him again. Considering that I, FOR SURE knew that I would not ever see my child again in this lifetime...it felt like a horse kick to the gut.

I wrote my friend back to tell her that my husband did not keep things from me and that although I was sorry someone didn't call her with every detail, I felt that considering the circumstances she could have found the information. I let her know that I didn't really have it in me to turn our life situations into a contest of whose life was the worst. She wrote back with more accusations and excuses, and the last contact I had with her was a response I sent expressing that though she had never asked for forgiveness. If she needed it, then I forgave her. I also said that I hoped she would forgive me for offending her during those first days of my grief. That was the last contact we had with each other for years.

Many years later we reconnected on Facebook. However, as much as I was ready to reconnect and catch up, she seemed very stuck in her feeling that I just did not understand and that until she felt I did understand, we could not have a meaningful relationship.

One of the things I am not able to handle very well to this day is the wasting of time. It is precious. And rehashing something that for me was put to rest long ago is a colossal waste of time. For all those years I was ready to accept that we would not see eye to eye on the events that happened between us over Cori's death, and move on. But my friend was not ready, and is not to this day. It saddens me, but it is not something I am willing to spend my strength and emotions on. Life is simply and truly too short.

*

TANISHA CALDWELL
Tanisha's 23-year-old son Tariq (Jay)
died in a car accident in 2015

The loss is still fresh for my family and I. We all have our days, and we all grieve differently. None of my relationships have been severely impacted, though I do think some have been strained. I am trying to be mindful that grief is different for everyone.

*

LYNDA CHELDELIN FELL
Lynda's 15-year-old daughter Aly
died in a car accident in 2009

There are two relationships that bore the brunt of our loss. The first was that between my husband and I. From the moment we met years ago, our connection was instant, strong, and beautiful. We rarely disagreed, and laughed frequently. He was my best friend, lover, husband and a wonderful father to our children. We made a great team, and I felt truly blessed.

When the accident happened, we clung to one another for dear life. Looking back, I could see that while my husband was always there for me, holding me as I wailed, I rarely saw him cry. About eighteen months after the accident I realized that somewhere along the line we had started to disconnect from one another. I was surrounded by lots of female support, but men and women are wired differently and my husband was afraid to allow his own grief. He and Aly were extremely close, but he had been raised to keep one's emotions in check, and to "move on." And so he kept his sorrow inside. Though our mutual love for each other never faltered, it was important for us to shore up the weakness, the disconnect that was becoming evident. For the first time since the accident, we decided to seek out counseling.

We went for about eighteen months and it wasn't terribly helpful. In the beginning, the counselor felt confident in her ability to help us, but child loss was clearly over her head. I had no strength left to find another counselor, and so we continued to see her.

And then tragedy struck our family again when my husband's grief got the best of him. One day after returning home from town, he suffered a terrible stroke leaving him permanently disabled. At first, I didn't know whether he would live or die. And if he lived, would he ever regain his speech or the ability to walk? Once again we clung to each other for dear life. Our whole focus at that point

220

became my husband's survival, and together we fought to regain all that the stroke had stripped from him. That reconnected us in a way that was unexpected, yet truly became a silver lining.

Today, our marriage is the best it has ever been. We again enjoy each other very much and laugh often. My husband will always be quite disabled from the stroke, and at times I still grieve for the husband I once had. But I feel incredibly blessed that we survived not one tragedy, but two. Now, with many years ahead of us, I look forward to enjoying all that life has to offer with my dear sweet husband by my side.

The second relationship that was impacted was our connection with my husband's parents. They live in Australia and didn't know Aly well. They arrived for the memorial service, and stayed for five weeks. They expected to be treated and entertained as guests. Sight-seeing was at the top of their list, along with proper meals each day. I was in a fog of shock, so my husband took them everywhere they wished and I did my best to host, though I failed miserably.

When the stroke happened, my husband's parents were very angry. They felt I was to blame for Jamie's poor health habits because I hadn't forced him to take better care of himself. They simply did not understand the far-reaching effects of profound grief. Their anger continues to this day, and it has caused a disconnect between us. Both my husband and I feel so sad about this; we simply don't understand their thought process. Their anger at me is like salt on a wound, but we remain hopeful that one day they will have better understanding and compassion.

*

MICHELLE DETWILER
Michelle's 19-year-old daughter Emily
died in 2014 due to congenital complications

Each of us had a unique relationship with Emily. Her disabilities were so profound that our lives revolved around her. For nineteen years we made her smile, and we held her during her hurts. We knew who we were, and who we were to her. But who were we without her? The stark reality of our daughter's death was like being in a sterile room. What were we supposed to do now? What were we supposed to talk about? We knew WHO we wanted to talk about. We wanted our daughter, our sister, our girl. It seemed that at the point of loss, we ourselves were lost.

Our emotions are raw, and at times we are on edge. Happy one minute and wanting to scream and collapse the next. We seem to know and understand that there will be days like this. Sometimes we snap at each other and then return to our senses. We're human and grieving.

There is a choice when you are lost. You can walk on and be found, or you can sit and remain lost. Together we chose to walk on. I don't know if we consciously decided, or just followed one another on instinct. But in the sadness that enveloped each of us there was also a compassion for every tear. So many tears have been shed, and we chose not to hide it. We covered one another in these tears. In our family there was and is no shortage of hugs. On days when we think we can hardly make it anymore, we hang on to each other. Our relationship as a couple and as a family continues. Even the ugly bonds of death cannot sever what we have. And what we have now is a new era. We are learning to talk about new things, learning to be happy about new things, and still open to sharing the deepest loss imaginable.

*

ANNAH ELIZABETH
Annah's son Gavin Michael aspirated on his meconium
during the delivery and died 26 minutes following his birth

I do not have any relationships that have been negatively impacted as a result of my son's death. That said, there are certainly associations that I've had to put into perspective. Shortly after Gavin's obituary appeared in our local paper, I received a pamphlet from a religious organization that said my child had been sacrificed for my sins. I initially felt a stabbing pain and an overwhelming sense of guilt. I quickly realized that I didn't believe that logic one bit, and I tossed that brochure into the trash. I still feel a little bit of anger toward this group's practice, because I believe it to be controlling (fear is a great motivator to keep us close) and hurtful. I could have chosen to stereotype all members of this faith as cruel and unreasonable, yet I chose to discard this sect's opinion, respect its members' rights to their own judgments, and then to accept that I do not have to adopt their beliefs. I have family members who, twenty years following the funeral, still refuse to acknowledge my son, even when his name comes up in conversation. In the early years, this felt personal, as if my struggle and pain were being ignored. It felt like my child's life was being denied. While I could have continued the conflict by feeding into these lines of thought and emotion, I chose to recognize that everyone grieves differently and that everyone suffers in their own way. By choosing to make their choices about them instead of about me, I found it easier to avoid being hurt as a result of their silence. Changing my own thoughts, and fully appreciating those who can and will share my son with me, have avoided the ultimate demise of those other associations. Choosing appreciation and choosing to share the joyous side of my son's life with others has allowed me to maintain those relationships in a way I can be okay with. It might be different from the connection I might have initially desired, but for me it is better than the alternative, which would mean relationships, or conflict-riddled one with these individuals.

*

WENDY EVANS
Wendy's 21-year-old son Kyle died in 2009
from diabetes when his insulin pump malfunctioned

My relationship with my daughter has been impacted the most. We have worked though several issues over the last two years. In the beginning there was mutual support. After she went back to school, the support for each other lessened. She wants her mom back, according to her.

223

*

BONNIE FORSHEY
Bonnie's 16-year-old son Billy died in 1993
from an overdose of prescription drugs

When I lost my son, I became so depressed that my daughter could not stand to see me that way. She was only eighteen, but she decided to move out and get her own place. She could not deal with my constant crying and depression. She was used to seeing me happy and strong, and it was too much for her to deal with. We all grieve in our own way, and she did what was best for her. We had many good memories in that house, but after my son passed away it was just too much for her to deal with every day. We have a close bond today. We have learned to deal with things and move on.

*

TALIA GATO
Talia's 8-year-old daughter Poppy
died in 2009 in a car accident

Here is the thing about grief over time. In the loss journey when you lose a child, your family has to start life over, and you have to pick and choose what works for you and your family. In grief, there are no rules even though counselors and books tell you things, yet you are the one living in it. If your heart doesn't feel it, don't do it. Being bereaved isn't about pleasing others. You now have to retell your new story.

In loss, we just don't have the energy we had before. We have to choose where we need to put our worthwhile energy. In order to survive since losing my daughter, I don't have the energy to invest in a less than authentic life. If I am not able to share my loss and talk about the good memories and sad memories with my friends, and if they don't want me to talk about it and shut me down by saying things meant to fix me, to make me better, then I know I can't be real with them. So I have to distance myself.

224

I would rather be with people who are raw and honest about themselves and life. It is a beautiful completeness of fellowship if one can do this with friends.

*

KORBY HAVE
Korby's 17-year-old daughter Taylor (Tayla)
died in 2013 in a car accident

I think all my relationships have been impacted. I no longer have the friends I used to, and I close myself off to making friends because I don't want anyone to know how badly I hurt. People who haven't experienced grief as severely as losing a child can't comprehend the loss, so they don't understand the struggle it takes just to get through the day. In order to avoid having to deal with what people think I should be doing or how I should be feeling, I just keep myself closed off and avoid situations where I might make someone feel uncomfortable. I even hide my feelings from my family so I don't make them feel uncomfortable either.

*

DEANA MARTIN
Deana's only two children, 25-year-old Amanda
and 21-year-old Logan, died in a car accident in 2011

Every relationship from my past has been severely impacted by my loss. No one in my family understands how badly I need their support or how I so desire them to understand how much pain I am in. I reach out in hours of desperation. I feel so alone. Of course I would never wish the raw excruciating pain I feel; some days it's all day long, even after almost five years, to be felt by anyone. It would be so nice to have someone hold me and tell me it's all going to be okay. It is an odd feeling to know intellectually that it will be okay, but emotionally to be dying inside at the same time, feeling as if every drop of blood has been drained from my body and every heartbeat stolen by some unseen force, my entire soul shredded to bits and there is nothing I or anyone can do. There are no magic drugs to make the pain go away or to help them to see. There is no sign I can hold up that says "I am hurting terribly today," or "Help me, please." There is nothing the grieving can do to help others who have not experienced the death of a child to know what we know. We can't show them pictures of what our pain looks like. There are no medical tests that spit out pictures of the pain, or tests that show the million pieces our hearts now lie in. There is nothing to show that our lungs can barely take breath; we gasp at air as if it were to be our last sip of life.

The soul, how can you measure the damage to one's soul? No one can even prove it exists scientifically. What test or proof do I have of the damage done to my soul by the death of my children? Besides the unseen excruciating physical pain I feel throughout every fiber of my life, I find myself angry that they can't see, or choose not to, and I feel hopeless that there is no one who tries to ease my weary soul. No arm around my shoulder, no hug, no kiss on my cheek.

I have one person from my past who I know, without a shadow of a doubt, will not let me slip into the nothingness, the huge empty void that is now my life. Thank god for her, my lifeline. No one from my past even barely acknowledges my children's birthdays, or how much I must be hurting on those days. Hallmark doesn't have "So sorry your child died, but happy birthday to him anyway" cards. I so long for someone to reach out and remember my children on those days.

There are hordes of new wonderful bereaved parents and others who are pure of heart who have graced my life since my children made their transition home. There are organizations that send me cards in honor of Amanda and Logan, and even though they are the same generic card every year, they are worth their weight in gold to me. I know I could reach out to anyone in the bereavement community and they would be there for me, day or night. Anything I need, they would do all in their power to rally around me. But my stubborn pride doesn't often allow me to tell them the truth of how much pain I am in. They know how much and they are in similar pain. I think it is an unwritten code that we choose not to burden others. What a quandary, because we know well the pain we both experience. I could be very wrong; I am sure that if asked, any one of these beautiful people would say, "Deana, don't be silly. We can only do this together!" Because they too know the loneliness and isolation after the death of a child. But there is something inside me that has always been a fighter, a survivor, and admitting defeat is so foreign to me. Just to think I could have possibly failed or am failing the biggest challenge of my life is more than I can bear. How can I dance with the devil during breast cancer and win, and face the myriad traumas I have faced in my life, to feel on some days that this one will take me, will finish me off, will pull me down into the abyss where all bereaved parents go who fail. Will I be one of the ones who end up there? Sometimes I don't know.

*

MONICA MIRKES
Monica's 30-year-old daughter Marisa
died in 2013 due to Cesarean complications

My friendships. The first year I just functioned from day to day. Talking to anyone was so exhausting for me. It still is, because there is nothing I want to share. Just emptiness. I have disconnected from my friends. Is it permanent? Temporary?

*

DENISE PURCELL
Denise's 27-year-old daughter Megan died
in 2011 from an accidental overdose

My other daughters felt I couldn't understand their loss as a sister, and I couldn't understand why they would think I didn't feel such a loss when Megan was my daughter. Unless you're a mom, you can't know. We still have limited conversations about Megan.

227

*

MARILYN ROLLINS

Marilyn's 37-year-old son Randy and 16-year-old granddaughter Sara
died in a car accident in 2006 during a family camping trip

I would have to say that the relationship most affected was with my son's wife and their two remaining children. It seemed to happen very gradually. The relationship with our daughter-in-law deteriorated after the accident. I will not go into detail, but there had been tension between my daughter-in-law and me. My son, Randy, was the buffer between us. With him gone, that buffer disappeared. We seemed engaged in a battle of who was grieving harder: she lost her husband and a child, I lost a child and a grandchild. One thing I want to make clear is that I take responsibility for my part in some of the awful things that were said back then.

We tried to maintain traditions for the sake of their surviving children, but I was never sure if this just made it more painful for them, not having their dad and sister there. As time went on, we rarely saw them except on holidays. But even then, it seemed like there was always an argument. My granddaughter eventually got married, and just a few from her father's side of the family were invited. It was very awkward. It also took place in the church where the funerals were held. I was very emotional. On my beautiful granddaughter's wedding day, I did not want the focus on me.

About a year after my granddaughter's wedding, my daughter-in-law remarried. I sent my RSVP with a note respectfully declining the invitation. It was not that I didn't want her to remarry; she was a young woman. But I was afraid it would be too emotional for me, and again I didn't want to draw attention away from her day. After the wedding, we stopped seeing them altogether. They no longer came over even on holidays. I bought my grandchildren presents anyway, and stacked them in the corner. A couple of times we picked up our grandson and took him to dinner. We did have texting and Facebook.

228

My great-granddaughter was born about a year after my granddaughter got married. My son had a grandchild! When I saw the first pictures on Facebook, I cried. I cried for my son, who would not see his granddaughter grow, but told myself that he had held her for nine months in heaven. On Thanksgiving, a short time after the baby was born, we were having dinner with my younger son and his children when a car pulled into the driveway. We watched through the window as my granddaughter got out of the car with her husband and the baby. When they came into the house and placed the baby in my arms, I sobbed. Vowing to have a better relationship, we later took all their Christmas presents to their house and went to lunch with them. We didn't see them again for over a year.

I had not really spoken to my daughter-in-law since her marriage, maybe a word or two when my grandson went to dinner with us. I can remember asking myself, "Is she still my daughter-in-law?"

Not seeing my son's children hurt. This last summer, we had a very strange day. First, I received a text from my granddaughter. She was having some personal issues and wanted to talk, so we texted back and forth for a while. I was glad she was confiding in me. She dearly missed her brother, who had joined the National Guard before his senior year, and was now at boot camp in Fort Benning, Georgia. My husband and I had just bought a TV that day. We were setting things up when a car pulled into the driveway. We watched in shock as my daughter-in-law got out. She had come to give us a letter our grandson had written us. She told us that she thought about us a lot, and remembered the good times we had over the years. We talked for a few minutes and then she left. My husband and I looked at each other like we were in the *Twilight Zone*. We had heard from three of them all in the same day.

I continued to communicate with my grandson while he was at boot camp through the summer. He is now home to finish his senior year, and recently we had a nice lunch with him. He wants to go into law enforcement. My granddaughter and the baby are spending more time with us. She even came and spent the night with us one night. I hope that we can all continue to maintain this relationship. I know my son would want it that way.

*

KATIE ROUSH
Katie's 26-year-old daughter Krystle
died in 2013 of accidental alcohol poisoning

My eldest daughter was horrible to me! When it came time to bury my daughter, my oldest got on the phone along with Krystle's father and basically they planned a funeral that Krystle did not want. Krystle's dad had been arrested four times for drug dealing. He had nothing and no money. So when my husband and I had plans for my daughter, the day we were to go to the funeral home, my eldest got out of the car and told me that Krystle's father had put a hold on her body. When I asked why, she said because Krystle's friends need to say goodbye. Krystle had lived here in Columbus for the past two years. She never wanted to go back home. She and her father had not communicated in three years. But because of my eldest daughter and Krystle's father, I could not go forward with her wishes. My eldest was excited because she got sixty new Facebook friends since Krystle died.

I signed off on Krystle's remains only when I knew that he had made funeral arrangements. But then he expected me to foot the bill for them. I said no. My eldest daughter called me all kinds of names, and even had a memorial page I made on Facebook turn into a horror show. It was all about her and what she wanted, not about what her dead sister wanted. I could not mourn my child in peace. Her friends tormented me, and Krystle's dad tormented me as well as his family. I don't know how I survived it all. Without my husband and my dog, I would have just given up. It was horrific.

*

SARA RUBLE

Sara's 19-year-old son Scott died in 1994 from a
combination of a seizure disorder, Strep throat and dehydration

When Scott died I had been married only nine months. I had gone through a divorce prior to that. Because of that chaos and all I experienced with friendships during that time, whether losing or gaining friends (it does happen), I think my friends who stood by me were very willing, cautious at times (yes), and supportive. They saw who I was becoming through all the emotions and pain and hung in there with me, for me. I did not lose friends as I know others have and my address book did not change as others have experienced. I am very grateful for that.

I do know there was always something in me that knew others could not really know how deep my pain and anguish was. I was angry and confused and needed more than anyone could ever provide me. I just wanted Scott. I sought out counseling early on to have that one-on-one support, and to try to understand who I was and everything else I was experiencing. My counselor would push me and I would respond with tears or strong words as anyone might…but perhaps that release in a safe setting gave me more to explore or contemplate as she guided me, pushed me, to do the heavy grief work. Not easy at all, but I see now that it brought me greater depth and understanding of death and all that it encompasses. If I was frustrated with work, or a lack of understanding there or with others, my counselor urged me to "educate, educate, educate." I knew this was important. Years before Scott's death, I had a friend whose baby died at six months and I had been at a loss to understand her continuing grief. I had been the one facing the grieving mother, and I knew that was not an easy place to be. Quite honestly, it was very hard not knowing how to help or what to say to her. So with Scott's death, I had a compassion within me that forgave more easily.

A mother's love for her child is like nothing else in the world.
It knows no law, no pity, it dares all things and crushes down
remorselessly all that stands in its path.
AGATHA CHRISTIE

*

CHAPTER TWELVE

THE FAITH

Love is the only law capable of transforming grief into hope. -LYNDA CHELDELIN FELL

Grief has far-reaching effects in most areas of our life, including faith. For some, our faith can deepen as it becomes a safe haven for our sorrow. For others, it can be a source of disappointment, leading to fractured beliefs. One commonality among the bereaved is that faith is often altered one way or the other.

*

STACY BERNDTSON
Stacy's daughter Cori Joy died in 2003, the day before her fourth birthday, from an undiagnosed genetic disorder

I consider myself doubly blessed that in addition to my relationship with my husband growing stronger in the aftermath of our daughter's death, so has my relationship with God. I have been a Christian since I was nine years old, and while there were times when I drifted far from Him, I have always believed in a God who held the world and all things in His hands. I believed that even when I didn't know the answers to the whys of my life, He did. I also believed and do believe with my whole heart that if He could

233

have fulfilled His plan for my life and the purpose of Cori's life to heal her, He would have.

Do I wish with every fiber of my being that she was with me today? YES! And I will miss her until that day when she is once again in my arms. But until that day I stand on the promises of God, throughout His word that He truly works ALL things together for my good.

When we moved to Washington state from California in 2001, because of Cori's special needs we were unable to attend church on any kind of regular basis. While in California we attended a large church, but because Cori was then an infant and young baby, she did well in the church nursery. We moved when she was eighteen months old and by the time she was two and beyond, it was hard to have her in the nursery. She was cognitively her age but the early toddler groups at churches were just not set up for a child who could not walk or talk and needed one-on-one assistance.

When Cori died it became very important to me that we return to church. My husband would later say that prior to Cori's death, he didn't know if his faith was real, but in her death he realized it was. Initially we did not socialize or engage in fellowship with other church attendees. We were so new in our grief, so we would come in a bit late and sit in the back. For me, this was a time when I could just pour out my emotions in song. I think I probably sang WAY too loud and I know I cried very hard at times, but it was what I needed. God met me there in those songs. His spirit gave me a comfort and a peace that I don't think I had when sitting in our home most of the time.

Through this church, I attended a grief support program called GriefShare. I attended for three sessions yet did not meet one person who had lost a child. But I did meet some beautiful women and a couple of gentlemen who will always hold a very special place in my heart. It was also through this church that we met the couple who would lead us to our adoption of Molly.

I can look back now and see God's hand in each step of our lives for all of Cori's life and after her death. There are still "whys." But as it was when I was a child, I have been able to lay those questions down for now in the belief that when I enter eternity those questions will be answered or the answer will no longer be important to me.

*

TANISHA CALDWELL
Tanisha's 23-year-old son Tariq (Jay)
died in a car accident in 2015

My faith has been my strength and has sustained me, though it has wavered. I try to understand how God could allow this happen and I struggle to find an acceptable answer. So I'm still trying to accept what God has allowed, and lean on him. There is purpose for this; I just don't yet know what that is.

*

LYNDA CHELDELIN FELL
Lynda's 15-year-old daughter Aly
died in a car accident in 2009

I've always been a strong spiritual Christian. I'm less inclined to follow organized religions, because some of what they dictate doesn't make sense to me. So I walk with my focus on God at all times, but not through any one church. My strong faith has never wavered. If anything, the accident has strengthened my faith even further and has provided an incredible source of comfort that I'm grateful for. I believe that everything in life has a purpose. Despite my tremendous emotional suffering, I trusted that God had a purpose that was much bigger than myself. I didn't always like or understand God's plan, but I've always trusted it.

I've never felt angry at God or the universe, and that is a tough one for others to understand. They wonder "Really? How can you not be angry?" I can't explain it other than to say that I trust in a higher purpose, and this trust has brought me tremendous comfort in my darkest times. When I find myself wailing in my bedroom, when the sorrow threatens to engulf me, I envision myself curled in a fetal position in the palm of God's hand. This vision brings me great comfort.

Why did God take Aly, an award-winning 4.0 student destined for the Olympics? A true leader who rooted for the underdog and exhibited a compassionate heart for the smallest of creatures? I don't question God, because perhaps the picture is bigger than myself. Perhaps God took Aly to help me learn lessons I wouldn't have learned otherwise. Perhaps God took Aly for reasons that had nothing to do with me. Was I happy that he took Aly to help me and others grow spiritually? Heavens, no! But I trust his judgment. I trust that God and the universe know better than I about what is needed. The idea of reincarnation came to mind frequently after the accident; it still does. Because the universe holds great mysteries, I believe that reincarnation is a distinct possibility. If Aly's accident was predestined to teach me a lesson about something, I vow to get it right so I don't have to endure this horrible lesson again. Ever.

As a bereaved mother, I also have seen firsthand the destruction that occurs when one is denied emotional support. Sometimes I wonder whether God puts into motion certain events so those of us who find ourselves on this journey can make a difference in the lives of others who are struggling. I find tremendous comfort in the belief that our loss has a higher purpose. I often counsel bereaved parents to volunteer within their own community because when we see the world through someone else's eyes, through the eyes of a homeless person or a battered mother, it helps us realize we aren't alone in our pain. And sometimes this awareness creates a compassion that helps our own heart to heal.

Also, our family and extended family have received many signs from Aly that cannot be attributed to coincidence. This further affirms that heaven, the universe, is a very magical place indeed. Some traditional Christians warned me that it was the devil in sheep's clothing. I don't believe God would allow the devil to behave in a way that would bring joy to our hearts. My neighbor's sister lost her teenage son two years before Aly's accident. Her sister's belief is absolute and unwavering: when you're dust, you're dust. Without some kind of afterlife to believe in, I wonder how she survives the sorrow. I want to wrap my arms around her, but her heart is tightly closed in this matter. So I just send prayers filled with love.

*

JACQUELYN CRUZ
Jacquelyn's 24-year-old daughter Jenna
died in 2012 from pulmonary edema

I never really looked at my faith as a disappointment, but I guess that's a good way to sum up how I feel. How I pleaded with God for those fifteen minutes in between the initial phone call and the actual call that gave me the devastating news. I begged him for Jenna to live, offered my own life in place of hers, anything I could think of, just let her live! I did a life review in my head of all the good I've done here on Earth; surely he wouldn't let that go unnoticed? That is why I live my life with love, kindness and forgiveness. What was the point if he was to take my child? How can someone I've prayed to for most of my life, someone I trusted to always guide me and help me, take my firstborn? Everything that I believed in vanished in an instant. I've had conversions with my priest about this and he says it's okay to be angry; God can take it. I sometimes find myself praying without even realizing it now; creature of habit, I guess. I was advised to pray to the Blessed Mother because she knows exactly how I feel, she saw her son die on the cross. My relationship with God now is complicated. I like to think that he took Jenna because he knew she was suffering here and he wanted to comfort her even if it meant hurting her family. I feel confident in knowing that someday I will be able to pray again as I once did, and I'm sure he'll be happy to hear from me.

*

MICHELLE DETWILER
Michelle's 19-year-old daughter Emily
died in 2014 due to congenital complications

My hope and trust is in God, the creator of heaven and earth. Death made this all the more real. Where I had blind faith before, there is now the reality of what I had once trusted in. After death we all meet our maker. I know my daughter is in heaven. I can trust that she is there. It is a lovely ending to a life that was often filled with pain. Each of us has a choice to know and follow the Lord. But what about people like my daughter who had severe brain damage? She couldn't choose anything. Did she know Him? Did she know she could trust Him? Did she know and understand she would see Him when she died? As her parent, I trusted in the Lord for her. There was no need to question her life ever after. None. God is as good as His word. He loved her.

It's all so real now. The Bible tells us that Jesus came to be the final sacrifice for sin. He is the Lamb of God and He chose to die for us. Can you imagine the loss felt by His family and those who were close to Him? And then he came back to life and walked around with them!!! Oh, my gosh! The thought of it sends chills through me. My daughter, whose body is dead, now lives because He chose to die. She is in the presence of the Lord! No more pain, no more tears, no more struggles. All of that is gone. There is my hope.

What if I had no faith? I'd be lost. My daughter would be gone and my life would be dark. Who could I turn to, who could I hold on to? Who would hold me up? My life has a sadness because I miss her, but there is no darkness in my faith. The one who knows our pain has taken her in His arms and given her new life. I can't wait to be there with them. I can only imagine the joy she has now, the joy I'll have when I arrive. Faith is something to hold on to even when you have nothing left.

*

ANNAH ELIZABETH
Annah's son Gavin Michael aspirated on his meconium
during the delivery and died 26 minutes following his birth

Yes. I no longer believe that God sits in heaven dictating what fortunes and misfortunes he will bestow upon each of us humans.

I have always felt a sense of paradox surrounding organized religion, but it wasn't until Gavin's death that I was able to articulate what I felt and thought. You see, there is this expression that "God isn't a cruel God, he's a loving God," but the very definition of the word "cruel" means to knowingly inflict pain on another. God would know how much suffering I would experience when my child died. Therein lies the contradiction.

Believe it or not, I didn't hit that proverbial rock bottom until almost seven years following Gavin's death; that climax came on the morning I discovered that my husband and one of my best friends were having an affair. Hours after sitting slumped against my washing machine, I knew that I had to get up and do something, ANYTHING, so I made a phone call, one that would lead me to one of the greatest gifts I received on my journey to healing. I was directed to a woman I didn't know. This theologian, whose body was riddled with something like multiple sclerosis, sat quietly across the room from me as I begged to understand why a loving God would continue to heap so much sh** onto one person's life. "God doesn't give us more than we can handle seems like some sick joke," I said to her, "and the joke is on me." Her response is forever burned into my brain: "God is always with us…divine intervention is rare. He was in the room with you when you encountered abuse; He was crying out in pain with you and screaming for it to stop…"

I felt giant, invisible arms wrap me in a compassionate hug and I knew…God is a loving God. As I wrote about that passage in my memoir, I had another epiphany: Just as my loving God screams out when there is injustice or tragedy, so too does he jump up and down for joy in celebration when good things happen.

*

WENDY EVANS
Wendy's 21-year-old son Kyle died in 2009
from diabetes when his insulin pump malfunctioned

Yes! Huge area of concern. Prior to Kyle's death I considered myself a person of faith and spirituality. I have since lost my connection to faith, as the answers about where my son has gone are not forthcoming. Because Kyle had not worked through his own questions about faith, I began to wonder where he was after death. After much prayer and talking with godly people in my life, I became numb. I still have not been able to find God again.

*

BONNIE FORSHEY
Bonnie's 16-year-old son Billy died in 1993
from an overdose of prescription drugs

I no longer attend church. I was crushed by my son's death. It changed everything about me.

*

TALIA GATO
Talia's 8-year-old daughter Poppy
died in 2009 in a car accident

My faith has definitely been altered. I grew up in the church, part of that was Catholic and then Protestant. I was immersed in it. I raised my kids with faith, we attended church all the time and led Bible studies for years. This didn't prepare for my loss, even though we prayed for others and their needs. I prayed and prayed the day of our accident, "Please don't take my little girl, please don't." But she died. I do have the assurance that she is in heaven and I will see her again.

I have been in my pool of loss for a few years. I will say that some people were kind and did nice things for us and prayed for our family. I am grateful for that. But people stopped coming over at about six months. I guess they thought we were cured or over it. Or maybe they were worried they would get catch my disease? Or maybe they couldn't handle how it had really changed me. I was grieving intensely, and was very free with my crying and verbalizing how I felt. My basic personality is vibrant, but I think I really became more intense and free with my thoughts.

My view of what I saw Christians do and say has changed me. It broke my heart and I wasn't prepared for that. I wasn't prepared for losing seventy percent of our friends. When I went to church, they couldn't look me in the eye, even those who attended our many dinners and parties. We could have used a hug or words of encouragement like "I still pray for you," or "I am thinking of you over the holidays," or "I miss Poppy." But instead most of the time people treated me like nothing had ever happened.

For a very long time I felt like I was a lone horse on a merry-go-round that kept on going but I stood still. I quit going to church for a while and I honestly was mad at God. Church culture doesn't know what to do or say to the bereaved. I couldn't tell anybody because I didn't want to scare them from their own faith; that wasn't my intent. I couldn't sing a hymn for about six years; it broke me and I'd cry at church. But after a while I did go, even though my daughter didn't want to go because her sister wasn't there.

I have returned to church, but how I view God, my thoughts on heaven, and some doctrines of faith and prayers too have changed. But I can't share it with others in my faith because I don't want to scare them regarding the truth of how I think now. Or worse, not be understood.

I have faith in God now and I am not angry anymore. But I do know there needs to be a change in our church culture to support the platitudes that she or he "is in a better place," or "you have to be strong." Being a Christian doesn't give you a free pass on pain and loss in this life. It's great that some never have pain or sickness, but it happens. So there needs to be a change. It's important how we treat each other, and how we care for our bereaved long term.

If church is to be a place or haven for the hurting or lost then we need to renovate and educate leadership on what really helps for a lifetime. If we continue to do what we do now, people will go (or not) to church but have to keep the hurt inside their hearts. They will keep it private and suffer in silence. Grief affects our health too, so if there is a change in grief and loss trauma education within the church culture, and who we are as community, then the next generation will be more equipped on how to care for the broken people. It is my greatest hope.

*

DAPHNE GREER
Daphne's 5-year-old daughter Lydia died in 2008 in a
car accident during a routine morning commute

Rooted in faith during my childhood, I was raised in the church. From Sunday school to worship to vacation Bible school and church functions, Sundays were devoted to God. Later, during my years of high school and college, I got a bit distant from God, rarely attending a church service or opening my Bible. My old Bible from childhood sat collecting dust on a dresser that I would occasionally glance at from across my bedroom. God was there. Sure, I knew that, but I didn't really understand or appreciate Him, seldom thinking about my faith. Little did I know what a role my faith would play later in life.

At first I despised the saying "Bad things happen to good people" as it was overly used in my mind. It was a feeble attempt made by others to console and bring comfort after my daughter died. Yet it never did. There was no reason, no plan for her to die. It just happened. In an instant, a car accident claimed my sweet girl's life. Did God do it? Was I being punished for things in my past? Was I a bad parent? Where was God? Why did He let this happen? So many questions plagued my mind for years. Yes, years.

Strangely, I didn't get angry with God. I was angry with myself. I just didn't understand. I knew he was not a punishing God, yet part of me couldn't stop the wavering and demeaning thoughts about what I did to deserve this.

At the accident scene, I prayed and prayed for Lydia's life to be spared, begging to trade places with her. Yet my prayers were not answered. Receiving the life-altering and horrific news that my daughter had died shook me to the core. I had no other option than to rely on that foundation of faith my parents had pressed onto me at an early age. As I said, I knew God, but didn't really KNOW him. I knew the basics, but never really needed him until after Lydia died.

Immediately, my heart turned to God. He was my only hope. I spent many nights alone in my bedroom closet, sobbing in complete loneliness and helplessness, searching for God's guidance and strength. I began to read my Bible daily, pray incessantly and turning toward Him in every direction. I knew this grief was bigger than me. I would not be able to survive it alone. After the rush of family left, people stopped dropping in, and the phone stopped ringing, there was no one left. I was alone.

Having my daughter die forced me to put life into perspective and examine my own. My eyes had been opened as I realized the fragility of our lives and found the purpose of Jesus' life. He died for me. For you. For all of us. Comprehending that deep of a love is unfathomable. When I think about it, it brings me to tears. For I am not worthy of such divine love. We are never alone.

God's grace is real. Tangible. I have felt it. Craved it. God has done so many incredible things in my life, and even since Lydia died, the blessings have been bountiful. By bringing people into my life at just the right time, opening doors while closing others, and making me a mother to five children, I am in awe.

I came to realize that there was no answer for such a tragedy. Accidents happen. God loves us and He is there to carry us through, picking up our shattered pieces and rebuilding us from the inside with an entirely new understanding and outlook on living. Lydia is with Him. So my hope remains in Him. Without Him, I am empty and remain nothing more than an empty shell. I am thankful, so incredibly thankful for His glory, sacrifice and promise of eternal life. I eagerly await the time until I can hold Lydia in my arms again.

Until then, I treasure this life. This grief and trauma I have endured has become the gift of a lifetime. Although part of me is elsewhere for eternity, my eyes have been unwrapped to see the glory of everyday things that we take for granted. Seeking to love others, sharing my hurt and finding my divine purpose is what my journey has brought me to. Beneath the pits of the blackest of black where no life can be found and finding that shimmer of light in the darkness can be life-changing, if we just believe.

*

KORBY HAVE
Korby's 17-year-old daughter Taylor (Tayla)
died in 2013 in a car accident

I wouldn't say my faith has been impacted by my loss. I truly do believe that when it is your time to go then it is your time to go. I know that Tayla is in a better place and someday I will get to see her again. What is hard is not knowing why it was her time to go, and why she couldn't have lived a full life. Losing my daughter has made me want to be better when it comes to my faith so that I will for sure be able to see her again.

*

DEANA MARTIN
Deana's only two children, 25-year-old Amanda
and 21-year-old Logan, died in a car accident in 2011

My faith has been shattered beyond recognition. I always had a very strong sense of a leading force in our lives. I was not raised religious. We were, as I recently heard a friend put it, of the C & E faith, Christmas and Easter. I had studied world religions and different cultures a great deal, plus ate up books on metaphysics in my thirties. I learned how to use the laws of attraction at amazing speeds and could manifest most what I wanted by believing it was part of my life. I found the power of the mind and the ability to heal one's physical body was nothing short of miraculous. I don't know that my God looked like others, my God was more a core energy that made all of this work. I dabbled in string theory and the belief that time was an illusion, that it was actually all going on at once. I believed in reincarnation. I also believed that the prophets of all the great religions were sent here to basically teach people how to play nice. Who they were sent by I did not know. Could have been the rulers of some advanced alien race that I was convinced put us on this earth, because the story of Adam and Eve just did not compute in my mind. Not to offend anyone, but I have a fairly scientific mind and I could not figure out how two people populated the earth, especially since one of the sons was slain and the other was told to go forth and procreate...well, with who?

My mind asks too many questions to have a strong belief in anything. I had enough exposure in my Methodist upbringing, and spent time as a Baptist and a Christian, that when my children died I first considered what horrible sin I could possibly be paying for. I felt I had paid back all that negative karma of my past. So I asked God, whoever God was, Why??? Why my children? I also begged and begged for "God" or the Reptilians, or the Pleiadians, Buddha, Brahma or the Aztec sun god. I did not care who, but someone needed to bring them back now!! The begging went on for a very long time! I still beg from time to time even today.

245

My belief in the laws of attraction pretty much went out the window because I can't manifest my kids back into life. The whimsical dreamer in me that believed dreams do come true died right along with my children. I often compare my relationship with God to the scene in *Forrest Gump* where Lieutenant Dan is up in the crow's nest during the storm having it out with God. Well, that's me most of the time, except I have legs still, at least currently. God or the aliens could take my legs at any given moment. Funny thing is, I believe having my legs taken would be a breeze compared to the current pain I feel.

So what do I believe today? I believe my children still exist, because energy does not die. I do not know where they exist, I call it heaven because that is the word that is most readily in my vocabulary. Some say heaven is a veil between this earth and the next. Some believe it is a tunnel that leads to grand pearly gates and streets of gold. Some say dying is just like being born, but you are being born back into where we originate from. Maybe that is the third star from the left, and straight on till morning. Maybe there is an unseen world right next to us, one that we do not see because it vibrates at a different rate. I believe my children will be there when I leave my body. Where is "there"? We have been through that.

I believe in near-death experiences and that people have seen the other side and come back. I believe in angels, but I am not sure if they are winged creatures, guides, helpers or just balls of light. I still believe in miracles, I suppose mainly because it was a miracle to have my children in my life at all, carrying a child in my womb and giving birth twice was a miracle. As hard as raising them by myself seemed at the time, it was all a miracle and a gift from somewhere and someone.

Where is hell? Hell resides in a bereaved parent's mind, heart and soul. We have seen hell, we have been there, stayed there for days and nights for long periods of time, and continue to visit there. Hell is second nature to us and we become quite comfortable there. Some are afraid to leave its warmth.

*

MONICA MIRKES
Monica's 30-year-old daughter Marisa
died in 2013 due to Cesarean complications

My faith in God has been absolute. I would want to know "why" Marisa had to fight so hard and for so long only to have it end the way it did. Was there something we were supposed to learn from this?

*

DENISE PURCELL
Denise's 27-year-old daughter Megan died
in 2011 from an accidental overdose

At first I cried out, Why??? But in my heart, I knew Megan wasn't having to struggle anymore. So I felt she was lucky to be picked first. And there is comfort knowing I will see her again. My faith is spiritual. There is no right or wrong answer for people to approach someone who has encountered a loss. Just acknowledge it, and help with the everyday things. That helps out a lot.

*

MARILYN ROLLINS
Marilyn's 37-year-old son Randy and 16-year-old granddaughter Sara
died in a car accident in 2006 during a family camping trip

My faith was very much impacted. I envy the parent who has so much faith that they immediately feel comforted by God when their child dies. From my experience as chapter leader for The Compassionate Friends, that is not always the case. As far as I was concerned, it was all God's fault and so I questioned Him. Why would He let this happen? Why not me? Why not the murderer in prison? Why not the awful and evil people we've heard about on the news? Why my beautiful boy and his beautiful daughter? They never hurt anyone. I was very angry at God.

247

After the anger, I decided that He was punishing me. I was sure of it. I was not a good mother. My son and granddaughter have paid for my sins. I spent hours lying in bed thinking of ways I could have been a better person, wife, mother and grandmother. I hated God. I hated myself. Things were not much better for my husband.

I returned to work. It was way too soon, but I was going crazy at home. I needed distraction. My husband had not returned to work yet. He had worked with my son, and now faced an empty desk each day. Every day I came home to find my husband curled in a fetal position on the sofa. I began to get angry at him also. The whole situation just made me more angry at God. He had taken a part of me, and now He was taking the rest. I knew that often a couple's relationship cannot withstand the loss of a child, and end up divorcing. Many days I came home to the same scene. A few weeks after the accident, I came home and again found my husband in a fetal position on the sofa. I was so angry and I said, "I think you died in that accident too!" He looked at me and said, "Why would God do this? What kind of God causes things like this to happen?" I said to him, "He didn't make it happen." He just looked at me and very flatly said, "There is no God." I screamed at him, "There has to be, because if there isn't, where are my kids?" I fell to the floor and cried. It was then when I realized that God didn't do this, and for the first time I said, "Oh, God, help me!" My husband embraced me, telling me over and over that they were in heaven, he knew they were in heaven. We just sat there holding each other for some time. I never found him curled up on the sofa again.

God gave us a great gift, the gift of free will. So many things had to happen the night of the accident to bring those vehicles to the same place at the same time. I believe that our days are numbered here on Earth, and though God may know the day we are going to die, I don't think He chooses the way we die. I don't think that we necessarily choose the way we die, but the choices we make lead us to that moment, just as His Son was led to Calvary. Maybe the way that we die leaves behind a lesson for the living.

After many years, I have found there are good things that have happened in our lives, things that would not have taken place if it weren't for the accident. Don't get me wrong, I would change it all in a heartbeat just to have one more day with either of them. I have spoken to others who also find this to be true. I like to think that God has put me back into His good graces, and He has forgiven me for my anger and doubt. I somehow think He understands, for He lost a child too.

*

KATIE ROUSH
Katie's 26-year-old daughter Krystle
died in 2013 of accidental alcohol poisoning

I yelled at God for taking my daughter. I hated Him for a while too. But I realized that He also lost a child. I prayed and talked to Him a lot. In a weird way, I started to see parts of the bigger picture. I accepted this as something I had to go through to understand and help people with later, maybe. No matter how I was feeling, I knew God was there with me, holding me close and sending angels to help me too. I value each day now. I pray each night and ask for blessings. I think I am more on a closer walk with God now than ever.

*

SARA RUBLE
Sara's 19-year-old son Scott died in 1994 from a
combination of a seizure disorder, Strep throat and dehydration

Faith? I did not have a strong faith at the time of Scott's death. I certainly had been to church a lot. I sang in the choir for most of my childhood (which was fun) and knew the prayers and responses by rote. I believed in a God...in ways that I just believed. Beyond that, there wasn't much depth to my faith.

Scott was Catholic because my first husband, his dad, was Catholic. So Scott's funeral was held in the Catholic church. It was a beautiful service, filled with love and prayers, as it needed to be for all of us. I did not know where God was on that day. But I remembered so clearly that I had thanked God profusely when our little Scott was born. "Oh, thank you God! Thank you! Thank you for Scott! Eight pounds and healthy!" I could not have asked for more. I was a mom!

So what did I do when Scott suddenly died at nineteen? His life was so meaningful and could have been even more. He was loved so greatly...and it all ended so abruptly. "God? Where are you?? This is not right! WHERE ARE YOU?" No answers...

And so basically, I set God aside. I said in my own way, "My grief and pain are too much God...I cannot deal with you right now. I do not know what to believe or not believe. I do not understand how this could happen or what your part has been in Scott's death. I am angry...confused...and I have to grieve...I must grieve... I cannot deal with you right now, God." And that worked for me.

In time...when the spirituality piece began to enter into my grief, a greater knowing, my healing, I began to know there is a God. With the signs and magnificent dreams that came from somewhere...I could not deny there was something bigger going on. I was being led down a path of trusting in something I could not see, that was showing me more in death and in life. It was a gradual knowing that Scott was still existing somewhere, and my faith in God, Spirit grew. As I look back now on my lack of a deep faith when Scott died, I am grateful I was not forced to believe in something that might have prevented me from coming into my own beliefs. It had time to evolve within me. So, so grateful.

*

CHAPTER THIRTEEN

OUR HEALTH

Health is a state of complete physical, mental, and social well-being, and not merely the absence of disease or infirmity. -WORLD HEALTH ORGANIZATION

As our anatomical and physiological systems work in tandem with our emotional well-being, when one part of our body is stressed, other parts become compromised. Has your grief affected your physical health?

*

STACY BERNDTSON
Stacy's daughter Cori Joy died in 2003, the day before her fourth birthday, from an undiagnosed genetic disorder

Caring for Cori was a sedentary way of life. I had very little respite and so, as has been a predilection of mine I guess, I ate to pass the time. I ate to make me feel better when I was sad about her condition and I got very little exercise. Having always been the "big girl with such a pretty face," the one who stands in the back row in every classroom photo (I could not even IMAGINE being one of the kids who got to sit cross-legged on the floor!), when Cori died I weighed the most I have ever weighed. Since then I have managed, plus or minus a couple of pounds, to lose eighty pounds. I am still a very big woman. I can't say that I tried really hard but I suppose it is true what they say: moving your body does wonders.

However, even so, I would say my health is not as good as it was when Cori was alive. I don't recall having issues with sleep and now more days than not while I may fall asleep, I do not stay asleep and I seldom feel like I've gotten a good rest. I cannot imagine that I slept well when Cori was alive either. I always kept a baby monitor in the room, and Cori was on an oxygen monitor that would beep if her saturations dropped, which it did at times. So perhaps this lack of sleep, feeling tired and unrested is an accumulative effect over many, many years.

In the early days after Cori's death, I did require an over-the-counter sleep aid for many months. I was in bed when my husband found Cori in her bed not breathing, and he screamed my name. Since then, far more frequently at first and then again when we brought Molly home from the hospital, I would have a dream in which Steve screamed my name again. Bolting upright with heart racing, I discover that it was in fact a dream.

As I was also an older mom, being thirty-seven when Cori was born and forty-five when we brought Molly home, I don't know whether to cast blame upon Cori's death for all my current aches and pains, high blood pressure, diabetes, etc. They were not something I had when Cori was alive. So perhaps her death and my grieving contributed to those issues on some level. Perhaps even more, because during Cori's life and the initial intense grieving, I did not take care of myself, let alone good care. Perhaps her death is not a contributing factor to these other things, but I am fairly confident that the sleep issue was born out of her life and death.

*

TANISHA CALDWELL
Tanisha's 23-year-old son Tariq (Jay)
died in a car accident in 2015

I wanted to lose weight, and I'm always trying to be more health conscious. Since Jay's death, I've lost twenty pounds. My stomach is often upset, and I can sometimes eat only once a day or not at all. Many days I feel drained and tired, but I push myself to keep going.

*

LYNDA CHELDELIN FELL
Lynda's 15-year-old daughter Aly
died in a car accident in 2009

Years ago, I shed over a hundred pounds by making significant lifestyle changes. My neighbor and I started walking every morning, I began healthful eating, and practiced good sleep hygiene. So when the accident happened, I was in excellent physical shape. Despite sticking to my routine, within weeks of the accident I began suffering from one illness after another. This is prominent in my mind because each time I became ill, what little coping skills I had took a nosedive. So early on, I understood the connection between emotional grief and physical health.

In the wake of the tragedy, everything in my life felt utterly out of my control. Being a good mom, loving my family and supporting them in their endeavors was not enough to keep a tragedy at bay. Suddenly I felt like NOTHING in my world was truly in my control. Except for my health. What I put in my body, how I treated my body, how I handled hydration and sleep hygiene was something I could control. Also, I made the correlation that the better care I took of myself, the healthier I felt. The healthier I felt, the stronger I felt. The stronger I felt, the stronger my coping skills became. Bingo, the light bulb went off….my health habits had a direct effect upon my ability to cope. Who knew?

I learned the hard way that when I gave in to my food addiction, the short-term bliss wasn't worth the shame and guilt that followed; which only hindered my ability to weather the storm of grief. I am protective of what little emotional reserves I have by avoiding my favorite sinfully delicious food triggers as much as possible, otherwise down the rabbit hole I go.

I've also noticed an impact upon my memory. I can remember moments and weird things like phone numbers from years gone by, but I can't remember what we just ate for dinner. This memory issue was a little scary at first. I would walk into the laundry room and completely forget what prompted me to go there in the first place. Had my grief induced some sort of dementia? Was I coming down with Alzheimer's at age forty-three? I found it embarrassing for the first few years.

I've since learned that short-term memory issues are common for those facing profound grief. Lists and notes help me manage, and my family has long since adjusted to this strange little quirk. I'm grateful for that, yet I still find it embarrassing at times.

*

MICHELLE DETWILER
Michelle's 19-year-old daughter Emily
died in 2014 due to congenital complications

One thing I've noticed since my daughter died is how tired I became. For many years my child needed twenty-four-hour care and the last two years were critical. When did I last sleep normally? When did I last eat normally? After Emily's death I had nothing but time on my hands. Exhaustion came in waves. My body seemed to want to make up for all the nights I stayed awake. Would I ever feel rested? It's been a year and a half and I continue to need naps. But I don't mind. I'm trying to give myself permission to take one every now and then.

*

WENDY EVANS
Wendy's 21-year-old son Kyle died in 2009
from diabetes when his insulin pump malfunctioned

I have absolutely had physical health changes since my son's death. I gained a lot of weight and began smoking a lot. I have experienced many symptoms of cold, flu and stomach viruses. Because it happens so frequently, and I still have very low energy, I feel like the physical symptoms may be stress and depression related.

*

BONNIE FORSHEY
Bonnie's 16-year-old son Billy died in 1993
from an overdose of prescription drugs

I was very healthy before my son's death. I worked out and was not on any prescription medications. Afterward, I fell into a deep depression and had to take antidepressants. I stopped going to the gym and stopped caring about everything. I had contracted hepatitis C in the 1980s from an infected patient I cared for and, after Billy died, it flared with a vengeance. My immune system was affected, and I developed rheumatoid arthritis, systemic lupus erythematosus osteoarthritis, diabetes, lung problems, cardiac problems, hypertension and more. It was as if my body had turned against itself.

*

TALIA GATO
Talia's 8-year-old daughter Poppy
died in 2009 in a car accident

I think I have aged, although nobody has told me this. I have a hard time sleeping and have physical pain, what feels like soreness of muscles, like I was run over by a truck. I am a very active person, and in the spring and summer I am a flower farmer. I find it very therapeutic.

I went to a retreat a couple of years ago for parents who had lost a child. By the time I left, I felt empowered. The retreat was put on by the MISS Foundation. I met many people there and I made friends, I am so glad I went. While there, we had sessions on yoga. Although I had heard of yoga, I didn't know much about it...after all, I am a church girl! In my circle, we didn't do yoga. I've since started doing yoga twice per week and now, for once, I can sleep like a baby.

I still have bad days, but nothing like before. I think I have posttraumatic stress disorder although have never been diagnosed, so there are things I am too afraid to do or see. But in some ways I think I have become more fit and healthier since my loss. I think I do more self-care.

*

KORBY HAVE
Korby's 17-year-old daughter Taylor (Tayla)
died in 2013 in a car accident

I find that I am more exhausted now than I ever was before. I don't sleep as well as I used to because I am constantly worried about my other children. I also know the exhaustion comes from having to hide my feelings all the time but that is the price I have to pay to make sure others don't feel uncomfortable.

*

DEANA MARTIN
Deana's only two children, 25-year-old Amanda
and 21-year-old Logan, died in a car accident in 2011

My physical health has suffered greatly since the death of my children and I worry what the continued emotional pain I experience will manifest into. I either don't eat or I gorge myself (comfort food). I don't sleep at night even with the help of sleeping medication, and then all I want to do is sleep all day. My gallbladder shut down shortly after their deaths and I had to have it removed. At the same time they took my ovaries because of my history of cancer. This left me feeling so very barren and hopeless, with no living children and now no eggs to produce any additional children. Even though they were probably old and shriveled, the symbol of still having eggs had some meaning that I was not aware of until they were gone.

My energy is so very low, I often feel I have aged many years in the five years since my children died. I try to tell myself I will start to do more things to take care of myself physically but it never sticks for more than a few days. My body hurts all the time, riddled with arthritis, and my heart truly hurts from being broken. I wear my emotions at the surface and it is very hard at times to keep them from overacting.

My short-term memory, focus and concentration no longer exist. People tell me I said things a day or two before and I do not remember. Also, I swear I did something I needed to do only to find out I didn't do it. I often feel like I am having an out-of-body experience, and my soul is no longer attached to my physical body. It is like a balloon flying high in the sky and I feel I need to pull it back into my being, but can't. It refuses to come back into my body because it is too painful in here, and much safer and more comfortable elsewhere.

I think a lot about death now. I used to be scared of dying, but now I count the days. Each morning I wake is one day closer to being with my children. If it were not for my granddaughter and my strong desire to care for her, I know my body would barely function. It functions now out of duty, and automatically advances to the next thing on the list. I fall into bed at night, so desperate for rest, only to stare at the ceiling and cry. The longing for my children is a true physical feeling in my body, it is not an emotion. It has physical symptoms that hold physical pain. Headaches and digestion problems are common. My weight will go up twenty pounds and then drop twenty pounds, sometimes within a month. I so desire fresh air and nature but can't seem to make myself go out into the world, even though my home feels nothing like my home since my children left. But at least it houses my bed, which is my haven, my security.

I also find security in my granddaughter's arms. But I spend so much time and effort being strong for her, it feels like a heroic feat some days, but I manage. Living life just to manage doesn't feel much like life anymore. But it is my life and I hear that as time goes on, I will adjust more and more to my new body riddled with pain and I will learn to live with this handicap. We will see. Each day feels like the next....some worse than others.

I continue to put one foot in front of the others and thank god for the new day to care for my granddaughter even though my heart is partly on the other side with my children. Sometimes the sorrow is so great my skin hurts. Grief takes a physical toll on your mind, body and soul that can't be put into words. All I know is that it is real, and big and baffling at times. Before the death of my children, if someone had tried to explain to me what I would experience physically, there would have been no way I could have comprehended the extent of it, just as it is impossible to explain childbirth to a woman who has never given birth. They are both very similar in the mystery of it all, but one brings great joy and hope for the future and one takes away all hope and leaves you feeling great sorrow. You're physically changed to your core.

*

MONICA MIRKES
Monica's 30-year-old daughter Marisa
died in 2013 due to Cesarean complications

My weight went way up. I would just eat mindlessly, not even realizing I was doing it. Being depressed and eating. Then doing something I had not done since grade school, biting my nails. You have no control over anything in your world anymore. Life is just spiraling farther away from you. Then you're left with the nightmare of trying to lose the weight.

*

DENISE PURCELL
Denise's 27-year-old daughter Megan died
in 2011 from an accidental overdose

I experienced anxiety and nightmares. I isolated myself from everyone. I started eating comfort food every night. I couldn't make healthy decisions for myself. I think I just didn't care.

*

MARILYN ROLLINS
Marilyn's 37-year-old son Randy and 16-year-old granddaughter Sara
died in a car accident in 2006 during a family camping trip

Very early on, I remember my chest hurting. I can remember wondering to myself, "Am I having a heart attack?" This is the first feeling that most parents who have lost a child describe. It is a pressure in the center of your chest, dizziness, a feeling of not being able to breathe. Emergency rooms even have a name for this, "broken heart syndrome." The stress of grief can cause the adrenal glands to send a surge of hormones to the heart, which can cause it to beat incorrectly. This will usually correct itself over time. So when we say we have a broken heart, it can be a very true statement.

I don't sleep well. It has been over nine years since my son and granddaughter died, and I still don't sleep well. When I do sleep, I have nightmares. Not necessarily of my son and granddaughter's deaths, just crazy nightmares. This, of course, leads to fatigue during the day. Some of the other things that I experienced are headaches, restlessness, muscle pain, stomach upset, bouts of crying, lack of concentration and forgetfulness. Ah, yes, forgetfulness. That one is still with me. I can set something down and thirty seconds later run through the house like a maniac trying to find it. I mentioned that I love to do scrapbooking. I have done one page in the last year. This is, I'm sure, due to my inability to concentrate. I tell myself that I'm going to the computer and I won't leave until I have at least picked out a picture and then a layout. I start looking through pictures, and the memories flow like water. And then I'm on Facebook scrolling through messages. I'll see something there that I need to look up online. This may lead to playing a game. Well, you see how it goes. I leave the computer an hour or two later with nothing accomplished.

When I know something has to be done, such as something for my Compassionate Friends group, I make lists and leave a lot of notes for myself. I also enlist the help of other parents in the group. If two or three of us have the information, we seem to be able to get the work done.

I also still suffer with a lot of anxiety. I have another son, along with six other grandchildren. If my son tells me he'll be here at a certain time and he isn't, I begin pacing. If he doesn't answer his phone or text me back, I am virtually unable to function until I hear from him. If a grandchild is sick, I will hover over them. I'll take their temperature every ten minutes and usually begin urging my son to take them to the emergency room. I'm a nurse and though my brain tells me this is illogical, my heart says otherwise.

Sometimes I look in the mirror and don't feel like I recognize the person that I see there. This person has sad eyes and dark circles under them. Her skin looks a bit pallid and when she smiles, there are wrinkles in her cheeks. Makeup can cover much of it, but she must work at not showing the sad eyes. She must put on that mask that we all wear. I vaguely remember the person she was before. I miss her.

*

KATIE ROUSH
Katie's 26-year-old daughter Krystle
died in 2013 of accidental alcohol poisoning

Oh boy! I hardly ate anything for the first few weeks. I could hardly sleep. I was so wounded, so raw. I was in a huge fog and my memory failed me a lot. I am five feet nine inches and dropped to

260

124 pounds. All I could do was cry. And cry. And cry some more. I was broken and realized just how someone could die of a broken heart. I had to force myself to eat. Anything and everything. I pushed myself to get up, shower and drive to work. I slowly gained my weight back. I slowly laughed again, and was shocked when I heard myself laugh too. I started to go out and do things again. Some were things my daughter did with me. I guess you could say I was not really depressed, but had posttraumatic stress disorder. I did not realize that....me, with the college degree in psychology! Imagine that. But PTSD is what I had. Any little thing would put me back to that moment of hearing my daughter died. I had to work hard, mentally and physically, to get back to the land of the living. I quit smoking. I gained my weight back. I shared in grief support groups, and I wrote. I wrote about and to my daughter. That saved me from a huge black abyss. I crawled through hell and came out okay. I am now 155 pounds and healthy. I laugh more and found myself again. I still cry. I let the tears fall when they come. I don't run from them or hide them, I just embrace them now. These are tears of love for my child. They are part of me. Just as she is.

*

SARA RUBLE
Sara's 19-year-old son Scott died in 1994 from a
combination of a seizure disorder, Strep throat and dehydration

As a pretty healthy adult, for years I would suddenly be disabled by horrendous headaches that forced me to bed, sometimes for three to five days. This was occurring even before Scott's death. Out of fear, I had a strong medication that I carried with me at all times. When I was working or at home, if I felt even a tinge of that frightening pain coming, I would take a pill...always as prescribed by my doctor. Even with much testing, scans and all, the doctors could never give me a reason for the migraines...only prescribe more medication. I was bound to it. After Scott's death, the headaches intensified. Coupling the overwhelming pain of grief with the physical pain I was forced to endure, I was screaming out for help. Neurologists, surgery, and even more medication that ultimately upset my stomach so greatly…I was desperate. I felt I had so little control over any of it. And then the medication started to cause rebound headaches, meaning that the medication I took for a headache actually created the next headache. How could that be??

I had to look for other ways to help myself. In my search I found a life-saving book in which a doctor wrote, "Get off all medications and take only aspirin." Oh wow…aspirin. I didn't think that would help, but I HAD to try. Actually, there was something rather powerful in pushing myself to be free of the medications. Something like…I'm taking back my body. Did I have a bit of control finally? I sought out the new. Massage, acupuncture, meditation, cutting out caffeine (big!), reflexology, walking on the beloved trails around my home and just being with nature, reading more spiritually based books, journaling, continuing with Jazzercise, and more.

The intense pain of the headaches did not leave easily. No, but I was on a new path toward healing my body, heart and soul. I was meeting new practitioners, making new friends, and growing spiritually. Each one gave me something new to try or the encouragement to continue seeking out the healthy aspects of my life. I do believe these headaches were a catalyst to my finding the deep spiritual needs I have in understanding Scott's death, life itself and the body, mind, spirit connection. I trust that anything that creates pain for us has greater meaning and shows up to insist we "Listen!" I turned to many of Louise Hays' books to further my understanding of all of this. There are answers sometimes!

CHAPTER FOURTEEN

THE QUIET

Heavy hearts, like heavy clouds in the sky, are best
relieved by the letting go of a little water.
-ANTOINE RIVAROL

The endless void left in our beloved child's absence remains day and night. When our minds are free from distractions there is a moment when sorrow fills the void, threatening to overtake us, unleashing the torrent of tears. For some, that moment happens during the day, for others it comes at night. What time is hardest for you?

*

ERICA GALE BELTZ
Erica's 5-year-old son Luke Jordan died in 2005
from a fallen banister in his aunt's driveway

The hardest time for me in the beginning was the morning. Even before I knew I was awake yet, I would open my eyes and there seemed to be this incredible space. First darkness and silence. Then I would hear the sounds of morning or see a glimpse of daylight coming through the blinds. It was as if I wasn't even in my own body, kind of like I was watching myself wake up from across the room. There would be confusion or, if I was awake, then more

263

confusion as to whether I was even alive. Once I realized it wasn't just a horrible nightmare, pain would fill every ounce of me and the devastation would set in again. That first hour was exhausting. I would close my eyes and beg God to turn back time, pleading with him to please take me instead of Luke.

*

STACY BERNDTSON
Stacy's daughter Cori Joy died in 2003, the day before her
fourth birthday, from an undiagnosed genetic disorder

In the early days of my grief the days were hardest because Steve was at work and I was home alone. I used to tell him that at least part of his life was the same, while my entire life was changed. From the people who used to fill my life before (physical therapists, occupational therapists, speech therapists, etc.), to my house being empty and my job being over. I felt as if I had been fired from the only job that I ever loved. Days were hard. I had pills I took to get through the night, but there was no pill to get through each day.

*

KARI BROWN
Kari's 2-year-old daughter Dominique (Deedee)
died in 2014 from obstructive sleep apnea

Immediately after the loss of our daughter, the nighttime was usually the difficult time. Dominique slept with us every night due to her medical needs. That very first night, we could not sleep because we felt so empty without her sprawled across the middle of the bed. For the first couple of months I had nightmares of her dying in our arms, and often woke up screaming "No!" The pain of her absence has eased up a little. We keep her toy in the middle of our bed still. If I am really missing her, we wrap her urn in her blanket and put it in the middle.

My day-to-day life has forever changed. It was hard going from staying home to working full-time and attending school. But filling my days with work and school has only strengthened my determination to become a Registered Nurse and help others like Dominique.

*

TANISHA CALDWELL
Tanisha's 23-year-old son Tariq (Jay)
died in a car accident in 2015

Although Jay is the first thing that I think about when I open my eyes, and the last thing when going to sleep at night, my hardest time seems to be at night. When everything in the world has quieted down, my mind seems to stay on Jay. I often wonder what he would be doing now. Would I have talked to him today? Would he have stopped by or texted? I'm not sure if it will change. I think I'll always miss him most and think about him most at nighttime.

*

LYNDA CHELDELIN FELL
Lynda's 15-year-old daughter Aly
died in a car accident in 2009

Every minute was excruciating. But nighttime was by far the hardest. For a very long time after the accident, every afternoon I could feel dread beginning to build as the day's light began to fade. I hated nighttime with every bone in my weary body; the house was simply too quiet and there was nothing to distract me from my profound sorrow. I don't recall the turning point, but eventually the dread subsided until dissipating entirely. Another hard time was dinner. We ate together as a family. We each had a dedicated place at the dinner table, and Aly's vacant chair was like an elephant in the room. Nobody sat there for a long time. Our table is trimmed in ornate carvings which, while beautiful, is a challenge to keep clean from crumbs. One day I was tediously cleaning the hollows filled with debris. Our oldest daughter became very upset

265

when I reached Aly's spot, because I was removing Aly's "food." Never again would Aly's crumbs grace her spot at the dinner table. It was such an empty feeling.

*

JACQUELYN CRUZ
Jacquelyn's 24-year-old daughter Jenna
died in 2012 from pulmonary edema

The most difficult time of day for me is early evening. For weeks after Jenna's passing, every night between 6:15 to 6:30, I felt like I couldn't breathe. I later found out this was the time she started to pass. I found it so amazing that my breathing would also be labored, as hers was. This is the connection between mother and child. Every night at this time I would lose my mind....I desperately want to see her face, hear her voice, anything to make this not real. I would work myself into such a state of hysteria, thinking about how she passed. Was she in pain? Was she scared? Did she understand what was happening to her? Did she think of me? Jenna will be gone three years in November and every night at 6:15 my breathing becomes difficult for a few minutes. I don't even have to look at the clock; I know it's 6:15. I also struggle when I get home from work around 3:30 p.m. Jenna and I both worked for the New York City public school system so we would often get home at the same time. We would prepare dinner and talk about our day, trade war stories, that's what we called them. We worked with special education students and Jenna had a real gift with working with the children who had autism. I was so proud of her! We would have dinner as a family. Chelsea usually worked 5 to 9 p.m. and most nights Danny would be home, and my husband David, and me and Jen. Something that families do all the time without even thinking about it, like myself, has become one of my most precious memories. So you can imagine how difficult those weeks, months and, yes, even years now, have become for me and my family. When the four of us sit down together as a family to eat, it just doesn't seem normal. Something is missing, somebody is missing.

*

MICHELLE DETWILER
Michelle's 19-year-old daughter Emily
died in 2014 due to congenital complications

Early morning has been the most difficult time of day for me because that was when Emily woke up. Usually around 2:30 or 3 a.m. I could hear her moving, coughing, breathing in her room. By 3:30 a.m. Dad was up. He would always go in and see her before he went to work. Occasionally she would go back to sleep, but not usually. So my day always began by 4 a.m.

Some days were easier than others, but the home of a child with disabilities and medical complications is always busy. Even through the busyness of each morning I had been able to set aside a quiet time where I would read the Bible and pray. Now that Emily is gone I fill the early morning hours that I would have been caring for her with caring for myself in quiet time. It seemed to fit, and has helped ease the anxious moments when I don't know what to do with myself.

*

ANNAH ELIZABETH
Annah's son Gavin Michael aspirated on his meconium
during the delivery and died 26 minutes following his birth

Twenty-five years have passed since Gavin's death and though there are some things that I can recall as if they happened twenty-five minutes or twenty-five days ago, there are other things that I can't resurrect. This is one of the latter. The first thought that came to mind when I read the question was "All of them." Every. Minute. Of. Every. Day. But I honestly don't believe that to be true. If I am to step back from the emotion and look at that timeframe objectively, the hardest part of the day depended on any number of random things. The constant ache in my swollen breasts was a stark reminder that my son was gone. How much sleep I had determined how much energy I had to get through the day and how much tolerance I had to face any reminder about the past or the future I wasn't going to have.

What song happened to be playing on the radio. Seeing a stroller someone had tossed to the curb like an unwanted baby might be left in a garbage can. Who phoned me to ask, "How are you doing?" What tone of voice in which that person asked, "How are you doing?" Who avoided the subject of my grief or my dead son. The second I spotted blood on my underwear and Lord only recalls how many hours following the start of my menstruation. Which meant I wasn't pregnant.

The Easter after my son's death, my husband gave me one of those electric bunnies that inch forward, squeak and wiggle its whiskers. I blubbered for hours, and I do mean snot-running-down-your-chin-and-onto-your-clothes sort of crying. My husband had no idea what to do to console me because he'd bought it with good intentions and a feeling that it would bring me joy. That bunny now has a special place on my bedroom bureau.

What I do recall, however, is that the silence of my thoughts was deafening in those early days and months. There were times when I desperately wanted and needed someone to show up and distract me from those torturous memories that replayed without end. And all too often the hours I spent holding on for dear life before someone arrived, or the heart-twisting pain left, were some of the most difficult.

*

WENDY EVANS
Wendy's 21-year-old son Kyle died in 2009
from diabetes when his insulin pump malfunctioned

After we first lost Kyle my hardest time was during the night, right after going to bed. Limited sleep for several months. As time moved forward my difficult time changed to morning. When I feel the sadness coming over me, the first thing I try is to close my eyes and do deep breathing until I feel calm again.

*

BONNIE FORSHEY
Bonnie's 16-year-old son Billy died in 1993
from an overdose of prescription drugs

There is no particular time that is the hardest. I think of him every day, at different times. He was in my life for sixteen years, but will be on my mind and in my heart forever. I cry at different times, even in the car alone. I can cry at the mall, just because I see someone who looks like him, or see some clothing that I know he would love. It does not stop, simply because he is not here. Every day is hard. The holidays and anniversary dates are agonizing. I have learned to go on, but it is not easy.

I miss him on Mother's Day, his birthday, holidays. There are constant reminders everywhere.

*

TALIA GATO
Talia's 8-year-old daughter Poppy
died in 2009 in a car accident

My hardest time of day would have to be the middle of the day when I am all alone going toward the season of winter. I feel much better after January with hopes of spring and summer ahead. I am normally really busy with my daughter, and now my mom is living with us. Still, when there is a free half day with nothing scheduled, I feel empty. And strangely enough I can't seem to focus even though there is a ton of stuff to do to be more productive. I feel more alone without my Poppy, and it is more pronounced on these days. After mid-October I get progressively sad throughout the major holidays and into January, just waiting for my worst month to pass so I can breathe again.

*

DAPHNE GREER
Daphne's 5-year-old daughter Lydia died in 2008 in a
car accident during a routine morning commute

Whether driving in the car or sitting on the couch at home, anytime of day when I am alone is the hardest. For so many years after Lydia died, I kept busy juggling children, work, and activities. I guess you could say I intentionally kept busy to soften the sadness. I became a master at avoidance. In those moments when life stopped, even if just momentarily, my mind immediately wandered to the events of that terrible day. Without fail, the tears would begin to fall like a torrential rain. The stillness held me captive, forcing me to remember, and to experience the reality. I could feel the emptiness as it encroached into my body. Knowing that Lydia wouldn't be walking through the front door every again was terrifying.

For years, being alone terrified me. It meant that I couldn't escape the raw pain; it brought me not only to a place of guilt, but also a place of profound sorrow. As the years continued, my "alone" time has slowly transformed into a peaceful retreat where I allow myself to process life, its purpose, and to replay memories of my beautiful girl. Now it no longer frightens me.

When the sun sets and the darkness arrives, I sometimes still shed silent tears while falling asleep, leaving evidence of those difficult nights on my mascara-stained pillow.

*

KORBY HAVE
Korby's 17-year-old daughter Taylor (Tayla)
died in 2013 in a car accident

I think the hardest time of day is nighttime. When I am done for the day and it's time to relax and go to bed, there is nothing to distract me. I haven't slept well since my daughter's passing because I often lie awake and think about her. Nighttime is when my grief is at its worst. There is no one around to hide the pain from, so it is really the only time I can express it without the fear of hurting or offending anyone.

*

DEANA MARTIN
Deana's only two children, 25-year-old Amanda
and 21-year-old Logan, died in a car accident in 2011

The hardest time of the day for me, almost five years later, is any time of the day that I am triggered or completely exhausted. I now care for my eight-year-old granddaughter and she is my world, my reason for going on every day, but being a new fulltime mom at fifty years old can be tiring. Evening times are very difficult. I am usually doing so many things, multitasking, trying to make dinner, help with homework, fold laundry, attempting to get my granddaughter to help me with things she is capable of doing. It is during this time I miss my daughter so very much, both of them really. I suppose it's more a self-pity and why are they not here to help. I know that sounds selfish, but before Amanda died she lived with me. She and I would do all these things together. Evenings were not only easier, but it was our time together. From when they were small, evenings were our time together. There was always dinner, homework, chores, a half hour for our favorite TV show, usually *Buffy the Vampire Slayer*, we watched it for years.

Even though we were always busy in the evenings with sports and daily routine, we were together. I remember the funny times of the evenings, like peanut butter and jelly sandwiches on the ballfield day after day, and telling Logan to go back to the shower and use soap this time. My mind jumps from year to year like a ping-pong ball. In some ways, my memory of them and their childhood becomes clearer all the time. I suppose my heart and mind are searching for them, and all I can find are memories and maybe for this reason the memories get more vivid.

To be most truthful, every minute of every day is still very hard. If I think about our lives together, my chest hurts as if being crushed by an elephant and I can barely write this due to the tears in my eyes. My heart and soul are shattered and empty without my children. I am only a very small part of who I once was in some respects and a thousand times the woman I was in others. It's all so confusing and all so hard. I miss them with my whole being! I hear again and again that they are here with me and I choose to believe this, but I do have to wonder if they are here and that is why it hurts so bad. Why can't they help more in the hard times? Why can't they whisper in Armaya's ear to be a good girl and not be so hard on Nana? If they do these things, do we not hear them or feel them?

Armaya is still very young. She seems as if she saw them many, many years ago and only a couple of times. Why? Why did she not see them a lot? Some bereaved parents say nighttime is hard, and it was for me in the beginning. I would lie in bed and cry and cry, and ask why and beg for their return until I cried myself to sleep. It never took long because of the sleep medication I took for severe insomnia. Mornings were hard too, waking up to the reality that it was all true. Almost like every day was *Ground Hogs Day*, for those of you that have seen the movie. Each day was just another reminder that they are gone. As hard as I try and as much as I believe they are not "gone," they are simply somewhere else. The sadness clouds my ability to hold on to this. I suppose in a lot of ways we are taught that dead is dead and for all purposes we better say it is or we are considered in denial and might be crazy. To me they are not dead. Their bodies are dead, but they are very much alive somewhere and this is hard, because where is that somewhere? Why can't I call or write? So now after almost five years the hardest time of the day is every minute of every day and the worst times of all are when I am sick or lonely or my resistance is down. When I am at my weakest, why can't they help hold me up? That is when I fall apart the most! It is then that my heart hurts so bad. Still today I can barely breathe, holding my breath between the tears. Every moment is the hardest thing I have ever done.

*

MONICA MIRKES
Monica's 30-year-old daughter Marisa
died in 2013 due to Cesarean complications

Night is the hardest time for me. I stay busy during the day so there is no real time to think. At night I just lie in bed replaying my last conversation with Marisa. Lying there awake...crying....trying not to wake my husband. I just quietly leave the room and go downstairs to watch TV, movie after movie, until I become so exhausted that I can fall asleep without thinking anymore. It has been two years and four months and I still do this. Sleep is just so hard for me.

*

DENISE PURCELL
Denise's 27-year-old daughter Megan died
in 2011 from an accidental overdose

Anytime of day that Megan would pop into my head. A song, picture, even grocery shopping, because that was a good time for us. And at night when I'm alone with my thoughts and silently I weep. It hasn't changed much. I don't think it ever will.

*

MARILYN ROLLINS
Marilyn's 37-year-old son Randy and 16-year-old granddaughter Sara
died in a car accident in 2006 during a family camping trip

Nighttime is easily the hardest for me. Though the nights were an absolute nightmare in the weeks following the accident, even after nine years they remain my worst part of the day. As I get into bed and night falls, the silence comes. With the darkness and the silence, my brain goes into overdrive. I think about my day, I think about tomorrow, I think about my family, and inevitably my thoughts turn to my son and granddaughter. I do most of my crying now at night. My husband always comes to bed after me, so I try to cry when he's not there. Sometimes that doesn't work.

273

One night not long ago, he was already asleep. As I lay there awake, my thoughts went to the night of the accident. I began crying silently at first, burying my head in the pillow so he wouldn't hear me. He woke up, walked over to the window and looked out. I struggled to keep my breathing even and not let him know I had been crying. He said to me, "Did you hear that?" Keeping my back to him, I said, "Hear what?" He said, "It sounded like someone was crying. It was so sad." It was all I could do not to sob out loud. I never told him it was me. I am seldom asleep before 2 a.m. and I am up around 7:30 a.m. I absolutely hate to sleep anywhere else. My physician does give me Ambien, a sleeping medication, in case I need it. I always take it if I am not home in my own bed. I don't like to take it if I don't have to. One night I took it and then ordered something off the internet. I don't remember doing it. I still get teased about that. I've tried meditation, prayers, and melatonin to no avail. When I do sleep, I have nightmares. Though the nightmares are not about the accident or Randy and Sara's death, they are nightmares nonetheless. If my mind does go back to the night of the accident, the memories are hard to stop.

We recently changed the look of our bedroom. There was a picture that used to hang on the wall at the side of my bed. It had hung there for many years. I remember lying in bed facing that picture night after night, after the accident. It finally dawned on me that it had become a trigger. I moved the picture and put some shelves in its place. I've found that if I watch TV, it distracts me and I actually go to sleep more easily. If my husband should turn the TV off, I wake up. He has learned to just leave it alone, turn the volume down and let me sleep.

I always pray that I will dream about them. In the nine years since they died, that has only happened a handful of times. When Randy used to stop by, he would see me and say, "Hi, Ma!" In one particular dream, I looked out my front window and saw him walk down the porch toward the front door. I threw the door open and ran out onto the porch. He grabbed me in a big bear hug, swung me around and said, "Hi, Ma!" I said to him, "Where's Sara?" He said, "Oh, she had to watch a movie." I said, "You have to watch movies in heaven?" That was it, but it seemed so real. A couple of years ago, near Randy's birthday, I again saw him in a dream but this time he was a toddler. I was lying on my back on the floor in the living room of the very first house that we owned, which was where we lived when he was a toddler. He was sitting on my stomach and we were playing. I could describe the pajamas he had on. He leaned forward, holding my face between his little hands, and kissed me. I could see his fuzzy little towhead, I could smell him, I could hear him giggle, I could feel the baby softness of him. Then I woke up. I was so angry! I tried so hard to go back to sleep and hold him again. I always like to think that he chose to come to me like that, because it was a happy, carefree time in our lives. I have only seen Sara in a dream once. It was from a distance, and she waved. She disappeared as I waved back. The nights are long. I'm working on better sleeping habits, but even after so many years, my son and granddaughter are my first thought every morning and last thought every night.

*

KATIE ROUSH
Katie's 26-year-old daughter Krystle
died in 2013 of accidental alcohol poisoning

Night is the hardest. During the day I am busy with work or have my husband home. At night, my husband worked and I was alone at home with my dogs and my thoughts. I don't know how many times I cried myself to sleep. I replayed my daughter's life over and over. I replayed her death too. I imagined so many things and even wondered if she was scared when she knew she was dying. It was torture. It was in these moments that I wrote, talked to her, and prayed to God. Soon, instead of fearing the night, I enjoyed it. It was my quiet time. It was also becoming a time for me to "visit" with my daughter. Tell her things I thought of, and talk as if she were right here with me. Sure, I cried some, but soon I began to laugh as well. I no longer fear the night. Now I embrace it.

*

SARA RUBLE
Sara's 19-year-old son Scott died in 1994 from a
combination of a seizure disorder, Strep throat and dehydration

Grief is not kind. I know it is there to allow us, or to be more honest, force us to express our pain, anguish, anger and all those emotions locked inside our shattered hearts. There was never one particular time of day for me that was the hardest. Life became totally unpredictable and shocking. I would wake up in the morning, if I slept, and know it was one more day without Scott. The agony was so great, so consuming...I felt I could not survive another day.

The evenings would descend on me and the darkness would envelop me. Every waking moment between morning and night could bring unexpected memories or brokenhearted dreams. I never knew if I wanted to be alone or be with others, go someplace or stay home. I was continually caught off guard, and each new day was a reality check. It was a very lonely place to be. In time, with help from my counselor, meeting other bereaved parents, becoming more aware of the depths of grief and the invasive physical aspects of the pain within, I learned to take one day at a time. I learned to open up more about what I was enduring, day in and day out, and to ask for help or just to be heard.

It took time, though, as days turned into years in which I was still caught off guard at times by any number of events such as startling words from others or the hardest days we must get through. But I worked at grief. It was a better alternative to me, rather than let it take over and complicate my already hugely complicated life. I worked for two years after Scott's death. This forced me to get up in the morning, to get out into the world and mingle (or endure) with those whose lives had not been changed forever. Hard? Oh yes. But my alternatives, I see so clearly now, most likely would have diminished me further. I could not stand to go any lower.

Today it has been over twenty years since Scott's sudden death. I trust that those most horrendous mornings, afternoons and nights of my grief were teaching me to hang on, not to give up. I found a strength within me that was deep, very deep, and pushed me to not only endure but to live with the unknowns that often took me down. Life is unpredictable. I have learned to expect the unexpected because that is where I had to live for so long. I will never ever forget how I got to this place. It was hell. And yet now I am strong, more compassionate, resilient and caring. It all has meaning.

*

Valentine's in Heaven
MARILYN ROLLINS

Are there Valentines in Heaven?
Are there Red Hearts everywhere?
Do they line the Golden Streets,
Or is that very rare?

I wish that I could send you one,
Right through Heaven's Gate,
To say how much we miss you,
On this special date.

I'd like to send a Candy Heart,
That is printed, "I Luv U",
And maybe you would whisper back,
"I know, I Luv U too."

*

CHAPTER FIFTEEN

OUR FEAR

The oldest and strongest emotion of mankind is fear, and the oldest and strongest kind of fear is fear of the unknown. -H. P. LOVECRAFT

Fear can cut like a knife and immobilize us like a straitjacket. It whispers to us that our lives will never be the same, our misfortunes will manifest themselves again, and that we are helpless. How do we control our fear, so it doesn't control us?

*

ERICA GALE BELTZ
Erica's 5-year-old son Luke Jordan died in 2005
from a fallen banister in his aunt's driveway

The thing I fear most is having to endure this loss again with my only daughter. The thought that I might lose her one day is paralyzing. It keeps you holding your breath, and a lot of times I just go through the motions in a tunnel or a fog. I'm not sure I realized that could ever happen again in the beginning, because I don't remember it consuming me like it does now. In the beginning I honestly didn't believe I would physically survive the loss of my son. I held my hand over my chest for at least six months; I feared it would burst right out of my body. I feared that I wouldn't live long enough to ensure that Luke would always be remembered and honored in the way he deserved.

Once I realized I would keep breathing, I feared I didn't have the strength to go on living without him. I was afraid of leaving behind my sweet daughter who I couldn't be there for. I feared never seeing my son again and that everything I was blessed with would be disgraced by my weakness. I feared I could never start to face the fact that I failed to keep him safe. I feared life would never have hope again. I feared everything. I feared waking up and repeatedly feeling the loss. I'm so thankful that these fears shift and change, for they keep moving you through the darkness. I fear losing Luke and the memories fading away. I fear finding the peace in things as they come. I fear falling short and not keeping my family safe now.

*

STACY BERNDTSON
Stacy's daughter Cori Joy died in 2003, the day before her
fourth birthday, from an undiagnosed genetic disorder

I am most afraid of losing Molly and Steve. My mom died when I was twenty-three. My dad died when I was thirty-six. My first husband walked away one day and never returned. Cori Joy died. As much as I fight not to dwell upon it, I do feel like all the people I love have left me. Without God's help I feel sometimes that I could easily take the slippery slope into paralyzing fear. Hardly a day goes by that I do not pray that God would protect my two remaining precious ones. I'm the person who has her husband call when he gets to his destination, whether that be a business trip to Seattle or taking the utility trailer to the dump! We pray out loud on our way to school each day that God will protect Molly.

Often I hear of someone who had one tragedy happen in their life, and then there is a second one. I do not believe I would be left standing if that happened to me. I know there are those who say the same thing about losing a child, and the answer always is, "It isn't like you had a choice. You just keep breathing even when you can't believe you could." But there is something in me that knows that should anything happen to Steve or Molly. Well, I just can't even really go there.

*

TANISHA CALDWELL
Tanisha's 23-year-old son Tariq (Jay)
died in a car accident in 2015

The thing I fear the most right now is losing another child. I have two left. Many days I get anxiety thinking about it. I fear for their safety many times. The fear has eased up a little. I'm learning to just continually keep them in prayer, asking that God just keep them safe. I can't even fathom the thought of losing another child!

*

LYNDA CHELDELIN FELL
Lynda's 15-year-old daughter Aly
died in a car accident in 2009

In the beginning, I was most afraid that the crushing sadness would never ease. My world had instantly become void of all color and beauty, and I was petrified they would never return. And then I became exceedingly afraid I would lose another child. When our youngest was in high school, I was terribly anxious until his car turned into the driveway at the end of each school day. Even though the kids are now adults, to this day I get almost unbearable anxiety when they are out on the road.

Less than three years after Aly's accident, my dear sweet husband suffered a debilitating stroke. So then, of course, I was petrified that I would lose him too. Initially, we didn't know whether he would survive. But he did, and after eighteen days in the hospital he was discharged home to begin outpatient rehab. I was petrified! While in the hospital, I knew he was in good hands. But when he came home, what if he died on my watch?! For months

I watched my husband sleep at night, nervous that he would quit breathing. My life was consumed by anxiety over losing someone else, though I fought hard to hide it from my family. They had been through so much already, they didn't need a "nervous Nellie" making things worse. It's been over six years since Aly's accident and three years since my husband's stroke. Although I don't allow it to dictate my life, I remain fearful that lightning might strike twice.

*

JACQUELYN CRUZ
Jacquelyn's 24-year-old daughter Jenna
died in 2012 from pulmonary edema

I am most afraid that people will forget about Jenna. They will forget about how funny she was or forget the sound of her great laugh. I'm afraid that my children will stop saying her name and stop telling stories about when Jenna was here. I fear they will not tell funny stories to their future children about how great their aunt Jenna was. I want them to tell their children what a great childhood they had together.

*

MICHELLE DETWILER
Michelle's 19-year-old daughter Emily
died in 2014 due to congenital complications

I am now more sensitive to loss of any kind. I don't want to be, but I guess once you've been there the fear of loss, at least for me, looms in the shadows. I know life is moment to moment, breath to breath. I don't want to miss any moments that can be saved. How does one keep from holding too tight to other family members? Life is in God's hands. I know this. Putting that knowledge into practice is more difficult. But new doors are opening and I'm learning. I don't want to be held hostage by the loss. So I choose not to. But it's a daily choice, and not always easy. This is where my faith in God

282

comes in. He is able to carry me, especially when I'm afraid. My fear is conquered in the knowledge that God lives, heaven is real, and neither life nor death can separate me from His love!

*

ANNAH ELIZABETH
Annah's son Gavin Michael aspirated on his meconium
during the delivery and died 26 minutes following his birth

This is a layered response. I do know, without a shadow of doubt, that we cannot—CANNOT—prevent tragedy or misfortune from happening. We can do everything right and still face devastating events. Every day random things happen, like planes landing on houses and killing someone who just happened to take a nap on the couch. RANDOM.

When my children were toddlers, many people made references that felt like they wanted me to smother my children, not allowing them to experience things, to learn their own lessons. People who knew about Gavin's death seemed to think that by becoming overprotective I could somehow shield my children from harm. I knew better and I didn't want my children living a life of fear because their brother died from some freak thing.

That said, if I dig deep into some of the emotion behind some of my decisions, it was the fear of something happening to them that drove my thoughts. Because I was so in tune with that line of thinking, however, more often than not I was able to stop that mind chatter from taking over.

*

WENDY EVANS
Wendy's 21-year-old son Kyle died in 2009
from diabetes when his insulin pump malfunctioned

I am most afraid my son will be forgotten, or losing another child.

*

BONNIE FORSHEY
Bonnie's 16-year-old son Billy died in 1993
from an overdose of prescription drugs

I am afraid of losing another child. It is so abnormal and very hard to cope with. I am afraid that I will never see him again.

*

TALIA GATO
Talia's 8-year-old daughter Poppy
died in 2009 in a car accident

I used to have a fear of our country going under financial collapse. Now I know I went through the worst: the loss of a child....that moment when your world, my world, collapsed. Everything has changed from that one life-altering event. Lots of worries I had before now seem trivial, and they still seem trivial: people complaining of this and that, their kids, politics, things like that. I have refocused on what is important. I guess I do fear losing my second daughter. But I try not to think of that, and take each day in stride and hope for the best.

*

KORBY HAVE
Korby's 17-year-old daughter Taylor (Tayla)
died in 2013 in a car accident

The thing that I am most afraid of is losing another child. I am constantly worrying about my other children, especially when they are out of my sight. I have a hard time allowing my oldest son to go off on his own and I always assume the worst when I can't get hold of them.

*

DEANA MARTIN
Deana's only two children, 25-year-old Amanda
and 21-year-old Logan, died in a car accident in 2011

It's been almost five years since my children were killed, and my fears are many. Fears of losing my granddaughter, as she is all I have left of my daughter; the fear is huge and real. Losing her to death is sometimes more than I can bear; I don't believe I would survive another funeral.

I also fear losing her to her father. His lifestyle can be destructive, and my daughter bore the brunt at times. I fought hard to hold on to my granddaughter. She has lived with me since before my daughter died, so this is her home and she would be beyond devastated to leave it. These fears are real. I promised my daughter, as she lay in her coffin, I would protect her daughter. I promised her brother as well, for he treasured this little girl. Why is life so hard?

I am also desperately afraid that my children will be forgotten. I work so hard to keep their memory alive. I know there are many in this generation who will always remember them, but then it is as if my life skips a generation. And I know there are very few in my granddaughter's generation who will remember my children vividly. One of their nephews was old enough, and he loved them so. But he alone cannot carry on the legacy of two people he loved but who died when he was in his pre-teens. There is no one after my children's generation that can carry on their amazing lives and spirits, not even my granddaughter, because she was three when they died.

I know that so many parents who have lost children face this fear. It almost makes me physically ill at times and paralyzes me. What does this mean? Does it mean that when their memories die, so do I? Does this mean I have nothing to leave the world, nothing to show for my twenty-five years of hard work during motherhood? I know I am the closest thing to a mother my granddaughter knows. She will remember me but, due to the age difference, her children more than likely won't know me well. The missing generation is like a missing link. My daughter always called me the strongest link in our family chain. Little did she know that a chain is broken no matter where it is broken, and each and every link is just as strong as the other. A family chain of three links that is missing two of its links is no longer a family chain. It is a broken heap of metal on the floor! There is no longer a chain to hold things together. We were only as strong as the sum of our parts.

Dear world, don't forget them, please!

*

MONICA MIRKES
Monica's 30-year-old daughter Marisa
died in 2013 due to Cesarean complications

What I was most afraid of has happened. I lost my child. There is nothing that can come close to that. The hardest part is trying to live without her. Hoping that I will be able to keep her memory alive for her son. How will he ever know his mommy? How hard she fought to have him. How she desperately wanted to be able to hold him and care for him. How am I supposed to do this?

My new fear now, as his daddy starts to date, is whether we will still be part of his life. Her brothers and sister want to be a part of his life too. The "what ifs" can be terrifying.

*

DENISE PURCELL
Denise's 27-year-old daughter Megan died
in 2011 from an accidental overdose

I have a fear that one of my other daughters will die. Going off to college in a different state, just allowing them to be on their own is fearful to me. I, as a parent, thought I could protect them. I did everything right and it still wasn't enough.

*

MARILYN ROLLINS
Marilyn's 37-year-old son Randy and 16-year-old granddaughter Sara
died in a car accident in 2006 during a family camping trip

I would have to say that my worst fear would be to lose another child or another grandchild. In my grief support group, I have heard people say that there is nothing that could happen to them that could be worse than what they had already been through. I can't agree with that, because I have another child and six other grandchildren. I know two people within that group that this has happened to. Yes, they lost two children at different times. It terrifies me!

My surviving son is forty-five years old, a grown man with four children of his own. But if he tells me that he will be at my house at a certain time and he doesn't show up at that time, I am a basket case. My mind fast forwards through every tragic plot that my mind will allow. I pace my living room, trying to reach him on his cellphone.

I am a nurse and I worked in pediatrics for many years and then for a family practice physician for many more. I used to be so calm during an emergency or if someone in my family was ill. This is no longer true. If one of the grandchildren runs a fever, or cough or has a rash, I panic. I tell my son that he needs to take him or her to the emergency room. While my brain still goes over the signs and symptoms and tells me it is not an emergency, my heart screams, "What if I'm wrong?!" Thank God my son remains calm.

I know that these are irrational thoughts and that they are typical of anxiety. I tell myself that I couldn't do it again. I couldn't bury another child or grandchild. Of course, I also know that sometimes it happens and we do keep on breathing. We get up each day and put one foot in front of the other.

Another loss that I fear is the possible loss of my husband, and that fear has been so much more exaggerated over the last few years. I don't know how I could survive without him. He has always been my protector, but now he is my rock. He knows what I feel because he feels it too. He buried a child and grandchild too. I can scream and cry and stomp, and he gets it. He just opens his arms, wraps them around me and holds me tight. We can share our memories and no one rolls their eyes. I look at him and know that this journey into grief has taken its toll. I wonder if he notices the same when he looks at me.

Last spring I attended a Cry For Me, No More grief recovery workshop. I actually went with a friend who had lost her son three years ago, and was having a very difficult time. One of the ladies who founded Cry For Me, No More is another co-author of this book, Deana Martin. I was so surprised at the feelings that came out over that weekend. After almost nine years, I thought I knew all about grief and how to get through it. But this was not just about grief, but about people and what grief does to them. They gave me tools I've never had before to deal with feelings that I didn't know how to deal with.

Many changes came after that weekend. I made some promises and so far have kept them, beginning with a date night at least once a month with my husband. I have been somewhat calmer, though I still have my moments. I would recommend this workshop to anyone who has lost a child. They are amazing people who know their stuff.

You do have to work at recovery. I think many of us just wait for our grief to go away, and that isn't going to happen. It is a lifetime sentence. We have to work at having a life again. Our children would want that, they do want that. I try to replace each bad memory of that awful night with a good one, from all the years we had together. Eventually, the good ones win out. There is no normal anymore. I don't even know if there is a new normal, but there is life and maybe it is time to live it.

*
KATIE ROUSH
Katie's 26-year-old daughter Krystle
died in 2013 of accidental alcohol poisoning

I am most fearful of not having enough time. Funny that I would say that now, huh? If I had been asked this two years ago, I would have said I am most fearful of losing someone I love. But time has acted like a salve over my broken heart.

Now I want to make sure that I make the most of the life I have left. I make sure I honor my daughter by living in the moment and living each moment well. I want to celebrate her short life by living fully with the people I love. So I am worried about not having enough time for me with those I love. I want to share everything with them. I want to make sure I am making memories with my grandchildren. I want to make sure I leave a legacy of laughter for my husband. I want to make sure each person who is dear to me knows without a doubt how much I love them. I always say "I love you" and do little things to make them feel it too. When my time comes, I want them to have had "enough."

*
SARA RUBLE
Sara's 19-year-old son Scott died in 1994 from a
combination of a seizure disorder, Strep throat and dehydration

Fear is such a big part of grief. There are so many ways to feel it. In the beginning of my journey into and through grief I was concerned for Scott's safety. I valued his life more than mine…I had to keep him safe. How do we do that after death? I knew so little and felt so much. My fears grew as I felt the distance between us grow. Where are you?! Are you okay? Are you with God, Scott…and safe? What are you doing? Can you hear me? Did I let you down? And so many more concerns that filled my day with angst and feelings of the unknown.

My biggest fear was Scott moving away from me. His being "somewhere else" and my not hearing from him, as I so begged for, scared me. And every year it seemed he could be further away from me, from our love, our connection. With Scott being my only child, it created such an emptiness in me…I felt incredibly desperate.

In time I began to see that Scott was somehow communicating with me. The signs and dreams came and showed me a bigger picture, inviting me to see that the connection Scott and I shared in life had not been severed as I had feared. My constant fears were lessened with each sign, and yet there was always that needy part of me wanting more. I grew to accept what was, because I had no control over the connection I had with Scott now…other than to love him. I knew he was directing the communication from where he was…and I knew it was truly spiritual.

My fears were fully present within me, I now know, to push me to accept the reality of Scott's death: his being "gone." As the signs and dreams revealed bits and pieces of our history, I could be more open to other aspects of our spiritual connection rather than the human connection I had known, loved, and desperately missed with my whole being. I guess I surrendered to that which was now providing me with answers. And as I did that, I was shown more of the mystery of the spiritual bond we share with our loved ones.

The grief journey is so complex, and I learned it is ever changing too. My grief turned to the spiritual because it provided me with so much more to hang on to, to see an ongoing relationship with Scott, to bring greater meaning to death, and what happens beyond when we leave our bodies. My deep fears were needed, I understand now, to push and literally shove me into looking for answers, to seek help, to listen, to believe in something new when I was so frightened of a future without Scott. I gratefully see more now and trust in an afterlife that has created an incredible new relationship for us.

*

CHAPTER SIXTEEN

OUR COMFORT

Life is made up, not of great sacrifices or duties, but of little things, in which smiles and kindness, and small obligations given habitually, are what preserve the heart and secure comfort. -HUMPHRY DAVY

Transition sometimes feels as if we have embarked on a foreign journey with no companion, compass, or light. Rather than fill our bag with necessities, we often seek to fill it with emotional items that bring us comfort as we find our way through the eye of the storm. What items or rituals bring you the most comfort?

*

ERICA GALE BELTZ
Erica's 5-year-old son Luke Jordan died in 2005
from a fallen banister in his aunt's driveway

Honestly, what brings me the most comfort is that I was chosen to be Luke's mom. I'll never understand why God blessed me with a love as great as Luke's. There were times when he was alive that it was truly like he was Jesus. He was precious and pure in heart. He was kind and had an old soul. I see him in all things. On sunny days and when the seasons change, he is always near. I celebrate Luke's life and share him any chance I have. I love to see his things.

I often speak of him and say the funny things that he would say. He appreciated every moment and it brings me great comfort to talk about him.

I spend a lot of time with Luke's cousin Preston. I like to hear the things that are going on in his life and think about how much Luke would love them too. I try to do the things that Luke loved to do and it keeps me close to him. I love to watch his other cousin play baseball and imagine what a game in heaven might be like. I guess it's changed in the years that have passed but keeping him a part of each day has kept me smiling.

I love to share Luke with my granddaughter and watch her play with his things. It melts my heart the way his second cousin Ryan loves him too. I have a quilt made out of Luke's favorite shirts and PJs that anyone can snuggle with at any time. I keep Luke's pictures in my current photos, so I see them often. I keep a CD of his favorite songs that I play as much as I can, especially when I am missing him. I have a special place in my heart for little boys who are around the age Luke was when he left this earth.

I love how my mama holds Luke's things as treasures, and always seems to surprise me with a trinket or toy I had forgotten about. I love to hear his Aunt Christy and Uncle Bill talk about him. They light up when they share a memory of Luke. I love to tell Luke about his sister's life and tell him what an amazing young woman she has become. I love that my boyfriend Adam loves Luke, Lakin and my granddaughter, Ava, the way he does.

*

STACY BERNDTSON
Stacy's daughter Cori Joy died in 2003, the day before her
fourth birthday, from an undiagnosed genetic disorder

I am comforted by the people I have met along the way who are also on this grief journey. In the early days, it was the women who were farther along in time than I was, those who told me the pain would not always take my breath away. I was able to put some measure of hope in the knowledge that if they had been where I was once, and they were doing better in "x" months or years, maybe that would be me too.

Now, since it has been nearly twelve years since Cori went to heaven, I still find comfort in knowing I am not alone in this thing called grief, and am thankful for social media giving us the ability to connect with other sojourners. Everyone in your life goes back to their own lives pretty quickly. For a few years, a couple of people would remember without me reminding them. Now, however, if I were not to remind them by my Facebook pictures or postings, I do not know if there is anyone who would remember Cori's "days." And, to be honest, sometimes when I post I worry that some may think it a plea for sympathy or something.

However, all the folks in the various grief groups I am part of, they GET it. I KNOW they do not think I am seeking sympathy but that sometimes I just need to SAY her name, in essence confirm out loud: SHE. ONCE. WAS.

Most of all, I am comforted by the biblical promises that I believe with every fiber of my being. That there is a place where she lives and breathes and that one day I will once again hold a real girl, MY girl, in my arms once again.

*

KARI BROWN
Kari's 2-year-old daughter Dominique (Deedee)
died in 2014 from obstructive sleep apnea

I carry some of Dominique's very small toys in my purse; that brings me some comfort. I also keep a picture of her in my car and at work, a visual reminder of the happiness that she brought into our lives. I also found writing to her on the days I miss her most helps to ease my aching heart. Though I don't get a response back, I feel somewhat better knowing I have something to remember our "conversations" by. Keeping a few of her things around our apartment has brought some comfort as well; they are a visual reminder of the things she loved. At first I did not want to share any of Dominique's belongings with anyone. But I found it brought bittersweet comfort; another child using or playing with her belongings creates a connection of sorts between that child and Dominique, as if I was sharing Dominique's love with that child and his or her family. I share now, because I want to see more of the connections that Dominique always had with people. She would share her things even if it was her favorite toy, and I felt selfish if I did not do the same. So most of Dominique's belongings bring comfort, especially her clothing that now hangs in our closet; they still smell like her.

*

TANISHA CALDWELL
Tanisha's 23-year-old son Tariq (Jay)
died in a car accident in 2015

I find comfort in praying and in reading God's word. I also find comfort in looking at photos of my son, and wearing his sweatshirts or his hats and caps. When wearing those things I feel like I have a part of him with me.

*

LYNDA CHELDELIN FELL
Lynda's 15-year-old daughter Aly
died in a car accident in 2009

In the beginning, what brought me comfort one day might bring me pain the next. There was no rhyme or reason to it. There was a time when going into Aly's room was comforting, but then it became painful, and now it brings me comfort again. I found that a nicely scented candle helped to soften the rawness, because Aly and I shared a love of candles. For years, my husband and I carried small blue glass hearts in our coat pockets.

One morning shortly after the accident while we were sitting in a daze on the concrete patio, my sister warmed a pair of luxury socks in the dryer and then knelt before me to put them on my feet. I had never owned luxury socks, so their warmth and softness felt incredible. It was such a loving gesture on my sister's part. To this day, I don a pair of luxury socks when my heart feels raw.

Aly always wrapped herself in a giant fuzzy blue blanket as her daddy drove her to 5 a.m. swim practice, and then she wrapped herself with it on the way home from evening practice. When I'm on my knees in grief, I wrap her blanket around me. In the beginning, I slept with that blanket for the longest time. I still sleep with one of her other blankets that she favored, but it isn't quite as big and bulky.

I love when someone brings Aly's name up in conversation to share a memory that makes us all laugh. I love seeing a new photo of Aly I hadn't seen before, a photo one of her friends might have stored in their phone and it just now comes to light. I love when I see butterflies, and I wonder if she is coming to visit me. I love getting a sign from her that encourages me to keep going.

What brings me the most comfort, though, is helping others. We all hold the power to make a difference in someone's life in a single moment by one word, one smile, one gesture. And offering a random act of kindness to someone in need is a powerful way to help heal my own heart.

*

JACQUELYN CRUZ
Jacquelyn's 24-year-old daughter Jenna
died in 2012 from pulmonary edema

Not many things bring me comfort. If I wear one of Jenna's T-shirts I feel sad. If I look at her picture, I cry. I still have a difficult time looking at pictures of her when she is an adult. I have a video on my phone of her that I've watched three times in three years. Some people can have pictures all around them, but I just can't yet.

I have a very small angel made from stone that says, "I will never leave you." My sister gave it to me; I carry it at all times. I have a small box (like a pillbox) with some of Jenna's ashes. I hope one day I will be able to watch all the videos we took of vacations, block parties, birthdays and holidays. For now, I'll just take comfort in knowing that she's always by my side.

*

MICHELLE DETWILER
Michelle's 19-year-old daughter Emily
died in 2014 due to congenital complications

Comfort is difficult to come by when you are grieving. Just as grief comes in different levels, so does my comfort. In the beginning I needed to find my daughter's scent. It was in some of her clothing and blankets, but it was quickly fading. At times I still hold on to her favorite stuffed animal, which helps to carry me through a rough patch. Comfort also arrives from family and friends. On days that are sad and almost too heavy to bear I send a note to a friend or two. They have been here where I am, and they understand. It helps that my friends also pray for me. I know that when I cannot hold myself up, they will.

We went on a mini vacation this year. I brought a bit of our girl with us, in a sense, by bringing one of her favorite Pooh characters. It was a miniature stuffed Piglet in a Tigger suit. His name is Tiglet. He was small enough to put in my purse to carry around, but it didn't take long for me to attach him to my necklace and wear him like a charm. Each time I saw something that I knew she would have liked I grabbed my Tiglet charm. And even when I cried, I could hold on to Tiglet and take comfort knowing that she is in her new vacation spot, enjoying the sun, enjoying her new life.

*

ANNAH ELIZABETH
Annah's son Gavin Michael aspirated on his meconium
during the delivery and died 26 minutes following his birth

Knowing that people care, that people are compassionate even if they haven't experienced what I'm going through is one of the biggest things that gives me comfort. For me, it's the little things that have the biggest effect: the phone call or the unexpected notecard that arrives in the mail, with messages that say, "Just thinking about you." Any gesture that says, "I remember Gavin. Gavin's life matters. I'll never forget." Probably the greatest comforts, though, were the connections and sources of inspiration I encountered. I now find solace in knowing that my story and my experiences have helped and continue to help others along the paths of their own journey to healing.

*

WENDY EVANS
Wendy's 21-year-old son Kyle died in 2009
from diabetes when his insulin pump malfunctioned

Information brings me comfort. Watching a podcast from The Compassionate Friends or talking with a fellow grieving mother is the most comforting to me. I also like to watch movies that are based on parents trying to get to a better place after the death of a child. *Down the Rabbit Hole* is a good example.

*

BONNIE FORSHEY
Bonnie's 16-year-old son Billy died in 1993
from an overdose of prescription drugs

I love photos of my son, they are all I have left of his life. My photos bring me comfort. My grandsons bring me comfort, because they look and act like him. My daughter brings me comfort because she is my child.

*

TALIA GATO
Talia's 8-year-old daughter Poppy
died in 2009 in a car accident

What gives me the most comfort? Going to the cemetery weekly, as Poppy is close by. Joining a support group. I go to three now, it's what I need. I don't get to talk much about loss in my family of friends, especially not with family. At times it's like Poppy never existed.

Gardening is comforting and therapeutic. Seeing her photos is heart-wrenching, but I am so glad I have them. Travel now is refreshing even though Poppy is missing, like the first half of every vacation feels sad although it's a nice distraction at the same time.

I like seeing Poppy's clothes and artwork in the rooms. Soon I will have a large photo up. In my garage I am painting a very nontraditional color for a garage. It is bright blue, and I write and paint poems that I find moving to my soul. They have to do with loss and grief, and it is wonderfully comforting to me. I am sure when people see it they think I am crazy. I am getting used to that though.

What brings me the most comfort is talking to others in the same boat as me. The real conversations of what it's like to be in the tribe of loss. Then I don't feel crazy anymore and that I am okay, that I will survive this. There is inner strength in this, though it takes a while to realize that you can survive. To have your voice heard and to be listened to without correction and without minimizing or to fix it is so healing. That's what comforts me.

*

KORBY HAVE
Korby's 17-year-old daughter Taylor (Tayla)
died in 2013 in a car accident

I find comfort in being able to decorate my daughter's grave with things she would have liked and by making sure that it stands out like she would. I love spending time searching for items to add to her grave, and maintaining it allows me to feel like I am doing something to help keep her memory alive. I also find comfort in rewatching the YouTube videos that were made in her honor. I love seeing her pictures and am grateful that she loved taking pictures of herself, so I have a lot of reminders.

*

DEANA MARTIN
Deana's only two children, 25-year-old Amanda
and 21-year-old Logan, died in a car accident in 2011

Very little brings me comfort now that my children are dead, and even less brings me joy. The only times I feel either, truly, without part of it being one of millions of masks I now own and wear, is when I hold my granddaughter or I am living my children's legacy by helping other grieving families.

I also find great comfort in being surrounded by those who love my children such as their family, my son's fraternity brothers and friends, my cousins who knew them. Since the death of my children, with the help of a beautiful woman we have created a nonprofit called Cry For Me, No More to help people who are grieving. Grief is a societal disease; the taboo of death and grief!

Often other countries have rituals, families and society rally around the grieving. They don't abandon them. I know this is not the experience of all. I don't mean to be exclusive here, but it is the experience of many. We are left isolated and alone in pain after the funeral. We are expected to go on as if nothing has happened. Often we are ignored because no one knows what to say or do. We are at times told to "get over it" and "go on." Can someone explain to me how someone who has lost a portion of her family or their entire family is supposed to do that? Take it from me, no one out there knows. They can sit and listen to you in offices from across a desk or room for large amounts of money. They can tell you it will get easier, they can tell you that your memory and energy may or may not come back. They can tell you that the severe insomnia, depression, anxiety and physical pain might be helped by this pill or that. They unfortunately cannot tell you what only we as grieving parents know: a part of us is dead, a part of us died the day our child or children died, this part will never return or heal.

If we are fortunate and work hard, a scab will form, but it is a delicate scab and the wound can easily reopen and it will at times. Only we know that we will not "get over it," we will not "go on." We will find some activities and actions that bring us comfort throughout the years. The things that bring us comfort today may not tomorrow, and at times we still will find no comfort on certain days. We have found our way out of the darkest pit that could ever exist in the human psyche. The only thing I can think of that could even compare would be the life of a prisoner in a concentration camp who watched as family members were taken away one by one, and have no idea of their own fate. Each day is faced with uncertainty and starvation. In their case it is starvation of the physical body and emotional will to live. In our case, it is starvation of our joy, hearts and spirits.

Going on five years since my children died, knowing that I can help one person in pain find that first step of that ladder out of that dark pit of despair brings me as much comfort as anything can. To coin a phrase by a dear brother in grief, Mitch Carmody, it is called "proactive grief." If one can find a way to channel the love of their child to others and to help others, through their own experience and the legacies their child left, this seems to bring many bereaved parents comfort.

I find hope in my actions of proactive grief, in my service to humanity through my children's love and life. Does this remove the pain? No. But after utilizing proactive grief and sharing my love and my child's legacy with those in pain, it can open slight holes in the scab, or it can irritate it a little. However, the knowledge of the healing paid forward slowly, slowly is causing healing to take place. I have the innate knowingness that the scar will always be there.

I have been told that a healed bone is stronger in the area where it broke than any other place on the bone. This healing of the broken bone happens around the five-year mark. I can see evidence of being stronger in some areas almost five years out, and doors have opened and people have come into my life who understand that there will always be that scar, and it will always be tender at times. And they know full well that if re-traumatized, it could be torn completely open in the blink of an eye. The knowing, wise people bring me comfort as well.

*

MONICA MIRKES
Monica's 30-year-old daughter Marisa
died in 2013 due to Cesarean complications

I have Marisa's iPod in my car. Listening to the music she liked and picked out makes me feel close to her.

*

DENISE PURCELL
Denise's 27-year-old daughter Megan died
in 2011 from an accidental overdose

Knowing that Megan is always with me brings me comfort. If I need to connect on a deeper level, I will hold her ashes, look at her photos and listen to a CD she made for me one Mother's Day. It is nearing the four-year anniversary. It just sits with me like a thief in the night, waiting to open the wound once again.

301

*

MARILYN ROLLINS

Marilyn's 37-year-old son Randy and 16-year-old granddaughter Sara
died in a car accident in 2006 during a family camping trip

This is a very difficult question. Comfort is something I don't seem to have had a lot of in the last several years. I am comfortable, I have enough to eat, I have a roof over my head, I have a vehicle and a monthly income. I have been comforted in the moment and over the years. But as I sit here, trying to figure out what brings me comfort, I draw a blank. I sat here in front of my computer for very long time. Finally, thinking that I wasn't going to come up with an answer, I began looking through files on my computer. I can be very easily distracted, especially if I'm dealing with something difficult. This was one of those times.

I clicked on different programs, games, and finally went to "My Files" to see what folders were there. Wow, I have a lot of junk on my computer. I clicked on "My Pictures" and saw the hundreds of subfolders that I had there. I clicked on the one named "Randy." It opened, and I immediately saw all his school pictures. I smiled as I saw his little kindergarten face staring back at me. I studied the pictures from kindergarten through his senior year. I reached up and touched his face on my computer screen. I opened the folder I had named "Sara" and I saw her shy smile as she posed with her third birthday cake. I saw the excitement on her face as she opened up the box with the shoe skates I had gotten her for her ninth birthday. My eyes overflowed with tears as I saw her with her sixteenth birthday cake, the last birthday we would have together.

That is when it dawned on me. It's the memories that bring me comfort. The memories of the everyday things. These pictures, and all these folders, open my mind to all the good times. As I looked through them, I remembered things that I thought I had forgotten. For a long time after the accident, I couldn't look at photos of them at all. It was over a year, maybe two, before I could look at them again. It was my scrapbooking that brought me back to them. It hurt so much at first, knowing there would be no further pictures. I began going through them and sorting them, because most of them were actual prints taken in the pre-digital era. As I went through the sorting process and began scanning them, I found a hunger that I didn't know I had. I wanted to see their faces, I wanted to remember every detail of every story that each picture told. These were it. There would never be another one. My son and granddaughter's lives were in these photos. Today, we have our cameras with us every day, on our phones. We snap pictures of everything, including ourselves. People take their picture taking and their pictures for granted. I am saving and protecting each and every precious memory. I have them on my phone, computer, an external hard drive, and in the cloud, not to mention the ones that I am scrapping. They may be all that I have left some day.

Yes, it's the memories that comfort me.

*

KATIE ROUSH
Katie's 26-year-old daughter Krystle
died in 2013 of accidental alcohol poisoning

When I am missing my daughter, I pull open the drawer where I have a few pieces of her clothes. Her scent is still in them. I will just hold her shirts up to my cheek and breathe her in. I close my eyes and just remember her face, her laugh, her voice, the way she tilted her head to one side as she thought about something. And yes, I cry. I cry for the things she was and will never be. I cry for the smiles and the laughter I will never see in person again. It is a bittersweet thing. I also carry her ashes in a memory necklace that I wear. I feel she is always with me, still riding along with me when I go to the craft store or just visiting places we used to go. I don't pull out that drawer much anymore. I don't want to cry anymore. I want to remember the silly things, the funny things that my Krystle was. I want to remember my daughter's life and celebrate that, not be stuck on her death.

*

SARA RUBLE
Sara's 19-year-old son Scott died in 1994 from a
combination of a seizure disorder, Strep throat and dehydration

I have found great comfort through the years from Scott's personal items. Sweet and funny cards he gave me in his teenage handwriting filled with our signature message…xoxoxoxoxoxo. I have his favorite football jersey hanging in my closet, Smurfs smiling at me all over the house, and one of his favorite stuffed dogs, Toby, on our bed. The list is endless, as I needed every item, every memory to be there for me to see, touch, remember. A huge source of comfort for me is a beautiful collage with twenty photos of Scott, ranging from his sweet baby pictures to the handsome nineteen-year-old he was. Seeing that collage every day, filled with his life experiences and smiles looking back at me, reassures me that this child came into this world and lived fully. As incredibly sad and devastating as it was in the beginning to know there would be no more pictures, memories, experiences, or laughter with Scott, I treasure this collage and all that Scott brought to me. He made me a mom. I'm forever grateful for what I had with him. In all the ways I found to feel close to Scott, there is one piece of jewelry I had made that has been so significant for me. It is a lasting source of comfort and still feels so perfect. Two aquamarine stones flank a center diamond in a beautiful yet truly meaningful ring. The aquamarines are Scott's birthstone and they represent his much anticipated March birth and his amazing life. These birthstones are the indicators of my joy, my never-ending love, my pain, my need to learn and grow, my reminder of the past and the present…all housed in one simple ring. When asked about this lovely ring, I am able to share about Scott, his death and his life. It opens up conversations and brings Scott to life again as well as allowing me to share my grief with others. I had not anticipated this, but the need to have something that would always be with me and would keep Scott close was my initial thought. I wear it every day and it is, for me, a perfect source of comfort. He existed. Yes, he was here.

CHAPTER SEVENTEEN

OUR SILVER LINING

Even a small star shines in darkness.
-FINNISH PROVERB

In the earliest days following loss, the thought that anything good can come from our experience is beyond comprehension. Yet some say there are blessings in everything. Whether one's loss reveals the kindness of a stranger or becomes the fuel to unfurl a new leaf, each silver lining, no matter how small, yields a light in the darkness. Have you discovered a silver lining in your loss?

*

STACY BERNDTSON
Stacy's daughter Cori Joy died in 2003, the day before her fourth birthday, from an undiagnosed genetic disorder

There is no day that I am not aware that my family is not whole. I will miss Corinne Joy Berndtson until the day in which I once again hold her in my arms (for I WILL do just that). However, there is also no denying that were it not for our loss of that precious child, the precious child I just watched do her math in the third grade classroom in which I was just volunteering, would not be called MINE. SHE is our silver lining.

305

Cori was our biological child after nearly ten years of marriage and various attempts at parenthood failed. Her birth was traumatic and her life was medically fragile. But JOY? That girl was the embodiment of her middle name. I once found a print of a blonde female figure and it was titled "She, who brings me joy." That was Cori Joy. A smile on her face for nearly every one of her three years and 364 days. Her death brought sorrow like I had never known before. Loneliness, despair. But it was the JOY she took with her that nearly did me in.

When Molly Faith was born just over four years later to another woman, and the nurse put her into my arms, JOY came back. If I could draw, I would draw a similar picture of a female figure and it would be titled "She, who brought joy back to me."

*

TANISHA CALDWELL
Tanisha's 23-year-old son Tariq (Jay)
died in a car accident in 2015

I haven't found a silver lining just yet, maybe because my grief is still so new. However, I do feel like I've grown closer to God. I also make sure I love my remaining two children more. Maybe my silver lining is baby Jacob, my second grandchild, who is scheduled to arrive in March. I am very excited to meet him!

*

LYNDA CHELDELIN FELL
Lynda's 15-year-old daughter Aly
died in a car accident in 2009

There are many silver linings that have revealed themselves since the accident. Our oldest daughter is now thirty, and she was a tough child to raise. Strong-willed with even stronger opinions, the accident drew us close enough to become best friends. I am very grateful for that.

Another silver lining is that my husband's stroke also saved his life. The grief was killing him. We both feel strongly that had the stroke never occurred, he would have died from his unhealthy coping mechanisms. And now our marriage is the best it's ever been, and that says a lot given that we've always had a great marriage.

The accident resulted in an entire change of career for me. But this new career, one dedicated to helping others, enriches my life in ways I never dreamed possible. I truly have a heart full of gratitude, and I take nothing for granted. Having survived the hell known as child loss, and danced with grief for years, I have so much more appreciation for the sunlight, the rainbows and even the rain clouds. For they all hold a purpose. For without the rain, there are no rainbows. Would I give it all back to have one more moment with Aly? Yes. I am human, and I will never stop missing my child. So you see, these silver linings are not taken for granted. I paid the ultimate price for the life I have now. I have a profound appreciation for the work that lies ahead. Maybe that is the best silver lining of all.

*

KARI BROWN
Kari's 2-year-old daughter Dominique (Deedee)
died in 2014 from obstructive sleep apnea

It took quite some time to recognize a silver lining from the death of my daughter which was sudden and unexpected. Her death definitely caused anger; it could have been prevented if the doctors had paid more attention. However, I found that by sharing my story with the families of other children facing the same syndrome, it seems to help them. I encourage them to speak up to the doctors, and urge them to take extra steps to ensure the health and safety of their children. I honestly wanted to crawl under a rock and to hide from the world, but I felt I would be dishonoring Dominique if I did. It took some courage and confidence to speak up and speak out. I no longer hold grudges, and instead offer positive thoughts when I can.

My relationship with my fiancé, Dominique's father, has also tightened. We are the only ones who truly understand the pain of our loss. My mother and I have also grown closer. Dominique taught her a lot about life with disabilities, and that there truly isn't a disability unless you choose to perceive it that way. Through a mutual friend, I was able to help a family that had many questions and didn't know who to turn to. I shared my experiences growing up and what Dominique experienced, and the parents found that tremendously helpful, and it guided them as they sought help for their son.

I have learned to embrace life in a different perspective: to always cherish happy moments and not dwell on pain or negativity from others, because that is not who Dominique was.

*

JACQUELYN CRUZ
Jacquelyn's 24-year-old daughter Jenna
died in 2012 from pulmonary edema

I haven't been able to recognize a silver, gold, or platinum lining in my loss as of today. That's like asking what good has come out of this. Not one damn thing. I sometimes think that mothers who have lost a child should receive some type of benefit. Two or more commuters get to use the carpool lane, there is parking for the handicapped, and discounts for seniors. But the grieving get nothing. If that were an option, what would compensate a broken heart? What would replace half of your soul? What would ease the constant yearning to hold your child for one more minute? Nothing.

*

MICHELLE DETWILER
Michelle's 19-year-old daughter Emily
died in 2014 due to congenital complications

For most people there is not and will not be any silver lining after the death of their child. For us, however, the situation is a little different. Emily had so many medical complications. It was excruciating to see the pain she was in at times throughout her life. Occasionally I hear a grieving parent declare how much they would give to get their child back, even if only for a day. My silver lining is that I will never wish to have her back. I miss her terribly, but never in a million lifetimes would I want her to come back to living with her multiple disabilities. She is healed now! That brings me so much joy. There was nothing I could do while Emily was alive to alleviate her pain. Every day I thank the Lord for healing her and taking her into His loving arms. Her body died, but she didn't. It's a beautiful silver lining to know that she is alive and well, and I'll get to see her in all her beauty some day.

*

ANNAH ELIZABETH
Annah's son Gavin Michael aspirated on his meconium
during the delivery and died 26 minutes following his birth

"Every cloud has a silver lining," is a quote as irritating as it is inspirational. You see, we often don't see a beneficial side effect of a difficult situation until after we've traversed that particular part of our grief journey. In the earliest days after Gavin died, and I do mean the immediate week, Warren and I wrote farewell letters to our son. Each of our letters said something along the lines of, "Your death has brought Mommy and Daddy closer together." We clung to that notion like it was some sort of lifeline, as if there HAD to be some kind of purpose in the unexpected, tragic death of our son.

I mention these things because I want you to know that it's okay if you're not in a place to see a silver lining. Shiny outlines and outcomes aren't mandatory when it comes to loss and grief.

That said, at some point along our journey we are likely to notice a sort of shift in our relationships, be it the connection with our self, our spouse, our family, our friends, or our hopes for the future, just to name a few. In my case, I knew pretty early on that I didn't want to spend a lifetime mourning my son and that I was going to figure out how to answer that one question most often asked in the face of adversity: "How am I going to survive this?"

In other words: How am I going to heal?

Were it not for Gavin's death I might never have pursued this work with The Five Facets of Healing. I have met so many beautiful people on this journey and I consider myself fortunate to have been able to effect something positive and inspirational in others' lives. My life is richer for the experiences I've stumbled into and the ones I've deliberately sought out. Sure, there is still some sorrow that shows up on a rare occasion but mostly I am grateful for the time I had with Gavin and for the many beautiful asides that have come to pass in the face of his untimely death.

One of the other side effects is that I am much more aware of life's fragility. As such, I've made it one of my mantras to try to stay in touch with life's little luxuries, those simple, fleeting moments that warm my heart or bring on feelings of happiness, hope, and healing. Not that I don't still get bogged down in life's minutiae from time to time—trust me when I say I still do—but I've tried to raise my awareness of life's many positive vibrations.

*

WENDY EVANS
Wendy's 21-year-old son Kyle died in 2009
from diabetes when his insulin pump malfunctioned

That is a very hard question. I suppose one silver lining is the fact that Kyle is not suffering from diabetes. All of the important relationships in my life have survived, although some are different. Possibly better with my mother and brothers. I did not have this realization until I read the question and had to think about it.

*

BONNIE FORSHEY
Bonnie's 16-year-old son Billy died in 1993
from an overdose of prescription drugs

There is no silver lining in losing a child. The loss of my son has been horrible for my daughter and me. We both witnessed his death and it has stayed with us. She had such a hard time watching me grieve that she moved out shortly after his death. Over time, we have been able to deal with the loss and become close again.

*

TALIA GATO
Talia's 8-year-old daughter Poppy
died in 2009 in a car accident

Well, this is my personal view. I don't think there is a silver lining to the death of a child. I just don't. It is not like other losses, like some illness and then surviving or a cure. You are alive, so you help others get to live again. But that is not so with the loss of a child. My child didn't come back. I am not cured. It didn't make me a better person. It did change me, though. It broke me. I am more truthful with myself and to others. I believe this world we live in is beautiful yet broken. Some very wonderful people still get sick and die and some children die. My card came up. I would do anything to get my daughter back. I am a believer in God. I am loyal to Him even though I was angry at Him for a while. Did it shake my faith? Yes. Did I have doubts? Yes. Do I want people to tell me the whys? No. I am okay now without knowing. I still believe I will see my daughter again.

*

KORBY HAVE
Korby's 17-year-old daughter Taylor (Tayla)
died in 2013 in a car accident

The only possible silver lining is that I am more determined to be a better member of my church so that I can be with her again.

*

DEANA MARTIN
Deana's only two children, 25-year-old Amanda
and 21-year-old Logan, died in a car accident in 2011

The silver lining around the dark ominous cloud of losing my children, my family, comes and goes. Some days the lining is bright and brilliant and I bless the heavens for the gifts that were bestowed upon me since my children's transition home. I praise the powers that be for the doors that have opened that have led to my living my life's dream of service to others in pain, and healing hearts and souls from the wounds of trauma. I raise my arms to the skies in gratitude for the authentic, loving and compassionate people who have entered my life by the droves that would not have done so had this chapter in my life never transpired.

Then there are the days where the clouds are so dark and there is no lining, and I can't even remember the last time there was one. The clouds are so big and black and take on a life of their own. I fear that at any moment it will rage into a horrible storm of mass destruction, taking out everything in its wake. Houses, cars, barns, trees, anything the storm touches it engulfs and destroys, shredding them into tiny unrecognizable pieces.

Then there are days when the lining of the cloud is there, but not very shiny. It is more a dull pewter, and by the look of the clouds it will more than likely bring drizzle. That cold, constant drizzle that zaps my energy and all I want to do is lie in my bed, with my head on my favorite pillow, covers tucked under my chin, and sleep. Sleep does not come easily at night, so these drizzly days with the pewter-lined clouds can be welcome. However, too many of these gray drizzly days will send me back into the pit of darkness from which I have struggled so hard to climb out.

Then there are days when the clouds really have no lining, but they are not dark either. These clouds are fluffy white, and sometimes I see signs in them from my children in the form of hearts, dragons, unicorns, music notes, something symbolizing them and what brought them joy here on earth. I like these days, the fluffy white cloud days. It is these days when I feel at most peace in connection with my children and I know they are not gone, they are just not here. When they let me see this by the images in the clouds, I sometimes cry. It is not always tears of missing them, it now can also be tears of joy for knowing they still live, for them showing me they are alive and with me all the time.

I have found the gifts they have left me, and I find new ones every day. It is as if every action, word and incidence years prior was leading to the ultimate day my life would change forever. I can see now how it was all connected. I can see how it was all a progression leading to today. And hear the words I type on this page, and the hearts I touch through my story and my experience.

People say my loss brings them hope; that somehow seeing that I have survived the death of my family in the blink of an eye gives them a feeling that possibly they can do it too. I am honest with them when they ask, "How do you go on? How can you survive?" They say, "I can't imagine losing all my children, one was more than I could stand." I tell them I don't know how I do it, but much like them, I just do. One moment at a time. I tell them about my blessings and my silver lining and how my children knew of my life dreams. In some ways it's as if they gave me that gift the day they went home.

I tell them of the dark ominous clouds and the raging storms. I tell them how this journey is an endless changing sky of clouds of all shapes, sizes, colors and configurations. Just like the weather in Florida, my sky can change many times in one day. I tell them about the days when it rains on one side of the street but not the other because the clouds are so isolated. I tell them when those drizzly days come, welcome them and rest your weary heart. If too many drizzly days come in a row and send you into the darkness and the fear creeps in, remember that the sun will shine again. And you will see a rainbow when the sun peeks through the clouds. It is at that very moment that one remembers that love never dies.

*

MONICA MIRKES
Monica's 30-year-old daughter Marisa
died in 2013 due to Cesarean complications

Now, two years later, I am trying very hard to look for something good in this unbelievable journey. As the mother of a chronically ill child, you have to stand by and watch as your child is subjected to all kinds of horrible treatments, all in the name of "you'll get better." You keep telling yourself and your child it's for the best, you'll feel better, it will be over soon. Yes, there are times when life resembles some kind of normality. No blood tests, procedures or doctor visits. You can breathe. For some of us it doesn't last very long.

Marisa wanted to have a baby, she was told it was safe, this would be the best time while her health was stable. She loved being pregnant, being able to experience what so many take for granted. Being in awe of her body and the life inside. Sharing that happiness with her father and me, her brothers and sister. All the while we were holding our breath and praying, praying, praying. Connor would be our silver lining. Our light in the dark. It's bittersweet, for Marisa is not here to see his "firsts." She is not calling us to share his antics. We cherish these happenings, this gift she has given us. Here on earth though, I know that good things don't always last.

*

DENISE PURCELL
Denise's 27-year-old daughter Megan died
in 2011 from an accidental overdose

I don't take time for granted. I tell my other daughters or anyone that I love, "I love you." Our relationships have become deeper. We have learned the hard way that we don't have to go through it alone. Even though they are away at college they will text me and say, "I heard Megan's favorite song and it reminded me of her and you, Mom, and I couldn't breathe." That's when I feel the pain through them. I just say, "She was letting you know she was around, and I love you." We are all connected, no matter how far apart. The time of year and dates that remind one, remind all of us.

*

MARILYN ROLLINS
Marilyn's 37-year-old son Randy and 16-year-old granddaughter Sara died in a car accident in 2006 during a family camping trip

I'm sure that some people who are new to their grief, especially after the loss of the child, look at this question and wonder how there could be a silver lining to losing a child. We have to remember that this loss changes our lives. It changes who we are, where we are going, our relationships, and even how we look at life. It changes our priorities and it puts life into perspective. It took years before I realized that there were good things in my life that would not be there if not for my son's and granddaughter's deaths. Without going into specifics, I have had wonderful things happen that would not have happened if Randy and Sara had not died. I know this because I would have not been in a certain place, at a certain time, if my life had not changed paths.

I have learned who my true friends are. I have removed people from my life and now know that they probably shouldn't have been there anyway. I have realized that the things that I used to think were important in life are not.

Are these silver linings? I like to think so. I have become a better person. I am so much more empathetic to people and their pain. My grief group, The Compassionate Friends, is the biggest silver lining of all. There is a bond there that I have never found elsewhere. These are wonderful, amazing people that I would never have known if not for Randy's and Sara's deaths. These people open their hearts and arms to complete strangers every day. There's no judgment, no disdain, only love and hope. You can look in their eyes and you can see that they know what you're going through, because they have been there. That brings comfort, knowing that you're not alone. When I first realized that they wouldn't be my friends if I hadn't lost Randy and Sara, I felt tremendous guilt. I wished I had never met them. I didn't want to know them. I wanted Randy and Sara back.

After thinking about this for a while I wrote a poem called "For My Compassionate Friends."

FOR MY COMPASSIONATE FRIENDS
How is it that I know you?
How'd you get into my life?
Sometimes when I look at you,
It cuts me like a knife.
I do not want to know you,
I don't want to cross that line.
Let's both go back into the past,
When everything was fine.
You've held me and you've hugged me,
And dried a tear or two,
Yet you're practically a stranger.
Why do you do the things you do?
Of course, I know the reason,
We are in this club we're in,
And why we hold on to each other
Like we are long-lost kin.
For us to know each other,
We had to lose a kid.
I wish I'd never met you,
But I'm so thankful that I did.

That was the best way I knew to word it. I hate the reason I know them, but I thank God each and every day that they are in my life and we are walking this road together. As their credo states, "You need not walk alone."

*

KATIE ROUSH
Katie's 26-year-old daughter Krystle
died in 2013 of accidental alcohol poisoning

There were so many times I wished that I could find a door to a time warp and go back to warn my daughter, Krystle, of what was to come. Just so I could change her path, change her direction, so she could be here longer. In that first year, I thought about just giving up and saying, "What the hell, what does it matter anymore?" But then I felt her kicking my ass and going, "No, Mom. You have to keep on. Don't do anything dumb and it will be okay." I did not believe that part, that everything will be okay. I mean, after all how can everything be okay when my little girl is dead? But, much to my surprise, it became okay. I took it one day at a time and just let time go on, as it should. As it will. Believe me, I did not want it to, but it had to.

There are no words to accurately describe how I felt when I was told my baby was dead. I don't think Mr. Webster had one for that, and I don't think he ever will. Unless you have lost a child, you would not and never will understand that. You can't. Period. There were times when I was so tired and cried so much that I did not think it was humanly possible to have more tears inside my body. I found it so hard to laugh. The colors I saw were just gray. The sun did not shine. The birds did not sing. It was just empty, a vast bridge of sadness so long and so tall that I almost drowned in it. It was filled with echoes of her laughter, her voice. And what once was, is no longer. Everywhere I went had, and has, a memory. Every song, every store, every road had my daughter in it. With me here, alive. My feet felt as though they were in concrete yet forced to walk again. I had to really reach into my soul to find strength and courage to face another day. And soon that day turned into two, then a week and then a month. I began to laugh again and to hear birds sing and feel the sunshine again.

I no longer hide and wish for night to come. I no longer look up at stars to try to find my child. I slowly began to live again. I picked up my paints and started to paint, draw, create. I started to care more deeply than I ever have before. I started to realize that this life is a gift...that she was a gift...and she had things to teach me even though her life was short. I learned how far I have come and I am proud of that, and I learned I have much farther to go. I began to understand the words "Everything happens for a reason," even though at first I did not understand. And did not want to. My daughter's death was my greatest teacher. It taught me how to love unconditionally. It taught me how to value the right things, cast off the wrong things. It taught me whom to trust, whom not to trust. It taught me more about people than I ever wanted to learn. It taught me to grab every moment possible because those moments will never come again. It taught me forgiveness from the soul, not just how to say the words, but how to do it and feel it and let go.

Her life is and was my legacy. I even started doll making again. It was something I used to do for Krystle when she was little. At first I started it to keep my sanity when she died and now it is a business that is growing. I bring smiles to people's faces. In a way, my daughter is right there with me doing that. She was my greatest accomplishment. I was honored to be her mom. Her death has taught me the value of my gifts and how to share them with others.

*

SARA RUBLE
Sara's 19-year-old son Scott died in 1994 from a
combination of a seizure disorder, Strep throat and dehydration

Unbelievably, there are many silver linings that have come to me. For years I was certain my life would not, or could not, have any great meaning, nor did I care. I was not able to see beyond the devastation and pain of my grief, for it was so consuming. But in all reality, I have learned that life can take even more twists and turns and show us more than we could have imagined.

A significant life-changing opportunity came to me unexpectedly. I was very surprised when I learned a local grief center was opening just a few miles from my home. Finally there would be help for those of us grieving and living within that pain and confusion. I felt a sense of relief that there was help on the way. I was even more surprised when I was asked to create and facilitate the support group for bereaved parents at the center. This was three years following Scott's death and I was still grappling with the intensity of each new day.

I wondered if I was ready to take on something this important. It was a giant step going forward. Could I do it? I was at three years, and some parents might be at one or two years since their child's death. Perhaps what I had already experienced and learned could help other moms and dads? So important too, we would have the much needed support of just being together.

Something in me insisted I take on this new endeavor.

I did it…cautiously at first, but dedicated. I worked very hard preparing for our monthly meetings, searching for tools and information that could provide the support and love I knew the moms and dads needed. I learned so much as well. I went on to lead the group for over seven years. I met amazing parents and watched as they found greater stability and understanding in their grief. Together we shared our stories and our lives. Friendships grew, and the support was profound. I was honored to be a part of the grief center and to see new aspects of my grief and life evolve. I know I thrived in that setting. A silver lining indeed.

Something I never could have seen happening was the creation of the Christmas Box Angel of Hope Children's Memorial in Stow, Ohio. Six years after Scott's death I heard the most unlikely words in my mind two different times: "Build the children's memorial." These words were heart-stopping as they flowed through my thoughts. I knew they were not mine! I tried to ignore them the first time, but the second time there was no way to ignore them. They were clear and bold. It sounds crazy, I know! And somehow I was certain it was Scott. I had never had an experience like that before. But I knew it was him.

What will we do for our children? I trusted him...and those four words were about to change my life. Suddenly I was incredibly driven. Parents from my support group joined me and we actually created the children's memorial after raising almost $50,000 in seven months. It was beyond incredible! We now have memorial bricks for almost six hundred children and have created a loving, serene setting for families to visit and remember their precious children. I had never done any fundraising in my life, and yet this project gave me and all the members of our committee great purpose to go out and change our community in a truly positive way. Another silver lining and, yes, life-changing.

My life now feels more balanced, meaningful, fulfilled. These "blessings" were filled with signs from Scott, and I knew I was not alone in anything I was doing. My grief was opened up and I have shared it. I have been rewarded with love, friendship, compassion, growth, purpose, and the knowing that I can be more and do more than I ever thought.

*

CHAPTER EIGHTEEN

OUR HOPE

Be like the birds, sing after every storm.
- BETH MENDE CONNY

Hope is the fuel that propels us forward, urges us to get out of bed each morning. It is the promise that tomorrow will be better than today. Each breath we take and each footprint we leave is a measure of hope. So is hope possible in the aftermath of loss? If so, where do we find it?

*

STACY BERNDTSON
Stacy's daughter Cori Joy died in 2003, the day before her fourth birthday, from an undiagnosed genetic disorder

My definition of hope is found throughout the book that I believe is the infallible word of God. Three Scriptures that best sum up where my hope is found are below.

Such things were written in the Scriptures long ago to teach us. And the Scriptures give us hope and encouragement as we wait patiently for God's promises to be fulfilled (Romans 15:4).

We were saved with this hope ahead of us. Now hope means we are waiting for something we do not have. How can a man hope for something he already has? But if we hope for something we do not yet see, we must learn how to wait for it (Romans 8:24-25).

Then I saw a new heaven and a new earth, for the first heaven and the first earth had passed away, and there was no longer any sea. I saw the Holy City, the new Jerusalem, coming down out of heaven from God, prepared as a bride beautifully dressed for her husband. And I heard a loud voice from the throne saying, "Look! God's dwelling place is now among the people, and he will dwell with them. They will be his people, and God himself will be with them and be their God. He will wipe every tear from their eyes. There will be no more death or mourning or crying or pain, for the old order of things has passed away." He who was seated on the throne said, "I am making everything new!" (Revelation 21:1-5). It is this last Scripture that I have held fast to for the last eleven years and 345 days (at this writing).

*

KARI BROWN
Kari's 2-year-old daughter Dominique (Deedee)
died in 2014 from obstructive sleep apnea

My definition of hope is still somewhat the same: that life will to get better even though the heartbreak will always be with me. I have a different perspective on faith though. My daughter's middle name is Faith. When Dominique was born two months early, we had faith that things would get better and she would become healthy. She did, and was healthier than the doctors expected her to be. We had faith that she would remain healthy, and she did until the day she passed. After, we had faith in ourselves to get through this, and to turn the pain into a bittersweet happiness. We have faith that Dominique was a blessing in our world; she taught us what love and life are about. We changed our perspective on life, and defined what our roles are. We are here to teach, to show that there is so much more than just living life on a day-to-day basis.

*

TANISHA CALDWELL
Tanisha's 23-year-old son Tariq (Jay)
died in a car accident in 2015

My definition of hope is looking forward to better days. I look forward to being able to live again with peace, joy, strength, and happiness while coping with the heartache of losing my precious son. I look forward to the day when I see his beautiful smile. My definition of hope is being able to still be all that God has destined me to be. Even through this, I know there is something good coming from it. I may not understand it, or even see it, but trust that one day it will all make sense.

*

LYNDA CHELDELIN FELL
Lynda's 15-year-old daughter Aly
died in 2009 in a car accident

My definition of hope has changed over time. Before the accident, my answer to this question would include mainly superficial, short-term things that affected only my world.

In the wake of Aly's accident, I felt robbed of all hope. So I fought hard to find it again. I looked for it in the sound of the birds singing outside. I pursued hope while splashing in the pool with our grandson on a warm summer day. I struggled to find hope as my husband's loving arms comforted my sobs.

It's been said that without grief, there would be no need for hope. So, now my definition of hope is much different. I hope to make a difference in the world so the next generation might have better bereavement support than this generation. I hope to help people share their story, because we learn so much by listening to one another. Finally, when it's my turn to go to heaven, I hope to leave behind some sort of legacy that continues to make a difference to those in need. And when I meet up with Aly, she will say, "Great job, Mom!"

*

JACQUELYN CRUZ
Jacquelyn's 24-year-old daughter Jenna
died in 2012 from pulmonary edema

The saying "Hope has no fear" has never been more right in my life. I fear nothing. Life is going to happen whether we worry or not. To me, hope is that voice you hear in your head saying it's going to be okay tomorrow, so the next day you get up and try again.

*

MICHELLE DETWILER
Michelle's 19-year-old daughter Emily
died in 2014 due to congenital complications

Our daughter's death brought me to a new definition of hope. I've been a Christian for many years and my beliefs are grounded on faith in the Bible and on Jesus Christ. He is my hope for life today and for eternal life. While this has been my way of living, it became so much more real the moment my daughter stepped into heaven. Knowing that she is there, experiencing the reality of what I've heard about and read about in the Bible has brought hope to me in a dark situation. Where my love extended to the four walls of her room as she lay in her bed, God's love has extended to her eternity. In this world death looks like an end to some people, but in my world it is an open door to hope and a future! And now I have a new hope, and a new reason to look forward to going to heaven!

*

ANNAH ELIZABETH
Annah's son Gavin Michael aspirated on his meconium
during the delivery and died 26 minutes following his birth

Hope is like a promise that we can achieve whatever it is we want to attain. It is the sense that we can realize some form of happiness when we are sad, we can shift our sorrow to joy, we can somehow make sense out of mayhem. It's knowing in our heart and in our gut that tomorrow has the ability to be different, somehow better. Hope is the belief that we can change our circumstances, resolve conflicts, and create a brighter and more fulfilling future.

*

WENDY EVANS
Wendy's 21-year-old son Kyle died in 2009
from diabetes when his insulin pump malfunctioned

Hope is feeling the ability to navigate through difficult challenges to arrive at a safe or better place. To feel that you have tools and resources to impact the outcome of a situation, to make it better in some way.

*

BONNIE FORSHEY
Bonnie's 16-year-old son Billy died in 1993
from an overdose of prescription drugs

Hope to me is being able to live a happy life and being able to deal with loss. It is about learning to be happy with the bittersweet memories, accepting the blessings in life and moving forward. Hope is knowing we will see our loved ones again.

*

TALIA GATO
Talia's 8-year-old daughter Poppy
died in 2009 in a car accident

I wondered if I was forever going to feel lost like the first two to three years, that feeling of ache and loss. Would I ever smile and laugh again? Yes, it did happen and, at times, I was happy and found some joy. Now I have learned that my mind and body enveloped my loss, and my soul grew a big callus so I could bear the weight of loss. Now I accept my loss and I am in a place of having some joy and sadness all at the same time.

*

DAPHNE GREER
Daphne's 5-year-old daughter Lydia died in 2008 in a
car accident during a routine morning commute

After experiencing the worst possible tragedy in life, all hope was shattered those first few months and year. My preconceived notions of hope went out the window when my daughter died, shattering my expectations for any type of future. Life as I knew it had ended.

Slowly, as the days and months progressed, glimmers of hope planted inside me. I started to appreciate life, recognizing the fragility of this brief stay on earth, and began to see the beauty in ordinary things. I found myself appreciating the sunrise and the majestic rainbow of colors in the sunset, studying the intricacy of insects and animals, and being thankful for having a roof over my head. I appreciated arguments with my children, and the piles of laundry and toys scattered around the house. Little things became big things. I no longer expected and waited for tragedy to strike me again. I would hear of so many others who were struggling much more than I. My soul felt their pain and I was humbled. My heart became full of compassion and love for others experiencing hardships, giving me an incredible urge to live my life differently. This life was no longer about me, but about what I could do for others.

Hope had arrived. It had miraculously floated in on a dewdrop one spring morning and landed in my lap, leaving a lasting impression. Little by little, I recognized just how blessed I really was.

Hope is having a positive outlook on life and not taking anything for granted. We don't have to live in the past. Conversely, we need to live this fleeting life expecting incredible things to happen. Praying, giving, receiving joyfully, and having a heart full of gratitude can transform your life in ways you can't imagine. Amidst the darkness, there is always hope.

*

DEANA MARTIN
Deana's only two children, 25-year-old Amanda
and 21-year-old Logan, died in a car accident in 2011

Hope is how we survive after the trauma of loss of a child. Somewhere, somehow, one must find hope. Hope is what heals the wounds of trauma of all types, whether it is the trauma experienced after the loss of a loved one, or the trauma of domestic violence, or the trauma of facing a possibly terminal illness. Hope is the antidote to quiet the fear, to slow the racing thoughts. Hope is to trauma as helium is to a balloon. Without hope we cannot fly again, we will not get back up after the tragic fall.

One can find hope most easily by living in gratitude. There is always something to be grateful for even when you cannot see it. Several years went by after my children's death, and most days it was a huge challenge to see anything to be grateful for or any reason to hope for a future. My future had been stolen from me. My life as I was supposed to live it, with many grandchildren, my children's spouses and their parents who would inevitably become my family, was all stripped from my soul. It was as if some thieving demon came into my world and took my future, my life, my identity, my reasons for living, and took it all far away to a place I could not go. I could not go because this demon left me one thing, one tiny little helpless life that needed me. The demon overlooked my precious granddaughter. God somehow hid her from him that day by placing her in the car behind the car that the demon would destroy in order to take my life.

I knew every day from that day forward that I had much to be grateful for because my granddaughter was alive. By the grace of God I had been spared one of my family members. As much as I knew this in my head and in my heart, my soul didn't fully understand. How was it a blessing to be left with a poor baby without her mommy? How was I, who was so broken, going to heal the poor baby's heart? How was I, who cried in the silence of the night, going to be able to hide my sorrow from this tiny soul? I had no earthly idea how I was going to care for her, and help her to heal, when I did not know how I was going to survive myself.

As I approach every other challenge in my life, I began to search for answers. If I did not know, someone out there did. So I searched the internet and found local support groups and books and Facebook groups, and I educated myself on my plight from those who had traveled this same journey before us. I found children's programs and children's books on death and heaven, and taught my grandbaby that her mommy and uncle were not dead, that their love and their spirit were very much alive. I taught my granddaughter that her mommy and uncle lived in a magical place now because their bodies stopped working the day the truck hit Mommy's car. I told her Mommy will always be her mommy, that it's okay Mommy is in heaven because heaven is a wonderful place where you can have all you desire by just thinking of it. I told her Mommy could ride unicorns in heaven and slide down rainbows, and that she could go there in her dreams and see Mommy anytime. I told her that Mommy was such a good mommy and loved her so very much that she made sure, before she had to move to heaven, that she left many Earth mommies here to care for her, and I named all the special women in my granddaughter's life. I explained to her how she was so lucky because most little girls have only one mommy, and she had many, one in heaven and many here on earth. And that someday when she was very old, she too would move to heaven and she would be with her mommy again. I explained to her how caterpillars turn into beautiful butterflies and that's how dying is. Your body is like a cocoon, and when your body stops working your spirit flies into the sky and becomes a beautiful angel. We talk about Mommy and Uncle Logan as angels that watch over us and help us live a good life.

My granddaughter is now eight, old enough to know my heart is broken. Through helping her to understand and by keeping her mother's and uncle's memory alive for her, I think it helps me find the hope and gratitude that eluded me and sometimes still does.

*

MONICA MIRKES
Monica's 30-year-old daughter Marisa
died in 2013 due to Cesarean complications

Hope? I actually had to look up the definition. To be truthful, because of losing a child, at least for me, hope has kind of lost its meaning. What are my expectations? What do I desire or look forward to with reasonable confidence? Nothing really. I take one day at a time. Enjoy the moment you have. Be in the moment. To laugh. Laughter would be my hope.

*

DENISE PURCELL
Denise's 27-year-old daughter Megan died
in 2011 from an accidental overdose

Hope is a possibility. Having. One. Personal. Epiphany. If you don't see any possibilities, then you have died right along with your loved one. And that's not what they want. They want you to smile again, love again, live. Just take that chance. If not for you, then for them.

*

MARILYN ROLLINS
Marilyn's 37-year-old son Randy and 16-year-old granddaughter Sara
died in a car accident in 2006 during a family camping trip

Hope: a noun, a feeling of expectation and desire for a certain thing to happen. After the accident, my first hope was that everyone in the vehicle was okay. When I realized that this was not true and that Randy and Sara had died, I hoped that they had not suffered. After the funerals were over, I hoped that I could just get through each day, one step at a time. When I started attending The Compassionate Friends meetings, my hope was that someone could help with my pain. At that time hope for me meant a smile, a helping hand, a kind word, a gentle hug, a touch or even a laugh.

Sitting in a meeting and talking with people who were much farther along in their grief gave me tremendous hope that I too could survive. Nine years later, and now a chapter leader for The Compassionate Friends, I hope that I am helping others who are just beginning their grief journey, or struggling along the way. There is an old Turkish proverb that says, "Things never go so well that one should have no fear, and never so ill that one should have no hope."

To me, hope is moving forward, not giving up. Without hope, we have no purpose. Hope is life.

*

KATIE ROUSH
Katie's 26-year-old daughter Krystle
died in 2013 of accidental alcohol poisoning

I remember watching a movie called *The Dollmaker* when my children were little. I remember the part when the little boy got run over by a train and the mother, played by Mare Winningham, just cried and screamed her heart out. I thought, "Man, I could never imagine that." It broke my heart as I looked at all three of my little girls and thought, "Oh, God! What would I do if that happened to me? How would I go on?" Hindsight, right?

On July 30, 2013, I got to play the starring role in a movie gone horribly wrong. I got to feel just how the mother in that movie felt. I got to be a member of a club no parent ever wants to join. I got to scream, beg, plead and even hate for real. I went through all the facets of dealing with the loss of my Kryssi...full force.

On one end of her life I was planning a baptism, and then suddenly here I was planning a funeral. What parent does that? I remember driving one day after visiting a friend. The pain was so immense, and I cried all the way home. I remember looking at the side of the road thinking, "You know, I can jerk this wheel of the Jeep just right and it will be all over. Kryssi and I can be together again." I didn't. I had too much to do, too much to live for. I think

330

that was my lowest point in all this. Yep, that was me. The upbeat-I-believe-in-magic-that-nobody-sees-but-me woman, the funny one who contemplated death for a split second.

I filled my days with busy stuff. I had to keep pushing and moving forward. I had to keep going, no matter how it hurt. I had to make sense of this somehow, some way. I knew there was a reason God did this...but did not see it at the time, nor do I see it now to be truthful, but there is one. I had to put the pieces of this shattered life together again...for me, for my husband, for Kryssi's sisters, my grandchildren. I had to just figure this out. Just as blacksmiths pound and reshape precious metals to create something new, I had to pound and reshape my life to make it stronger and new. My husband gave me strength. He let me cry and scream when I needed it. He held me when it became too much...and made me laugh at just the right time. He was my true North Star, guiding me back to myself.

I found out who true friends were: they were my laughter and my let's-go-do-something-before-I-break-again sisters. Dondi Deskins and Cristal Allen, you also were my stars guiding me home. You did not know it at the time, but you both were.

I slowly emerged from this deep dark pit with a bigger heart, a more profound sense of being and a deeper love for important things....the small things that make life worth living. I have learned to really embrace life with all its ups and downs, tears and laughter, pain and sorrow. Through all this, I have learned the true meaning and value of life. It is not who has the biggest bank account, biggest house, better car or job. It's not about the one-upmanship, it is not about false promises one gives to another. It is not about trying to drag people down. It is about the little things like a smile, a kind word, a flower blooming. It is about helping your fellow man. It is about love and having a good pure heart.

It is about the dash...the point between your birth and death. Because when it is your time to go, when you look back at your life with God by your side, you want it to filled with love, laughter and good works. You want others to remember you for your heart, for your caring and good character. Funny, this is how my daughter, in her short twenty-six years of life lived. So in a sense, I am beginning to live as she would have, as she did. Any of you who knew her can attest to that. She was good, kind, funny and had a pure heart. She had problems, yes, but she still always had time to help someone. Even when she did not want to, she did. She did it with a laugh and a joke. I guess I am like her in a lot of ways. This is how I choose to carry her with me, until we meet again.

Do good. Love with all your heart, even if it is not returned. Laugh and dance like nobody sees you, no matter how silly you might look. This is my message of hope, for all of us.

*

SARA RUBLE
Sara's 19-year-old son Scott died in 1994 from a
combination of a seizure disorder, Strep throat and dehydration

Before Scott died, I'm not sure I ever knew what "hope" was. I hoped for lots of things…and then hoped they would all come true. Death, being so invasive, broke into my heart and soul. Suddenly "hope" seemed impossible. The impossible task of bringing Scott back could not be. Where do we send our heartfelt hope? To God? I wasn't sure where God was in all this now. Scott had died! Where was God? Does God hear our hopes and with a magic wand of sorts let us have what we hoped for? Hope seemed to be meaningless. But then I hoped for Scott's friends to be safe. I hoped my mom could survive seeing her beloved daughter in such great agony. I hoped my marriage of just nine months could survive as well. Hope continued to run through me…even when it confused me.

In my most devastated state I had the hope that Scott would show me he was still around me somehow. Hope is a dream…and it takes us to a place of trusting that good or healing or the positive can still be…that more can come and allow us to survive in the hardest of times.

We put hope out there, never knowing for sure if it will be answered. And yet in my twenty years of grief and, yes, healing, I know hope is important. If we hang on to the possibilities being possible, we can grow and see a bigger picture of life and even death. Will there still be disappointment? Yes. We cannot always stop what comes. But now I am truly able to see more in my life of pain and growth and everything I have experienced. I know hope pushed me to figure that out...to not give up...to love and help others and to accept that life is unpredictable. Hope is a part of who we are, I believe. A deep spiritual peace within us.

*

Hallmark doesn't have
"So sorry your child died but
happy birthday to him anyway," cards.
I long for someone to reach out and remember
my children on those days.
DEANA MARTIN

*

CHAPTER NINETEEN

OUR JOURNEY

Be soft. Do not let the world make you hard. Do not
let the pain make you hate. Do not let bitterness steal
your sweetness. -KURT VONNEGUT

Every journey through loss is as unique as one's fingerprint, for we experience different beliefs, different desires, different needs, different tolerances, and often we walk different roads. Though we may not see anyone else on the path, we are never truly alone for more walk behind, beside, and in front of us. In this chapter lies the participants' answers to the final question posed: What would you like the world to know about your grief journey?

*

ERICA GALE BELTZ
Erica's 5-year-old son Luke Jordan died in 2005
from a fallen banister in his aunt's driveway

A friend of mine, Glen, lost his battle to cancer on Christmas Day. Glen was my boss at Taco Mac and he was my buddy. I signed in at his memorial service and hesitated when I saw his wife and young daughter standing by the casket. I had heard how they put their recent divorce behind them and she cared for him until the end. Friends lined up to say goodbye. It was so sad losing Glen.

Everyone loved him. He was a big old teddy bear, and he was too young for cancer to take his life. I had no idea what I would possibly say to comfort his family. I began to pray for courage. There was this light that surrounded them both, they were the ones comforting others. It was beautiful. I can still feel the love that poured from them in that moment eleven years later. When I got home, I shared with my mama the experience. I asked her, "How can one endure the pain of watching someone die? How can you plan a funeral so soon after? How do you tell a little girl that her father is gone?" I explained what I witnessed. I was truly blown away. My mama listened to everything I said and then - I'll never forget her response - she said, "Erica, that is God's grace!"

Mama said she had seen it before and that God steps in and carries us when we no longer can. She said that they say you are in shock during those first few months. That it is your mind's way of protecting itself from the horrible pain your mind wouldn't be able to recover. I was so humbled by the experience. I got a beautiful card and sent it to Melinda. I told her things I witnessed that night at the funeral home. How her beauty was such a gift to Glen and their daughter. I also shared what my mom had told me about God's grace, and how moved I was. It was so spiritual. My prayer was that it would never leave her and would carry them.

She came to the funeral home to comfort us. It was very surreal seeing her. She thanked me for the card. She got the news about Luke just before getting home, the day he passed. When she checked the mail later that night, my card was in the mailbox. She looked me in the eye. I could see her pain now; it wasn't guarded, it wasn't beautiful, it was full of sorrow. She said, "It doesn't feel much like God's grace though, does it?" She was right: this could not be God's grace. The chaplain who opened my car door at the emergency room was Patrick's dad. Patrick was a friend who died by suicide around the time Luke was born. A young mom whose five-year-old son was murdered by her boyfriend came to the funeral home. She said, "I heard about your son and wanted to give you this book." It's called *Safe in the Arms of God*. She had found comfort in the pages and Scripture and hoped I would too. It was so moving and brave. It touched my entire family and continues to today.

For as long as I can remember when I shared my experience, I told the story about God's grace and seeing Melinda afterward. My days did get dark and eventually I had no will to live. I have always referred to that time as my darkest days. I had failed God. God had chosen me to be Luke's mom. His gifts were so pure in heart, so special. Shock became my reality, my protective mechanism where my mind went to take cover. I got completely wasted after the funeral and woke up vomiting in the trashcan in my mom's kitchen in the wee hours of the morning. My mom doesn't drink, and I can't imagine how hard it was seeing me like that. I drank a lot more, though, in the days that followed.

I never lost my faith. I know many parents who have. I was never mad at God, a question I have been asked over and over. I planned to kill myself as soon as I could assure that Luke's life wouldn't be in total vain. I would need a baseball stadium, something huge for people to know about his kind heart and gifts.

God was carrying me, I had no idea. Through the trenches, valleys, and to the top of the mountain, I dug my way back to life. I found hope. The tragedy of losing my little Luke has softened somewhat over time.

*

STACY BERNDTSON
Stacy's daughter Cori Joy died in 2003, the day before her
fourth birthday, from an undiagnosed genetic disorder

There is a phrase that is often used in death. I think I may sometimes even use it in reference to Cori Joy's death. One will say, "They lost their daughter." When Cori died, we reached out to our old pastor. When the first neurologist told us that Cori had cerebral palsy at just six weeks old, we drove straight to that pastor's office. He prayed with us and gave us encouragement through Scripture.

When Steve told him we had lost Cori Joy, he told us, "I don't like to use the word 'lost' when you know where someone is." That stuck with me. She is not lost. I know where she is. But she is not with me. And for a very long time, I was most definitely LOST without her.

No amount of platitudes can fix that. If you have never experienced a similar loss, do not say, "It will get better in time," because YOU do not know that. Don't tell a grieving parent that their child is "in a better place," because even though I believe heaven is a better place, when Cori first died there was NO better place than in my arms. Acting as if she never existed by never talking to me about her was the worst thing someone who cared about me could do. If someone you know has lost a child, SPEAK that child's name. TELL the mother and father your memories of that child. What he or she meant to YOU. How their life impacted you. Write the days on the calendar and send a card or write a note. Private message them on Facebook to let them know you are thinking of them. Not just the first year but for as many years as you can.

When my mom died, my dad heard from hundreds of people with cards of sympathy and calls. But it was the one or two people he did not hear from after her death that had the most impact. I have a friend who was unable to fly when Cori died. She got on Amtrak and traveled for three days to get here in time for Cori's funeral. To this day she signs cards and notes "Love to you, Steve and Molly and Cori Joy too." I will never tire of seeing someone else write her name or speak her name.

Journey is the perfect word to explain what grief is. There is a definite starting point. And from this point, one can and often does travel forward and backwards, gaining and losing ground. For me, there will come an end to my journey. But until my final breath is over, my journey of grief will never end.

One does not "get over" grief. Like a journey, grieving is a process. Some sights, sounds and feelings along the way are easier to maneuver through than others. The best part of the grief journey is who you meet along the way. Fellow sojourners. All with their own private pain and yet you are instantly connected to them. The grief journey is not a sprint. It is a marathon.

There is a song that I listened to back in the late 1970s. A lyric in it was a paraphrase from a Robert Browning Hamilton quote and truly sums up where I feel I am at in my personal grief journey:

I walked a mile with Pleasure;
She chatted all the way;
But left me none the wiser
For all she had to say.
I walked a mile with Sorrow;
And ne'er a word said she;
But, oh! The things I learned from her,
When Sorrow walked with me.

*

KARI BROWN
Kari's 2-year-old daughter Dominique (Deedee)
died in 2014 from obstructive sleep apnea

The journey through grief is an especially hard experience to go through. There is never an end to the journey, and the pain will always be there. It is up to me to decide what to do with the lessons I've learned through challenges. I have learned that it eases my pain to teach others and share my experience. I am still a parent, and I have the experience of raising a child for two years and four months. I have learned not to take it personally when someone says I don't have experience, because they also don't have the experience of what I've been through. It is up to me to decide how to react with regards to my daughter's death. I ask for strength similar to Dominique's to get me through the day, and for her comfort when I am having a hard day.

I miss Dominique every single second, and I long for her to be here with me. I know she is watching over me; I see signs of her everywhere almost daily. I try not to look for her, but I do keep my mind open to the love she sprinkles throughout the day. Doing so helps me get through the hard times.

I don't pay attention to what people say about how long it should take to "get over" Dominique's death. There is no expiration on grieving or missing someone; it may take one year or thirty. I will always miss the daughter who came into our world, and left too soon. She taught me more about life and love than I could have ever imagined. I am forever grateful for the short time she was here with us, and will cherish the time we had.

Mama and Daddy love you and miss you so much. We are forever blessed to have you and we think of you every single day.

*

TANISHA CALDWELL
Tanisha's 23-year-old son Tariq (Jay)
died in a car accident in 2015

My journey has shown me that one can never truly understand the depth of loss and grief until it happens to you. It has definitely been eye opening for me! I'll never say the wrong thing to another person who has lost a loved one. I have learned that life truly is short. Never in a million years would I have thought I would lose my son and be participating in a book about grief! You don't have to be old or sick to die. I've learned, and continue to learn, that my hope remains in Jesus Christ. He is the only who has seen me through. Without him, without my relationship with him, I don't know where I would be. My life has been forever changed; I'll never be the same. I'm still adjusting to Jay being gone. I still get sick when I think about Jay not ever coming back. My days have been long, lonely, dark, rough, sad, and tiresome. But I'm still making it...day by day, hour by hour, minute by minute, second by second. It's all I can do. With God, I can handle it, and so can you!!!

*

LYNDA CHELDELIN FELL
Lynda's 15-year-old daughter Aly
died in a car accident in 2009

I would like people to know that it's okay to talk about our losses; in fact, it's imperative to our well-being and should be viewed as a critical piece of recovery. When we share memories or sad emotions, it doesn't mean we're stuck, it means we're processing a very complex transition, and that's healthy. Past generations tend to believe that openly discussing our sorrow is a sign of wallowing in self-pity. I hope our generation turns that thinking around, because those who stifle their sorrow are the ones we should be concerned about. They are in the danger zone of failing to thrive after loss, not the other way around.

*

JACQUELYN CRUZ
Jacquelyn's 24-year-old daughter Jenna
died in 2012 from pulmonary edema

Everything I've read about grief is true. But when you're the one grieving, you have to multiply it by a thousand. You read about the waves of grief and how they come and go but you really can't understand the depths of the water until you're standing in it, drowning. You can't explain it to anyone who hasn't lost a child.

I remember in the first weeks of grieving I was so lost. I kept saying, "I don't know how to do this, please someone tell me how I do this." So, like any other somewhat educated woman, I read. I read everything about grief and losing a child. I walked, I meditated, I read some more, but at the end of all that, Jenna still wasn't here with me. People have to understand that you never get over losing a child. All the self-help books and meditating in the world doesn't bring them back. What I have learned is how to ride the waves now, how to avoid certain places and people. I cry every single day for Jenna. Sometimes it's just one tear that slips out and other days I get in the car alone and go somewhere where nobody can hear me. The crying has to happen, it has to be released, it cleanses my heart for the next day.

*

MICHELLE DETWILER
Michelle's 19-year-old daughter Emily
died in 2014 due to congenital complications

For many days and weeks after our daughter was gone I lived in a fog. I didn't know I could hurt so bad and still be alive. At times it took the breath away from me. And then a day passed, and then the next day, and then the next. And soon a week passed. I was still alive. I didn't want to be here! I wanted to be with my girl! My friends and family carried me along. They provided support when I could not possibly do anything for myself. I often thought, "How can I survive another day?" But I did.

For those who are reading these lines because you have lost a child, I'm here to tell you that you can make it. Your grief will never be over, but it will change. It's a journey that is difficult to go through, and it seems like no one else can understand the pain. I can. I've been here for over a year now and I thought I would not get through it. What is helping me through it? My faith in God, my family and friends, and my grief support group. While it felt like I would be forever hurting, forever struggling, I am now moving forward. My life has changed. It won't always be days filled with sorrow. There are days when the sun does actually rise! Grief is a journey, not a destination. Follow the path, lean on loved ones and continue to look forward. There will be a better tomorrow.

*

ANNAH ELIZABETH
Annah's son Gavin Michael aspirated on his meconium
during the delivery and died 26 minutes following his birth

Which one? I ask, for there are many paths that bring about grief, and I've traveled the terrain of many types of loss, from death to disaster, from miscarriage to mental illness, from infidelity to an inferno that destroyed our family's business and rattled our financial security. My grief journeys and my quests for comfort unearthed many grief event recovery tools, a collection of which I've assembled into a resource I call "The Five Facets of Healing."

What I'd like you to know about my journey is something everyone needs to know: We can go on to live our best personal, professional, and philanthropic lives, even in the face of adversity. The five most important things I discovered are:

1. Chinese philosopher Lao Tzu once said, "A journey of a thousand miles begins with one step." We need to begin a new conversation around the meanings of and the autonomy between loss, grief, and healing. We need to know that healing doesn't mean that what happened to us is okay; it merely means that we can somehow be okay in the face of our adversity.

2. In order to heal, we need to identify the type(s) of loss we are experiencing as well as the minor misfortunes that we tend to overlook. I call these "The 5 Ds." They include death, despair, disaster, disease, and dysfunction.

3. We have everything we need to heal. In fact, we are each born with everything we need to triumph over tragedy. Though the details look differently on each one of us, WE ARE ALL BORN WITH THE SAME FIVE FACETS. The five facets are our academic ability to learn; our ability to feel emotion; our physical environment and the physical body we are born into; our ability to connect, to relate to others; and the spirit that resides in our very epicenter.

4. There are five steps to help us systematically make the transition from grief to healing. Whereas we often are not in control when faced with adversity, healing is a choice that empowers us. The five Steps of Healing are: Choose grief. Choose acceptance. Choose your facets. Choose healing. Choose vitality.

5. Platitudes, quotes and clichés like "Time heals all wounds" and "Everything happens for a reason" all have meaning, but each and every one of them holds a different meaning for every one of us. Whereas one phrase might bring great comfort to you, it might elicit great angst in another. The reason for this is that we each bring to the table different experiences, different expectations, and different belief systems. We need to create our own set of power mantras, personal sound bites that feed our souls and fuel our inspiration. By establishing our own power mantras, we establish inspiration that we, as individuals, can live by.

*

WENDY EVANS
Wendy's 21-year-old son Kyle died in 2009
from diabetes when his insulin pump malfunctioned

I would like the world to know that my grief journey has no end. I will always miss my son. I will always wish the outcome was different. My love for my son goes on even though he is not here.

*

BONNIE FORSHEY
Bonnie's 16-year-old son Billy died in 1993
from an overdose of prescription drugs

There is no quick fix when you lose a child. Everyone grieves differently and there is no time limit. I lost my son twenty-two years ago and I still grieve. I still cry when I see someone who looks like him or hear a song that he liked. You never get over it, you just learn how to adapt and keep going.

*

TALIA GATO
Talia's 8-year-old daughter Poppy
died in 2009 in a car accident

I don't dream of my sweet daughter often, I wish it was more. Recently I did have a dream that we were all in church. It was an older church, smaller, with light-colored wooden pews. In my dream my husband and I were closer to the front. There was a choir performing and singing, only it was odd that the choir was facing away from the congregation. I thought it was strange. The choir included people of all ages young, old and middle-aged, maybe about twenty-five people. In the middle there was a beautiful girl wearing a white dress, singing and smiling. I knew immediately it was my daughter Poppy. I urgently had to see her face and look into her eyes; I had to! I said, "Rodrigo, it's Poppy! Let's go see her!" We ran to her and Rodrigo picked her up and twirled her around and around....it was her! I saw her face, we were so happy! It was then I realized why the choir was facing away from us, they were singing to God and I was in heaven.

I would like the world to know my story on how I picked up the pieces of my life. In fact, I am still doing this. I believe it takes a lifetime of picking up pieces and putting them together again with my daughter and husband. There is not a manual on how to overcome loss, we have to learn to bear it. Like a farmer getting calluses on his hand and building muscles for digging, we learn to adapt. There is no timetable for this. If each of us got to tell our real stories on how our life is on this journey, this living without our child, it is so different from other losses, and here is why. We have to learn to absorb our grief, compartmentalize our loss, learn to "bear" it rather than run away from it. Maybe when we feel loved through the pain, we can have the feeling of surviving one more day. Just being understood in itself is healing. I am thankful for all the people I have met along the road called grief whom I most likely would have never met before. The meaningful connections that made a huge impact made my heart feel validated. When I walk

345

away from these deep conversions, I walk away so empowered in a way that I had never before experienced. It's a sense of heightened fulfillment which I've never experienced before in my life. For this, I am thankful and blessed. To be in that moment of truth is healing. I am not healed, but it is a healing experience. People say, "You can't let that define you." Oh, but it did! How can surviving a car crash but losing a child in that crash not change you? But what happened that day helped me to understand what is worthwhile, more authentic. And that, in itself, is freeing.

I would like to end with a quote:

> *Pain deserves acknowledgment, not repair.*
> *We need to start telling new stories of bravery*
> *in the face of pain that can't be fixed. The path*
> *of bearing witness is the true path of love.*
> *You are not helpless in the face of someone's pain.*
> *Hearing someone's pain and letting*
> *them have it is an amazing gift.*
> MEGAN DIVINE
> "Refuge in Grief"

*

KORBY HAVE
Korby's 17-year-old daughter Taylor (Tayla)
died in 2013 in a car accident

That grief isn't cut and dried as people make it out to be. My daughter has been gone for almost two and a half years and my heart and soul still hurt as much as they did when I found out she had been killed. I still have a hard time getting through each day and life seems hopeless without her. Time does not heal all wounds and just because she is in a better place doesn't make losing her any easier.

*

DEANA MARTIN
Deana's only two children, 25-year-old Amanda
and 21-year-old Logan, died in a car accident in 2011

Where would I start on what I would like the world to know about my grief journey? I personally would like the world to know it is very hard to live with this pain, and that it is a real and physical pain. It is emotional and physical and it is a journey with no destination. When someone has faced such a profound loss as the loss of a child or children, your identity as that person's mother is gone. And there is no way to describe how it feels to lose your identity as a mother. I spent my entire childhood wanting children, wanting something, someone to love me who could never leave me. Then I spent twenty-five years of my life loving my children with everything I had and doing my best with no direction or much help, raising them and trying to teach them how to fit into this crazy world of ours and how to keep their individuality and what makes them special and unique at the same time. That was a superhuman feat when I had no earthly idea on how to do it myself. But it had worked for the most part. My children, like anyone, had their own individual issues in life. But they were, and are, amazing people. They managed for the most part to learn to fit into society but still maintain their beautiful uniqueness. They taught me so much!

I look back at some of the silly disagreements we had and how much of their lives I took for granted or issues I thought were huge and none of it mattered. Who cares that Amanda thought wearing cat collars to school was cool, or that Logan could care less if he smelled like a horse or dirty gym socks? None of that mattered. The only thing that mattered is that they knew I loved them with my entire being, and that I was there for them no matter what. I would not help them if they would not help themselves, and we lived through many years of tough love and had many, many disagreements.

347

They had manipulated me, cheated me, lied to me, stolen from me, hurt me terribly with their guilt trips, and boy, did they know how to push my buttons. They knew without a shadow of a doubt that I would never bail them out of jail, so they better not end up there. Because if they had done something that deserved going to jail for, then jail is where they needed to be. They knew that when I died what my last wishes were, and they had to carry them out, although they were silly and ever changing. At one point, I was to be buried in the sky like the Indians on a platform. But I didn't want the birds to eat me, so I needed to be in a glass box like Sleeping Beauty. I was to be in my pajamas, on my side with a blanket pulled up over my shoulder like I was sleeping.

You see, my children were also my best friends. And I shared these silly things with them while dealing with my own fear of death while battling breast cancer. It was my way of making them laugh and finding joy in something that could end up very devastating and painful. They, however, did not reciprocate. When it came time to make their final earthly arrangements, I had no clue. Along with motherhood also comes this naiveté about death. You never think in a million years that your child could die - at least I didn't. I feel as if there are a million or possibly a billion things I want the world to know about my journey. However, I would never want them to know it well enough. I wouldn't want them to know the pain, isolation, hopelessness and fear associated with it. I would not want them to know how difficult it is to function or how lonely it is. Losing a child goes against the natural order of life, leaving an endless battle for your brain to make sense of something so senseless. When I lost my children a part of myself, a big part, went with them. Where my heart once was now stood a huge black hole. As I mentioned before, none of the trials and tribulations with a child matter! All that matters is love! Don't let a day go by without saying "I love you" and kiss and hug loved ones as often as you can! Make sure they know how special they are in your eyes and what a gift from the gods they are to you! Because if you are sitting here in my chair typing this, nothing else will matter.

348

*

MONICA MIRKES
Monica's 30-year-old daughter Marisa
died in 2013 due to Cesarean complications

This is a hard road to walk. We see so many things that are just not right. I had a wonderful little girl who didn't let her burdens weigh her down. She was like a turtle making her way. Life would flip her over and leave her on her back, but she would right herself and, without complaining, continue without missing a beat. To lose a child is the end of your life as you knew it to be. My life is forever changed. I miss her. I will miss her until my heart stops beating.

*

DENISE PURCELL
Denise's 27-year-old daughter Megan died
in 2011 from an accidental overdose

My grief journey will never end. It will always hurt a little. I will cry a little. I will even wish a little. But I know Megan can't come back. I know she loved me. She made a difference in so many people's lives for the years I did have the privilege of being her mom. As a parent, that day is forever etched in our memories. But since that day, Megan is etched in every part of my life, my thoughts, my heart. I smile because she gave me the greatest gift of all: her unconditional love. And to have hurt so deeply also means to have loved so deeply.

*

MARILYN ROLLINS
Marilyn's 37-year-old son Randy and 16-year-old granddaughter Sara
died in a car accident in 2006 during a family camping trip

I guess it would be that grief is indeed a journey. There is no textbook that can tell me what stage of grief I should be in, or how long it should take me to get through it. There is no end to it, you do not "get over it." It is lifelong. I believe this to be especially true when a child dies, whether it be an infant, child, teen or adult child. This is not what we've learned in our whole lives, about the "cycle of life." We've learned that our children are supposed to bury us, not the opposite. I can remember my husband saying this over and over again at the wake: "We're not supposed to bury our children."

Our futures changed. Sara will never marry or give me a great-grandchild. Randy was the one who was going to take care of health, aging and end-of-life issues for his father and me. It raises real questions and fears for us.

The person that I was before the accident is gone. I am, however, very aware of the person left behind. I wish I could say that I'm completely satisfied with the person I have become, but I continue changing and growing every day.

Yes, grief is a journey. A journey with so many ups and downs that I've heard it described as a rollercoaster ride. I have been at the top, only to crash before the day is over. As time goes by though, things are leveling off. I think the old adage of "time heals" still stands. But we do have to remember that with any healing wound there is a scar.

*

KATIE ROUSH
Katie's 26-year-old daughter Krystle
died in 2013 of accidental alcohol poisoning

It is going on three years since my youngest daughter, Krystle, died. And I have no clue how the hell I did it, but here I am. Three birthdays, almost three Halloweens, two Thanksgivings, two Christmases, and two Easters and two angelversaries. I have new words I use now: survivor language; Angelversary, deceased daughter, before you died, after you died, memorial, crematory jewelry. I have walked through the pits of hell, a place few know about. It's where your heart goes after being shattered into a million pieces. The place where memories of replaying a day of death lived and haunted me. The place where fear, darkness and emptiness live. I was there for a while. The fires of that place molded me into this person you see now. I had to stay there to become strong. I cried hot tears that never seemed to stop. That beginning pain of death was so much bigger than life at that moment. I felt as if I walked in shadows waiting for a replay, waiting to wake from this horrible nightmare; for the world to stop moving; for the shock to wear off; for the pain to subside; for the tears to not fall so much, and for life to come back to me.

When the door to life opened again, I came through it with new knowledge. It's stuff that only parents who have had to face a death of their child know. How to answer questions like "How many kids do you have?" or "How old is your youngest?" or "What are your children's names?" How to silently celebrate birthdays and to get through them when my heart is silently breaking. Why? Because the day that once was joyous is now a permanent reminder of loss. Hearing my child's name or seeing her name on mail brought me to my knees. I had so many worries to overcome. I worried about whether she was scared when God took her home and if she was scared because I was not there; if she struggled when she died; if she was okay on the other side. I worried about whether I was a good enough mother, and worried if I could have done more. I worried about whether Krystle knew just how much I loved her.

Now, new worries: am I going to forget her voice, her laugh, her smell, how the sun made her hair sparkle, or the look of her smile? Will I forget how it felt to hold her or if my daughter will forget me. These are "grown-up" worries.

The "old me" is slowly returning. But a piece of my broken heart pierces through and I cry, though it too has changed. It is subtle and soft and soundless. I cry at old memories now: watching a movie, hearing a song you loved, or going to a place that we used to visit. I have broken down looking at a pair of ear buds. Those times are becoming fewer, but they are still there. These are part of the "new me." The old and new parts are melding.

351

I feel as if I am learning how to walk again. I am stronger, but weaker. I never thought I could continue on after she died. I learned slowly. I whisper to her when I look into the stars at night. I hope she is proud of this new and improved version of her mother that her death helped me to become. I visit Krystle in memories and in my dreams, and we laugh, cry, and talk until morning comes. I don't fear mornings anymore. My daughter said that tomorrow is never promised, and today is a gift; that is why it is called a present. I unwrap each new day with joy and welcome laughter now. With all of the ups and downs, the greatest joys and the most sorrowful sorrows, it is still a beautiful world. I live each day now in the present, in this gift.

I love you, Krystle, every second of every minute of every day. I will carry you with me, proudly. You are my child who taught me how to love even more after your death. I carry you in my heart always. I just hope I live up to my daughter's legacy.

*

SARA RUBLE
Sara's 19-year-old son Scott died in 1994 from a
combination of a seizure disorder, Strep throat and dehydration

I have written about my grief and many aspects of my life in the last twenty years since Scott died. I have the knowing and even the advantage of seeing more outcomes, my wisdom growing, and my spiritual growth sustaining me. I knew so little about a spiritual path before my son died. For many years after his death I only knew that "spiritual" went above and beyond the knowing of something. I was limited, but became more curious as I desperately needed answers that again went beyond conventional thinking. Scott pushed me to seek out more by sending me signs and messages, and coming to me in vivid dreams. It was impossible for me not to know he was continuing his relationship with me. It was life-sustaining, mysterious, magical, and not at all logical. I had to understand how, in death, these kinds of things could occur and bring such great assurance of continuing relationships with our loved ones. And so I have grown into a new belief system that includes knowing that we plan our lives before we are born. Nothing is random, but filled with meaning. I hated thinking Scott's death was random. I now know his life and death were, and continue to be, filled with meaning and purpose. This brings me great peace of mind and definitely contributed to my ability to truly invest in healing my broken heart...and in life again.

Bigger picture, greater meaning...going way beyond what I knew before. I believe in God and trust there is always more than I can see. I know my own journey has great meaning too, as I have seen it evolve over these last twenty years. I have a rich and remarkable life knowing that Scott and I came into this lifetime together for all the experiences, lessons and love we shared...and it continues now in beautiful spiritual ways.

*

One hello can change a day.
One hug can change a life.
One hope can change a destiny.
LYNDA CHELDELIN FELL

*

CHAPTER TWENTY

FINDING THE SUNRISE

One night in my own journey, I had one of *those* dreams: a vivid nightmare that stays with you. I was running westward in a frantic attempt to catch the sun as it descended below the horizon. Advancing from behind was nightfall; ominous and frightening. It was a pitch-black abyss. And it was coming directly for me. I ran desperately as fast as my legs could go toward the sunset, but my attempt was futile; it sank below the horizon, out of my reach. Oh, the looming nightfall was terrifying! But it was clear that if I wanted to see the sun ever again, I had to stop running west and instead walk east to begin my journey through the great nightfall of grief. For just as there would be no rainbow without the rain, the sun rises only on the other side of night.

The message was clear: it was futile to avoid my grief; I had to allow it to swallow me whole. Then, and only then, would I find my way through it and out the other side.

I remember reading in a bereavement book that if we don't allow ourselves to experience the full scope of the journey, it will come back to bite us. I couldn't fathom how it could get any worse, but I knew I didn't want to test that theory. So I gave in and allowed the grief to swallow me whole. I allowed myself to wail on my daughter's bedroom floor. I penned my deep emotions, regardless of who might read it. I created a national radio show to openly and candidly discuss our journeys with anyone who wanted to call in. And I allowed myself to sink to the bottom of the fiery pits of hell. This, in turn, lit a fire under me, so to speak, to find a way out.

Today I'm often asked how I manage my grief so well. Some assume that because I have found peace and joy, I'm simply avoiding my grief. Others believe that because I work in the bereavement field, I'm wallowing in self-pity. Well, which is it?

Neither. I miss my child with every breath I take. Just like you, I will always have my moments and triggers: the painful holidays, birthdays, death anniversaries, a song or smell that evokes an unexpected memory. But I have also found purpose, beauty and joy again. It takes hard work and determination to overcome profound grief, and it also takes the ability to let go and succumb to the journey. Do not be afraid of the tears, sorrow, and heartbreak; they are a natural reaction and imperative to our healing.

As you walk your own path, avail yourself of whatever bereavement tools ease your discomfort, for each one was created by someone who walked in your shoes and understands the heartache. While there are many wonderful resources available, what brings comfort to one person might irritate the next. Bereavement tools are not one-size-fits-all, so if one tool doesn't work, find another.

Lastly, grief is not something we get *over*, like a mountain. Rather, it is something we get *through*, like the rapids of Niagara Falls. Without the kayak and paddle. And plenty of falls. But it's also survivable. And if others have survived this wretched journey, why not me? And why not you?

On the following pages are the baby steps I took to put hell in my rearview mirror. At first they took great effort and lots of patience. But like any dedicated routine, it got easier over time, and the reward of finding balance in my life was worth every step.

1. VALIDATING OUR EMOTIONS

The first step is to validate your emotions. When we talk about our deep heartbreak, we aren't ruminating in our sorrow or feeling sorry for ourselves. By discussing it, we are actually processing it. If we aren't allowed to process it, then it becomes silent grief. Silent grief is deadly grief.

Find a friend who will patiently listen while you discuss your loss for fifteen minutes every day. Set the timer, and ask them not to say anything during those fifteen minutes. Explain that it is important for you to just ramble without interruption, guidance, or judgment. You need not have the same listener each time, but practice this step <u>every</u> day.

2. COMPASSIONATE THOUGHTS

Find yourself a quiet spot. It can be your favorite chair, in your car, in your office, or even in your garden. Then clear your head and for five minutes think nothing but compassionate thoughts about yourself. Not your spouse, not your children, not your coworkers, but yourself. Having trouble? Fill in the blanks below, and then give yourself permission to really validate those positive qualities. Do this every day.

I have a _____
Example: good heart, gentle soul, witty personality

I make a _____
Example: good lasagna, potato salad, scrapbook, quilt

I'm a good_____
Example: friend, gardener, knitter, painter, poem writer

People would say I'm _____
Example: funny, kind, smart, gentle, generous, humble, creative

3. TENDER LOVING CARE

While grieving, it is important to consider yourself in the intensive care unit of Grief United Hospital, and treat accordingly. How would nurses treat you if you were their patient in the ICU? They would be compassionate, gentle, and allow for plenty of rest. That is exactly how you should treat yourself. Also, consider soothing your physical self with TLC as an attentive way to honor your emotional pain. This doesn't mean you have to book an expensive massage. If wearing fuzzy blue socks offers a smidgen of comfort, then wear them unabashedly. If whipped cream on your cocoa offers a morsel of pleasure, then indulge unapologetically.

Treating our five senses to anything that offers a perception of delight might not erase the emotional heartache, but it will offer a reminder that not all pleasure is lost. List five ways you can offer yourself tender loving care, and then incorporate <u>at least three</u> into your day, every day. With practice, the awareness of delight eventually becomes effortless, and is an important step toward regaining joy.

TLC suggestions:
- Shower or bathe with a lovely scented soap
- Soak in a warm tub with Epsom salts or a splash of bath oil
- Wear a pair of extra soft socks
- Light a fragrant candle
- Listen to relaxing music
- Apply a rich lotion to your skin before bed
- Indulge in a few bites of your favorite treat
- Enjoy a mug of your favorite soothing herbal tea
- Add whipped cream to a steaming mug of cocoa
- _____
- _____
- _____
- _____

4. SEE THE BEAUTY

Listening to the birds outside my bedroom window every morning was something I had loved since childhood. But when Aly died, I found myself deaf and blind to the beauty around me. My world had become colorless and silent. On one particular morning as I struggled to get out of bed, I halfheartedly noticed the birds chirping outside my bedroom window. My heart sank as I realized that they had been chirping all along, but I was now deaf to their morning melody. Panic set in as I concluded that I would never enjoy life's beauty ever again. Briefly entertaining suicide to escape the profound pain, I quickly ruled it out. My family had been through so much already, I couldn't dump further pain on them. But in order to survive the heartbreak, I had to find a way to allow beauty back into my life.

So on that particular morning as I lay in bed, I forced myself to listen and really *hear* the birds. Every morning from that point forward, I repeated that same exercise. With persistent practice, it became easier and then eventually effortless to appreciate the birds' chirping and singsongs. Glorious beauty and sounds have once again returned to my world.

Profound grief can appear to rob our world of all beauty. Yet the truth is, and despite our suffering, beauty continues to surround us. The birds continue to sing, flowers continue to bloom, the surf continues to ebb and flow. Reconnecting to our surroundings helps us to reintegrate back into our environment.

Begin by acknowledging one small pleasantry each day. Perhaps your ears register the sound of singing birds. Or you catch the faint scent of warm cookies as you walk past a bakery. Or notice the sun's illumination of a nearby red rosebush. Give yourself permission to notice one pleasantry, and allow it to *really* register.

SURVIVING LOSS OF A CHILD

Here are some suggestions:
- Listen to the birds sing (hearing)
- Observe pretty cloud formations (sight)
- Visit a nearby park and listen to the children (hearing)
- Notice the pretty colors of blooming flowers (sight)
- Light a fragrant candle (scent)
- See the beauty in the sunset (sight)
- Attend a local recital, concert, play, or comedy act (hearing)
- Wear luxury socks (touch)
- Wrap yourself in a soft scarf or sweater (touch)
- Indulge in whipped cream on your cocoa (taste)
- Enjoy a Hershey's chocolate kiss (taste)

5. PROTECT YOUR HEALTH

After our daughter's accident I soon found myself fighting an assortment of viruses including head colds, stomach flus, sore throats and more, compounding my already frazzled emotions. Studies show that profound grief throws our body into "flight or fight" syndrome for months and months, which is very hard on our physical body. Thus, it becomes critical to guard our physical health. Incorporating a few changes into our daily routine feels hard at first, but soon gets easy. Plus, a stronger physical health helps to strengthen our coping skills.

Below are a few suggestions to consider adding to your daily routine to help your physical self withstand the emotional upheaval.
- Practice good sleep hygiene
- Drink plenty of water
- Take a short walk outside every day
- Resist simple carbohydrates (I'm a food addict, so I know that avoiding simple carbs is worth its weight in gold)
- Keep a light calendar and guard your time carefully, don't allow others to dictate and overflow your schedule

6. FIND AN OUTLET

For a long time in the grief journey, everything is painful. In the early days, just getting out of bed and taking a shower can be exhausting. Housecleaning, grocery shopping, and routine errands often take a back seat or disappear altogether. As painful as it is, it's very important to find an outlet that gets you out of bed each day. Finding something to distract you from the pain, occupy your mind, and soothe your senses can be tricky, but possible. Performing a repetitive action can calm your mood, and even result in a new craft or gifts to give.

Beginning a new outlet may feel exhausting at first, just remember that the first step is always the hardest. And you don't have to do it forever, just focus on it for the time being.

Possible activities include:
- Learn to mold chocolate or make soap
- Learn how to bead, knit, crochet, or quilt
- Volunteer at a local shelter
- Learn a new sport such as golf or kayaking
- Create a memorial garden in a forgotten part of the yard
- Join Pinterest
- Doodle or draw
- Mold clay
- Learn to scrapbook
- Join a book club

Grief is hell on earth. It truly is. But when walking through hell, your only option is to keep going. Eventually the hell ends, the dark night fades to dawn, and the sun begins to rise once again.

Just keep going, and you too will find the sunrise.

Lynda Cheldelin Fell

Hope is like the sun, which, as we journey toward it,
casts the shadow of our burden behind us.
SAMUEL SMILES

*

MEET THE WRITERS

There's a bright future for you at every turn,
even if you miss one.

*

*

ERICA GALE BELTZ
Erica's 5-year-old son Luke Jordan
died in 2005 from a fallen banister in his aunt's driveway
lukeslove5@gmail.com

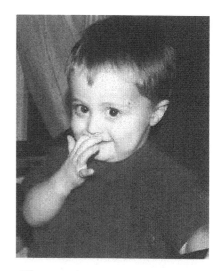

Erica Gale Beltz was born in Herrin, Illinois, the youngest of three. The family moved frequently, finally settling in western Georgia when Erica was eight. At eighteen, Erica gave birth to her daughter Lakin who was born fighting for her life. Five years later Erica gave birth to Luke. Struggling through alcoholism, drug abuse, and domestic violence, Erica worked backwards to find her footing. Erica has been a general manager at J. Christopher's in Marietta, Georgia, for the past three years and been with the company for eight. Despite her daughter's serious medical needs, Erica has volunteered extensively for The Compassionate Friends including serving as group leader, co-leader, facilitator instructor and event coordinator. She also volunteers for Kate's Club, a club for grieving children. Erica is co-author of *Grief Diaries: Surviving Loss of a Child* and *Grief Diaries: How to Help the Newly Bereaved*. Her first grandchild, Ava Kate, was due on Luke's Angel Day, and has brought a joy into Erica's life that keeps her heart singing. She and her fiancé just bought a home where they reside with their English bulldog MollyGirl.

365

*
STACY BERNDTSON
Stacy's daughter Cori Joy died in 2003, the day before her
fourth birthday, from an undiagnosed genetic disorder
stacylindy1@comcast.net

Stacy Berndtson was born and raised in Bellingham, WA. She moved to California in 1987, where she met and married her husband, Steve, in 1989. After ten years of infertility, Stacy gave birth to her daughter Corinne Joy in 1999. They moved back to Washington in 2001.

In 2007, nearly four years after Cori's death, Steve and Stacy adopted their daughter Molly Faith. They live in Blaine, Washington.

*
KARI BROWN
Kari's 2-year-old daughter Dominique (Deedee)
died in 2014 from obstructive sleep apnea

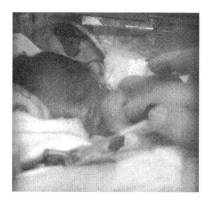

Kari Brown was born in 1988 and raised in Gray, Maine. She moved to Austin, Texas in 2008 with her fiancé Brandon.

Kari was born with Treacher Collins Syndrome, a genetic congenital disease she passed on to her daughter Dominique who was born on December 28, 2011. This was a true blessing in Kari's life and enabled her to be a stay-at-home mom while attending college to obtain her nursing degree.

*

TANISHA CALDWELL
Tanisha's 23-year-old son Tariq (Jay)
died in a car accident in 2015
ladytee73@gmail.com

Tanisha Caldwell was born and raised in Detroit, Michigan. She is the mother of three children and one grandson, and is expecting her second grandson in March 2016.

Tanisha enjoys making people look and feel good, and is currently pursuing an education in the beauty field.

Tanisha plans to continue to speak out about her grief, as she feels people need to know how grief really is. She believes that everything happens for a reason, and that this is the path that God has placed her on. Tanisha resides in Michigan with her husband Tremayne.

*

LYNDA CHELDELIN FELL
Lynda's 15-year-old daughter Aly
died in a car accident in 2009
www.lyndafell.com * lynda@lyndafell.com

Born and raised in the Pacific Northwest, Lynda Cheldelin Fell is a mother and grandmother who treasures moments of joy, laughter, and the little things in life. In 2009, Lynda and her beloved husband lost their third child, a fifteen-year-old competitive swimmer named Aly, in a tragic car accident while coming home from watching the U.S. Open in Seattle.

Surrounded by love and support, Lynda was determined to overcome the overwhelming darkness, and was just finding her footing when her forty-six-year-old husband suffered a major stroke leaving him with permanent disabilities. Seeing the world through the filter of sorrow, Lynda found comfort by helping others who were struggling, and this fueled her passion to create a legacy of help, healing and hope.

*

JACQUELYN CRUZ
Jacquelyn's 24-year-old daughter Jenna
died in 2012 from pulmonary edema
Jcruz62jackie@aol.com

Jackie Cruz is a fifty-three-year-old native of Staten Island, New York. She has been married to her husband, David, for twenty-nine years.

Jackie is the mother of three children: Danny, twenty-four, Chelsea, twenty-two, and Jenna, who would have been twenty-eight this coming February. Jackie was a stay-at-home mom until Chelsea entered kindergarten, at which time she began working as a special education para-professional for the New York City school system. Jackie enjoys baking, reading and gardening.

*

MICHELLE DETWILER
Michelle's 19-year-old daughter Emily
died in 2014 due to congenital complications
mdetwiler@yahoo.com

 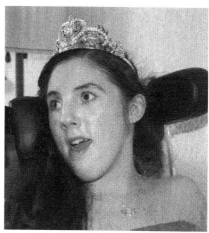

Michelle Detwiler and her husband, Jeff, have raised four children in Washington state. Former foster parents for seventeen years, they adopted two of their four children through the state. Michelle's career experiences have been varied.

Aside from foster care, she was also at one time a medical assistant, an electronics technician, and a regular contributing writer for *Preemie* magazine. Michelle owns an embroidery business and works as a professional embroiderer. She also loves all kinds of crafts, especially making mini scrapbooks.

*

ANNAH ELIZABETH
Annah's son Gavin Michael aspirated on his meconium
during the delivery and died 26 minutes following his birth
www.TheFiveFacets.com * thefivefacets@aol.com

Annah Elizabeth is an author, speaker, and the creator of The Five Facets Philosophy on Healing™, a groundbreaking guide that helps us live our best personal, professional, and philanthropic lives, even in the face of adversity. She authored the book, *Digging for the Light* and is co-author of *Grief Diaries: Surviving Loss of a Child* and *Grief Diaries: How to Help the Newly Bereaved*.

Motivated by personal tragedy, the death of her firstborn — and other big and little life grievances including miscarriage, infidelity, and severe depression — Annah Elizabeth set out to uncover the secrets that allow some people to triumph over tragedy. Through her explorations of loss, grief, and healing, Annah not only discovered that the answers are as universal as the mystery itself, but also unearthed essential grief event recovery tools which she assembled into an innovative program, one that teaches us how to solve grief puzzles by identifying, evaluating, and refashioning conflicts with intent and purpose. Annah's work pioneers a new discussion and provides the roadmap that helps us make the transition from grief to healing. Born and raised in North Carolina, Annah currently lives in upstate New York with her husband and numerous pets, in a soon-to-be empty nest, but that is just geography. Annah feels at home wherever her life and work lead her. Got Grief? Get Healing.™ with Annah Elizabeth and The Five Facets.

*

WENDY EVANS
Wendy's 21-year-old son Kyle died in 2009
from diabetes when his insulin pump malfunctioned
wendyconley1976@gmail.com

Wendy Evans was born in Middletown, Ohio, in the late 1950s. She is happily married with two children and two stepchildren.

Wendy has worked in the staffing industry since 1987 in a variety of roles. In 1996, Wendy and her family moved to Atlanta, Georgia, for better job and education opportunities.

*

BONNIE FORSHEY
Bonnie's 16-year-old son Billy died in 1993
from an overdose of prescription drugs
bonnieforshey@msn.com

Bonnie Forshey was born in Lewistown, Pennsylvania and grew up in New Castle, Delaware. She later moved to Swainsboro, Georgia, where she attended Emanuel County Junior College. She earned the Science Merit Award and graduated with her A.S. degree. She later attended Gordon State College in Barnesville, Georgia, earning a B.S. in Nursing.

Bonnie spent most of her career in medical-surgical, rehabilitation, geriatric, and long-term care facilities. She also raised two children and worked as a nursing assistant, unit secretary, and in medical records, while putting herself through school. Bonnie currently splits her time between Port Royal, Pennsylvania, and Brandon, Florida. She has two grandsons.

*

TALIA GATO
Talia's 8-year-old daughter Poppy
died in 2009 in a car accident
Talia can be contacted via lynda@alybluemedia.com

Talia grew up in the country with animals and gardens and orchards, the opposite of how her parents were raised; they both grew up in wealthy homes in the city. She married later in life to a wonderful and ambitious man with great values and a tender heart.

Talia has been very involved in school PTA programs and auctions. Before the loss of her daughter, she was very active in church leadership and led small groups and education classes for many years. She also started the first local support group for moms who had children with allergies. Since the loss of her daughter, she took time off from leadership roles to focus on caring and advocating for disadvantaged children. She continues to run a summer business, which is therapeutic and she loves the creativity it offers. Talia plans to pursue grief education courses. She facilitates a local support group for bereaved parents, and has led community events including balloon releases and candlelight vigils to advocate for grief awareness and to support the bereaved. Helping others facing loss gives Talia comfort and she hopes that in time our culture will be more open to discussing pain and loss which will lead to healthier communities.

Talia and her husband have two beautiful daughters, one here and the other in heaven waiting. Talia worked right up until giving birth to her oldest daughter, but once they had children, Talia devoted all her time to them. They live on a large plot of land in the country with fruit trees, animals, and lots of gardens.

*
DAPHNE GREER
Daphne's 5-year-old daughter Lydia died in 2008 in a
car accident during a routine morning commute
www.grievinggumdrops.com

Daphne Greer is a native of eastern Oregon, where she continues to reside with her husband, Jake, and their four living children where she enjoys the country lifestyle and love for the outdoors. She spent thirteen years as an adult parole officer.

Following the tragic death of her daughter in 2008, Daphne found a new purpose and passion in life. She cofounded a nonprofit organization in memory of her daughter, Lydia, which provides birthday celebrations to children in need. She blogs at www.grievinggumdrops.com and writes about finding hope amidst grief and loss. She is a member of the Oregon Christian Writers Association, and also served for five years on the steering committee of The Compassionate Friends in Salem, Oregon. She has contributed to two books: *Miracles and Moments of Grace, Inspiring Stories of Survival* by Nancy B. Kennedy, and *The Mom Quilt*, compiled by Paula Rollo, Becky Mansfield, and Jodi Durr. Daphne's memoir in progress was a finalist in the Cascade Writing Contest in 2015. Daphne also volunteers with Ellie's Way, a nonprofit organization proving hope and outreach for the bereaved.

*

KORBY HAVE
Korby's 17-year-old daughter Taylor (Tayla)
died in 2013 in a car accident
peaches2404@hotmail.com

Korby Have is a single mom struggling to raise her sons and deal with the devastation of losing her only daughter in a car accident. She was born and raised in Utah where she continues to live with her family.

*
DEANA MARTIN
Deana's only two children, 25-year-old Amanda
and 21-year-old Logan, died in a car accident in 2011
www.CryForMeNoMore.com * deana@cryformenomore.com

Deana Martin is a childless parent, who lost her only two children in a tragic auto accident in 2011. A third young man, Deana's future son-in-law, was also killed in the car. Miraculously, Deana was spared her only granddaughter who was in the car behind them. Since the death of her children Deana has become a certified grief specialist and has channeled the love for her children to other families facing loss. Before this life-changing tragedy, Deana was a project manager in the pharmaceutical industry and had enjoyed a twenty-five-year career with several Fortune 500 pharmaceutical companies, starting with Eli Lilly in 1988, the year her son was born.

She is vice president of Cry For Me, No More, co-author of *Grief Diaries: Surviving Loss of a Child* and serves on the board of the National Grief & Hope Coalition. She has faced many adversities in life and feels each one makes her stronger. She is a breast cancer survivor, and is no stranger to trauma. She hopes to help people heal by showing them how to find the strength and courage needed along the journey.

*

MONICA MIRKES
Monica's 30-year-old daughter Marisa
died in 2013 due to Cesarean complications
monica.mirkes@yahoo.com

Monica Mirkes was born and raised in Texas. She had four children, two boys and two girls, and juggled all the "mom" jobs including carpools, Boy Scout den leader, Camp Fire leader, church, pets, and home. She did this with endless energy and humor. Through it all she cared for a medically fragile child. Monica could always find a way to make you laugh no matter what you were doing.

After raising her own children, Monica found herself working with preschoolers, which led to her becoming a Montessori teacher. Her gift for making each child feel special, along with their families, makes her a very special person.

*

DENISE PURCELL
Denise's 27-year-old daughter Megan died
in 2011 from an accidental overdose
psunshine07@hotmail.com

Denise Purcell was born in Syracuse, New York. The oldest of seven children, Denise became a mother at the early age of sixteen, and had five daughters by the time she was thirty-one.

Denise is an artist with pieces on display around the northeast. She is also a published poet and is co-author of *Grief Diaries: Living with DID*, to be released in 2016.

Denise is a strong advocate for many injustices, and lives her life according to her own truth. Her children bring her great joy, and is she now proudly tackling empty nest syndrome with the last of her children now in college. Denise views life as a chance to see the beauty in adversity, and is trying to heal her broken heart since her daughter died in 2011.

*

MARILYN ROLLINS
Marilyn's 37-year-old son Randy and 16-year-old granddaughter Sara
died in a car accident in 2006 during a family camping trip
roll@netnitco.net

Marilyn Rollins was born in East Chicago, Indiana, and raised in Hessville, Indiana. She attended Morton Elementary and high school in Hessville, and graduated with a Licensed Practical Nurse diploma from Purdue University.

Marilyn began her nursing career on the medical floor of a hospital, eventually moving to nursery and then pediatrics. She spent the last twenty years of her career in family practice before retiring following the deaths of her son and granddaughter in 2006.

Marilyn attended The Compassionate Friends grief support group after their death, eventually taking leadership training and becoming a chapter leader herself. She is married and has one living son and six living grandchildren.

Marilyn feels it is important to help others on the grief journey and is co-author of *Grief Diaries: Surviving Loss of a Child*. She does intend to step back from leadership in 2016, after ten years in the organization. She and her husband, Bob, intend to do some traveling. They love road trips.

*

KATIE ROUSH
Katie's 26-year-old daughter Krystle
died in 2013 of accidental alcohol poisoning
Kroush0405@gmail.com

Katie Roush is a wife, mother, grandmother, dog lover, motorcycle rider, and doll maker. She is fifty-three years old and married to her best friend. She has three children. Thirty-three-year-old Samantha has twelve- and ten-year-old daughters, Haley and Paige. Katie's daughter Nicole is thirty-one and has one eight-year-old son, TJ. Katie's daughter Krystle was twenty-seven years old when she passed, leaving behind a daughter, Olivia, who is now ten.

Katie loves her grandchildren dearly. She and her husband, Griz, have two fur babies, Scooter, an eight-year-old Jack Russell terrier and a four-year-old American bulldog named Samson. Katie and her husband ride motorcycles for leisure.

Her husband owns a trucking business and Katie watches her grandson so her daughter can work. They are a family who laugh a lot and enjoy one another's company. Katie and her husband prank each other all the time, as well as their daughters and grandchildren.

*

SARA RUBLE
Sara's 19-year-old son Scott died in 1994 from a
combination of a seizure disorder, Strep throat and dehydration
www.deathteaches.com * Sara@deathteaches.com

Sara Ruble lives in Stow, Ohio. She graduated from the University of Akron with a degree in Elementary Education. She taught fifth and sixth grades, fulfilling her dream of working with children. When her son Scott was born, Sara chose to be a stay-at-home mom. Nothing was as amazing as that dream come true. As Scott entered kindergarten, Sara went back into the workplace as a sales representative for Maybelline cosmetics. On May 20, 1994, Sara's life changed forever when Scott suddenly died in his sleep. Her only child, the great love in her life, died at age nineteen. Life became much less meaningful and was a daily struggle. But, never one to give up, Sara found her way back into teaching, this time creating a support group for bereaved parents. It opened up a whole new future. In 2001, Sara and her committee created the Angel of Hope Children's Memorial in Stow. She co-authored *Surviving and Thriving: Grief Relief and Continuing Relationships*, as well as presenting at The Compassionate Friends National Conferences, Bereaved Parents of the USA National Gatherings, and Now-Childless Conferences. Her blog is titled Death Teaches...from a mom's perspective.

*

DENISE SHELTON
Denise's 22-year-old son Nicholas died in 2010
when he struck a steel cable while riding an ATV

Denise Shelton married her high school sweetheart in Indiana. She graduated with honors from Purdue University with a B.S. in psychology. Denise worked as a social worker for ten years. By then, she and her husband were blessed with two beautiful children, a daughter and a son.

Soon after, Denise quit her job to stay home and take care of their children. Their family was of utmost importance, as it is in most families. She and her husband tried to keep family traditions, as well as add some new ones such as the No-Sin Sunday sundae, apple picking, bonfires, vacations, valentine hunts with clues, themed birthday parties, family game night, and so on. Both Denise and her husband were very involved in their children's lives and education; never missing a sporting event, play, or a chance to volunteer at the school.

Denise is currently working as a teacher and continues to love her job. She and her husband are blessed to have their daughter, son-in-law, and granddaughter live nearby.

THANK YOU

I am deeply indebted to the writers who contributed to *Grief Diaries: Surviving Loss of a Child*. It required a tremendous amount of courage to pen such painful memories for the purpose of helping others, and the collective dedication to seeing this project to the end is a legacy to be proud of.

I very much appreciate author Annah Elizabeth's assistance in framing the start of each chapter. I'm also grateful to our Grief Diaries village and the very lovely souls I consider dear friends, collaborative partners, mentors, and muses. I treasure each and every one of you!

There simply are no words to express how much I love my husband Jamie, our children, and our wonderfully supportive family and friends for being there through laughter and tears, and encouraging me at every turn. None of this would have been possible without their unquestioning love and support that continues to surround me.

Finally, I am indebted to our daughter Aly for being my biggest cheerleader in Heaven. Her bright star continues to inspire me, and I can feel her love through the thin veil that separates us as I work to offer help, healing and hope around the world. My dearest Lovey, I love you to the fartherest star and beyond. XO

Lynda Cheldelin Fell

Shared joy is doubled joy;
shared sorrow is half a sorrow.
SWEDISH PROVERB

*

ABOUT

LYNDA CHELDELIN FELL

Considered a pioneer in the field of inspirational hope in the aftermath of loss, Lynda Cheldelin Fell has a passion for creating and producing ground-breaking projects that create a legacy of help, healing, and hope.

She is the creator of the 5-star book series *Grief Diaries*, board president of the National Grief & Hope Coalition, and CEO of AlyBlue Media. Her repertoire of interviews include Dr. Martin Luther King's daughter, Trayvon Martin's mother, sisters of the late Nicole Brown Simpson, Pastor Todd Burpo of Heaven Is For Real, CNN commentator Dr. Ken Druck, and other societal newsmakers on finding healing and hope in the aftermath of life's harshest challenges.

Lynda's own story began in 2007, when she had an alarming dream about her young teenage daughter, Aly. In the dream, Aly was a backseat passenger in a car that veered off the road and landed in a lake. Aly sank with the car, leaving behind an open book floating face down on the water. Two years later, Lynda's dream became reality when her daughter was killed as a backseat passenger in a car accident while coming home from a swim meet.

Overcome with grief, Lynda's forty-six-year-old husband suffered a major stroke that left him with severe disabilities, changing the family dynamics once again.

The following year, Lynda was invited to share her remarkable story about finding hope after loss, and she accepted. That cathartic experience inspired her to create ground-breaking projects spanning national events, radio, film and books to help others who share the same journey feel less alone. Now one of the foremost resilience experts in the United States, Lynda is dedicated to helping ordinary people share their own extraordinary stories of survival and hope in the aftermath of loss.

Because of that floating book her daughter left behind, Lynda understands that the dream she had in 2007 was actually a glimpse into a divine plan destined to bring comfort, healing and hope to people around the world.

lynda@lyndafell.com | www.lyndafell.com | www.griefdiaries.com

ABOUT THE SERIES

It's important that we share our experiences with other people. Your story will heal you, and your story will heal somebody else. -IYANLA VANZANT

Grief Diaries is a ground-breaking series of anthology books featuring true stories about real life experiences. The collection of stories highlights the spirit of human resiliency, explores intimate aspects of each experience, and offers comfort and hope to those who share the same path. The series began with eight books exploring losses shared by people around the world. Over a hundred people in six countries registered, and the books were launched in December 2015. Now home to more than 450 writers spanning the globe, Grief Diaries has 17 titles in print with 13 more due by the end of 2016. Another 20 titles are set to be added in 2017.

Now a 5-star series, a portion of profits from every book in the series goes to national organizations serving those in need.

Humanity's legacy of stories and storytelling
is the most precious we have.
All wisdom is in our stories and songs.
DORIS LESSING

*

ALYBLUE MEDIA TITLES

PUBLISHED
Grief Diaries: Surviving Loss of a Spouse
Grief Diaries: Surviving Loss of a Child
Grief Diaries: Surviving Loss of a Sibling
Grief Diaries: Surviving Loss of a Parent
Grief Diaries: Surviving Loss of an Infant
Grief Diaries: Surviving Loss of a Loved One
Grief Diaries: Surviving Loss by Suicide
Grief Diaries: Surviving Loss of Health
Grief Diaries: How to Help the Newly Bereaved
Grief Diaries: Loss by Impaired Driving
Grief Diaries: Through the Eyes of an Eating Disorder
Grief Diaries: Loss by Homicide
Grief Diaries: Loss of a Pregnancy
Grief Diaries: Living with a Brain Injury
Grief Diaries: Hello from Heaven
Grief Diaries: Grieving for the Living
Grief Diaries: Shattered
Grief Diaries: Project Cold Case
Grief Diaries: Through the Eyes of Men
Grammy Visits From Heaven
Faith, Grief & Pass the Chocolate Pudding

FORTHCOMING TITLES (PARTIAL LIST):
Heaven Talks to Children
Color My Soul Whole
Grief Reiki
Grief Diaries: Through the Eyes of a Funeral Director
Grief Diaries: You're Newly Bereaved, Now What?
Grief Diaries: Life After Organ Transplant
Grief Diaries: Raising a Disabled Child
Grief Diaries: Living with Rheumatic Disease
Grief Diaries: Through the Eyes of Cancer
Grief Diaries: Loss of a Client
Grief Diaries: Poetry & Prose and More
Grief Diaries Life After Rape
Grief Diaries: Living with Mental Illness
Grief Diaries: Through the Eyes of D.I.D.
Grief Diaries: Living with PTSD